Music Therapy and Group Work

of related interest

Groups in Music
Strategies from Music Therapy
Mercédès Pavlicevic
ISBN 1 84310 081 9

Improvisation
Methods and Techniques for Music Therapy
Clinicians, Educators, and Students
Tony Wigram
Foreword by Professor Kenneth Bruscia
ISBN 1 84310 048 7

Community Music Therapy
Edited by Mercédès Pavlicevic and Gary Andsell
Foreword by Even Ruud
ISBN 1 84310 254 4

A Comprehensive Guide to Music Therapy
Theory, Clinical Practice, Research and Training
Tony Wigram, Inge Nygaard Pedersen and Lars Ole Bonde
ISBN 1 84310 083 5

Music Therapy and Group Work
Sound Company

Edited by Alison Davies and Eleanor Richards

Foreword by Marina Jenkyns

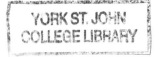

Jessica Kingsley Publishers
London and Philadelphia

First published in the United Kingdom in 2002
by Jessica Kingsley Publishers
116 Pentonville Road
London N1 9JB, UK
and
400 Market Street, Suite 400
Philadelphia, PA 19106, USA

www.jkp.com

Copyright © Jessica Kingsley Publishers 2002
Printed digitally since 2005

Library of Congress Cataloging in Publication Data
A CIP catalog record for this book is available from the Library of Congress

British Library Cataloguing in Publication Data
A CIP catalogue record for this book is available from the British Library

ISBN-13: 978 1 84310 036 2
ISBN-10: 1 84310 036 3

Contents

Part 2 Music Therapy Groups with Children

Part 3 Group Work in Supervision and with Music Therapy Students

...a phenomenon of so manifest and universal a reality as is music...a phenomenon without which, for innumerable men and women, this plagued earth and our transit on it would probably be unbearable.

George Steiner
Errata (1997)

Foreword

Marina Jenkyns

'Both music and psychoanalysis are constantly concerned with questions of meaning', posit the editors in their introduction to this book. Aristotle spoke of 'works of imitation', by which he meant art forms, as 'gathering the meaning of things'. While reading this book I found myself thinking of *The Tempest*, Shakespeare's last play, in which we see demonstrated the elements that go to make up the individuation process of a human being. It is full of music. Music is a central force through which the meaning of the play reaches its audience, on many levels. It is music that Prospero calls on in *The Tempest* to bring about the final change and revelation that ushers in the denouement of the play. It is through music that those who have wronged him in the past will come to understand; it is through the use of music that reconciliation will be made possible. Music and language come together to help us to experience the process of individuation, the meaning of a man's life being gathered. It is one of the enabling forces of the plot, bringing characters together, ushering in events and tuning the audience in to the internal psychological shifts of the central character, Prospero, as he makes sense of his own life and reflects to us our own.

> But this rough magic
> I here abjure and when I have required
> Some heavenly music – which even now I do –
> To work mine end upon their senses, that
> This airy charm is for, I'll break my staff,
> Bury it certain fadoms in the earth,

And deeper than did any plummet sound
I'll drown my book.

(Act V sc. i)

Magic and language give place to music. It is music that must begin the process of transformation. There are numerous instances in the play where meaning cannot be expressed in words alone and where the deep unconscious and forgotten memory can only be made accessible through music, and as such it is central to transformation.

This is the very theme that this book addresses as it draws together psychoanalysis and music therapy. Shakespeare's use of music is an art form within an art form. Through music the drama can be fully realized. What the writers of this book consistently do is to explore the place of music within a psychoanalytic theoretical perspective and invite a consideration of the relationship between the two forms of healing and communication, and the part played by this marriage in transformation.

As musicians, they are aware of form and structure, and I am fascinated by the way in which the form of this book echoes the structure of both therapy and analysis and of therapist training. It begins with the section on work with adults. It then moves into considering music therapy with children and ends with looking at the implications for training. I felt I was being invited to think that only by becoming children, unlearning what is safe and known as adults, can the trainee begin the arduous journey towards becoming a therapist. Once there, it is vital to maintain the facility to be able not to know, but to allow oneself to discover through creative playing with both people and music, and stay and struggle with the difficulties and challenges which that can present. The book is moving in the way the therapists reveal the challenges of group work in music therapy. Winnicott is shown to be at the heart of much of the work, whether this is stated explicitly or not; his notion of potential space and its relationship to the music therapy group is allowed to echo and re-echo in the reader's mind. And Foulkes (who, as the authors remind us, used the word 'conductor', rather than 'facilitator' or 'analyst') is used to help the therapist keep constantly in mind the group matrix as central to an individual's growth.

In their chapter on working with adults with learning disabilities Eleanor Richards and Hayley Hind tell us how '…the music felt 'mad' at times, as though both consciously and unconsciously there was no expectation that anyone might hear, understand or respond to anyone else or hope to be heard herself.' This deep hopelessness reminded me of Caliban, disabled and abused, who carries the unconscious shadow of Prospero. In his anger and rage he tells Prospero: 'You taught me language and my profit in't is I know how to curse.' Yet when Caliban thinks of the music on the island it is to him that Shakespeare gives some of the most beautiful language. For me this links with the use made in Chapter 8 of Adam Phillips' notion of therapy restoring the artist in the patient. Music enables Caliban to speak with aesthetic form and meaning.

> Be not afeard; the isle is full of noises,
> Sounds and sweet airs, that give delight, and hurt not.
> Sometimes a thousand twangling instruments
> Will hum about mine ears; and sometimes voices,
> That, if I had then wak'd after long sleep,
> Will make me sleep again: and then, in dreaming,
> The clouds methought would open, and show riches
> Ready to drop upon me; that, when I wak'd,
> I cried to dream again.

(Act III sc.ii)

The notion of acoustic dreaming thought about in the chapter by Rachel Darnley-Smith helped my free association to lead me to this passage. I had already made my links with *The Tempest* when I arrived at the final chapter by Alison Davies and Sue Greenland. The book ends with a reference to the storm and seeing the group as a boat. One of the exciting aspects of this book is that it has a way of reaching out into the unconscious of the reader so that we find our own metaphors with which to respond, just as the group conductor of the music therapy group can be in touch with the unconscious of the members through the music. It is as though the interplay of conscious and unconscious between people, made accessible through the art form in the music therapy group, is replicated in the relationship created between writers and readers in the book.

The interplay between group analysis and music is eloquently presented; after reading it I was left thinking: who better to be a group 'conductor' than a music therapist trained in psychoanalytic approaches to the dance between conscious and unconscious communication of the group? Time and again, contributors to the book show how the client and, indeed, the therapist, are enabled to grow within its matrix and to discover more about themselves as communicators aided by the centrality of music and of the understanding of the importance of silence.

Form replies to form and thus meaning is gathered. As a dramatherapist with a particular interest in dramatic literature I found myself replying to the music therapists' writing with the art form which is closest to me as I thought about writing this foreword. That I should have done so was, I think, prompted by the spirit of this book. That I should have been asked, as a dramatherapist who integrates psychoanalytic perspectives, rather than a music therapist, to write this, says something about the approach the editors have put out in the world by producing this book. It is through relationships with others that we find ourselves, and through paying attention to difference we can be enriched. The music therapy group is not a desert island onto which we take our eight records and have control over what we play but no-one to play and listen and talk with; it is not a comforter for the absence of others. It is an island, like Prospero's in *The Tempest*, where chaos and confusion are discovered to have a hidden order, where one form relates to another, where we improvise to discover the latent structure and where, through sound and silence and the presence of others, we gather our meanings.

Part 1

Music Therapy Groups with Adults

CHAPTER I

Introduction

Eleanor Richards and Alison Davies

There is a story of a rabbi who asked to be shown the difference between heaven and hell. He was taken to a room with a big table. In the centre of the table was a bowl of food and round it sat a group of starving people. Each one held a spoon. They could reach out to the food, but their spoons were very long. They could not turn them round and put the food into their mouths. They were in hell. Then the rabbi was taken to another room. Here again there was a table with a bowl of food and round it a group of people holding long spoons. But these looked cheerful and well fed. They were in heaven. And the difference? The second group had learned to feed one another, and no one was hungry.

This book raises some questions about group music therapy. There seems to be a great deal of group work going on in music therapy at the moment. Within any institutional setting in particular, many of us, from our first experience as students on placement onwards, have found ourselves invited or simply expected (and expecting) to work with groups. But why and how have we responded?

The contributors to this book repeatedly return to two connected issues. First, what might be the rationale for engaging in group therapy of any kind? That involves looking at some well-established theoretical ideas about group therapy and seeing what they mean to us now. Second, how can those ideas be related to working with music? In other words, why do we choose to be music therapists?

The thinking about group music therapy represented here is predominantly in the analytic tradition. Many of the authors draw upon some of
the most well-established strands of analytic and developmental thought
of the past 100 years, including the work of Klein, Bion, Winnicott,
Bowlby and Stern. Alongside that is a debt to the tradition of group
analysis, most represented here by Foulkes, Bion and Yalom. In these
accounts and discussions of work with a wide range of different client
groups, it emerges clearly that music therapists are turning increasingly to
these ideas as a framework for their thinking about the therapeutic
process.

But a question remains: what is the basis for working with music? The
mainstream analytic tradition assumes the use of language as its fundamental currency ('the talking cure'), so what links can be authentically
made with music? Perhaps this question has some of its roots in the
limited account taken of music in the early psychoanalytic tradition. Late
in his life, in 1936, Freud described himself as a 'ganz unmusikalischer
Mensch' – a 'quite unmusical man' (quoted in Jones 1957, p.226). The
prevailing mythology suggests that he found little active pleasure in
music and was little drawn to speculation about it, although Leader
(2000) amongst others, is beginning to contest that commonly held
assumption. Certainly Freud has much more to say about the visual arts;
perhaps because they share with verbal language the possibility of some
initial consensus, however broad, about what words or images may
represent. In the abstract world of music, or auditory experience, enquiry
into meaning is necessarily more speculative from the outset. Indeed
perhaps music, while it may be increasingly fascinating for psychoana-
lysts, is also in some ways innately subversive of the traditional analytic
process. It defies translation and demands to speak for itself.

A growing mutual interest has emerged, however, between music and
psychoanalysis in the past 60 years. In the field of musical scholarship, for
instance, a tradition of analytically informed thinking has begun to
develop. That has included not only consideration of what might be the
unconscious processes involved in composition and improvisation, but
also a recognition that both music and our responses to it emerge from a
psychobiographical context. Musicians, whether performers, theorists or
historians, have begun to acknowledge that their investigations cannot be

concerned simply with the music's idiom or structure or place in a line of stylistic development. Just as important are its sources in the experience and inner world of its creator, and the associations it arouses in those who hear, perform, or study it. In other words music, like all human activity, is open to a multiplicity of interpretations. Both music and psychoanalysis are constantly concerned with questions of meaning. What is being communicated and why? What does it mean to us, and why (Feder, Karmel and Pollock 1990)?

In spite of Freud's own apparent distance from it, associations with music have been present in analytic writing from early on. Words with strong roots in the vocabulary of music – 'dissonance', 'harmonious', 'resonance', 'theme' – appear frequently in accounts of analytic theory and practice. What is important too is not only what happens, but when. Music moves through time and we experience it within an imposed time frame, like the analytic session. The pattern of events within that time frame is all important. What is repeated? What appears once and never again? What is repeated with variations? What is transformed? Where are the silences?

Music and psychoanalysis have ready common ground in that both are fundamentally concerned with emotion, and above all with the communication of emotion. Both call for active listening. We refer readily enough to 'the talking cure', but, perhaps even more importantly, psychoanalysis is 'the listening cure'. The good therapist in any tradition is alert, both consciously and unconsciously, to far more than the surface material of sounds or words

If music is about the communication of feeling, then it is immediately connected to something that is part of our experience from the start. Much has been said about the significance of the carer's gaze, the mutual gaze of carer and infant, and the infant's need to find herself mirrored in her carer's eyes. If that gaze is withheld or unavailable, the infant is at a loss and left with the terrifying sense that there may be no recognition or containment of her intense feelings. The same can be said of sounds. An existence in which the carer relates to her child in silence, or what the child experiences as silence, is equally traumatic. When the carer cannot listen to or be moved by the baby's voice, she and her baby together cannot develop the idiosyncratic shared vocabulary of sounds that needs to be at the heart of their interactions. At that early stage the overwhelming need is for communication, recognition, response and sharing of feeling, long before there are words available to make statements or explain ideas. Daniel Stern (1985, p.142) turns, significantly, to the word 'attunement' when he discusses the absolute necessity for the infant that her carer should respond to her gestures. He adds crucially that these responses must go beyond mere imitation or verbal description of the infant's behaviour and confirm for her that the parent has understood her state of feeling: 'Imitation renders form: attunement renders feeling.' It is this that gives the infant a sense of the possibility of an encounter on an intersubjective level.

The acute isolation manifested by many people who come into therapy may be often the result of a failure, at that early stage, of attunement. Therapy may be the first place in which the patient can feel that someone else is actively seeking to enter into his experience. The music of the therapist or of the group may, like the well-attuned mother, offer a means through a medium other than words by which the patient can feel recognized. That recognition also allows things to move forward: 'Attunement is a distinct form of affective transaction in its own right' (Stern 1985, p.145).

Adam Phillips, among many others, points out that the young child lives an intense, passionate emotional life which in the moment she is unable to conceive of articulating in words and for which, in later life, it may be very difficult to find words to recall. He goes further and suggests that the child's acquisition of language, often eagerly welcomed by the adults in the family, involves not only gain but loss:

> Learning to speak is not the same as learning another language. It would be misleading to assume that young children are involved in an act of translation; words are not merely translations of sounds, so what is translated? It is not simply one life in terms of another, because that passionate life had no terms. It was articulated without words... From the point of view of the infant and young child, language is not missing (what is to be mourned is the pre-linguistic self). But what the adults call intense feeling is present and unavoidable. (Phillips 1998, p.47)

Perhaps another aspect of the 'pre-linguistic self' that is to be mourned is the capacity for inventiveness. At a stage when she does not share the apparent fluency of the adults, the child nonetheless desires powerfully to be heard and understood. Part of the struggle towards that involves the endless search for ways to make her mark, convey her desires and experience, and create a shared non-verbal vocabulary with those around her. That makes demands on the adults too. If they are to be in touch with her they must let go of their dependence upon the generalities of a common verbal currency and seek to enter into her idiosyncratic gestures of communication and the feelings that drive them. In the same way in therapy, perhaps, the use of some medium other than words not only takes us back to an intense sense of our pre-verbal selves, but also reawakens our capacities for invention and imagination, in the interest both of articulating something of ourselves and of making sense of the communications of others. One thing that the small child never does is to deal in clichés; in the non-verbal world there are no short cuts and we cannot so readily assume that we know what is meant. The immediate 'surface meaning' of words is not even available; we have to enter in imaginatively and intersubjectively at a deeper level. In the same way in improvised music we find that we must experiment and struggle to find a means of expression which both reflects our experience and is accessible to those around us. So the business of music therapy is not simply about observing musical material (or verbal content) and making surface connections, but rather about the value and meaning of those elements as means towards some much more profound intersubjective encounter. The dreamlike (in the broadest sense) atmosphere of improvised music can facilitate a way into split off or repressed areas of feeling which may in turn be most valuably contained and responded to in non-verbal terms. The interactions of improvised music allow something of the group process, conscious and unconscious, to be made audible.

Susanne Langer talks about the capacity of music to embrace emotional complexity and contrast. She goes further and suggests that the very ambivalence of music, its resistance to being directly translated into words, means that it can be 'true to the life of feeling in a way that words cannot' (Langer 1942, p.243).

> Music is revealing, where words are obscuring, because it can have not only a content but a transient play of contents. It can articulate feelings without becoming wedded to them … The assignment of meanings is a shifting, kaleidoscopic play, probably below the threshold of consciousness, certainly outside the pale of discursive thinking. The lasting effect is … *to make things conceivable* rather to store up propositions. Not communication but insight is the gift of music; in a very naïve phrase, a knowledge of 'how feelings go'. (Langer 1942, pp.243–4)

And maybe a knowledge of 'how feelings go', 'outside the pale of discursive thinking', is the crucial ground in therapy. Langer points out that even when experience seems at its most chaotic, there is some deeper coherence that brings it together and, once again, gives meaning to each of its apparently disparate elements because of their underlying (and unconscious) relation to one another:

> The great office of music is to organise our conception of feeling into more than an occasional awareness of an emotional storm, i.e. to give us an insight into what may truly be called 'the life of feeling', or subjective unity of experience. (Langer 1953, p.126)

If we share Foulkes's view that 'all phenomena in an analytic therapeutic group are considered as potential communications' (1973, p.226), we can perhaps move beyond assumptions about the supremacy of words. In the context of improvised group music, there are also phenomena of other kinds. There is not only the spirit and events of the music itself, but also the questions arising from its creation. What is implicit in each person's choice of instrument, manner of playing, level of involvement (or not), and so on?

As several of the contributors to this book remind us, Foulkes's concept of the group matrix has some immediate musical parallels. He suggests that our actions, sounds or utterances do not take place in isolation, but rather in the context of, and as responses to, a network of events. It is their context that gives them meaning. To musicians that is a wholly familiar idea. A sound, melodic line, chord, pause, silence, or anything else in the texture of a piece of music acquires both its expressive and its structural function from what is going on around it. It makes no emotional sense on its own. Similarly, the meaning of what is going on in the group, both for individuals and for the group as a whole, resides in the essential interrelatedness of all the various elements. But this is more than just a useful musical metaphor for an aspect of group analytic theory. Through the activity of jointly improvised music, relationships and changing feelings within the group can be powerfully played out and the potential 'meaning' of individual acts can be considered and acknowledged. Furthermore, improvised music is something that the group may engage in together. Verbal exchange is necessarily sequential. Only one person (usually) speaks at a time and while other non-speakers may be full of feeling, it cannot at that moment be directly expressed. Group improvisation, on the other hand, offers utterance to the group as a whole. George Steiner writes eloquently about the relationship between music and language:

> As I see ('hear') it, one of the ways we can pay our debt to music, to its role in our lives, is to keep asking. How is it… that we are driven to, that we somehow can conceive of the inconceivable, of that which denies the words, the grammars of discursive understanding? Music bears insistent witness to the question. In the face of music, the wonders of language are also its frustrations…verbal discourse remains linear, sequential in time. It is handcuffed to the avarice of logic. (Steiner 1998, pp.65–6)

Is it often logic that prevents a 'letting go' for patients. Can there be greater freedom through music? Could music be the beginning of the disruption of some of the crippling patterns that patients present with? If music has the power to disrupt, can it also have the power to challenge assumptions and accommodate conflict? Steiner suggests that it may 'house contradictions, reversals of temporality, the dynamic co-existence within the same overall movement of wholly diverse, even mutually denying moods and pulses of feeling' (1998, p.66) He adds: 'Can music lie?' We could ask ourselves as music therapists whether can music conceal. If it reflects feeling, whether resistance to it or immersion in it, can improvised music impart more of someone's state of being and relations with those around him than the approximations of words? Do our patients want us to know the 'beyond words' of themselves that Steiner says is beyond logical or rational explication?

In *The Group as Therapist*, Rachel Chazan (2001, p.179) reminds us that 'there is a need for cultivating ethical relating in the modern world'. In groups this does not mean taking a moral position, but rather helping to develop a 'sensitivity to the feelings and needs of others, their awareness of the nature of their own way of relating to their fellow-men' (Chazan 2001, p.183).

Patients often come to therapy because they feel alienated from others and isolated and estranged from the world – a sense of disconnection. Children may feel distanced from their peer group. People with disabilities may feel apart from others and that the disability is lodged in them. Groups may help to bring awareness that disability is not so much in the individual but a problem between one person and another and thus a shared responsibility. Deafness, for instance, is a problem for both the deaf person and the speaker; autism isolates both the individual and whoever reaches out to him. It is communication that is disturbed. Closeness and intimacy are ordinary human needs, and human contact the most basic of all. Difference and uniqueness are as much an aspect of relatedness as are similarity and universality.

One of the issues that groups raise is the place of responsibility to others. We can think about this in relation to society and see a parallel in a group. Steve Gans (1999, p.204) draws our attention to how Emmanuel Levinas, the French philosopher, speaks of 'the one for the other' as opposed to 'the one against the other'. In a music therapy group, and through shared vulnerability and a desire for a sense of connection, a group member, whether child or adult, can have two languages – music and words – through which to experience herself in relation to others. This experience may bring her closer to that of being 'for' rather than 'against' the other. Gans (1999) in his writing about ethical sensibility, talks about returning to the between of relatedness, in order to attend to the suffering of the other. He speaks of the Levinasian phrase 'give me your hand' as the gesture of attentiveness that is at the very heart and soul of psychoanalytic therapy:

> 'Levinas', 'give me your hand' is the gesture of attentiveness to the other that is perhaps at the very heart and soul of psychoanalytic therapy. Compassion for the suffering of the other transforms the useless suffering into suffering that has meaning for me, for it is my

non-indifference, my responsibility for the other, the 'one for the other', that constitutes the *between* of human relatedness' (Gans 1999, p.215)

Subjectivity, the mental space of how we perceive and feel about ourselves in relation to others, can be explored in an alternative way in improvised music. This feeling network of sound constitutes another sort of relatedness. Expressions of suffering and sorrow, anger and frustration, as well as joy and delight in others are only a few of the emotions that music can elicit and where we can be touched at a deep level. Above all, there is a particular sense of belonging when a musical improvisation is shared in a group where the instruments and many voices of sound seek a place to be alongside each other, affecting or resonating with each other rather than being indifferent. Here the uniqueness of the individual sound or instrument makes up the meaning of the whole. Members of a music therapy group, irrespective of verbal skills or the availability of words, can have an enriched experience, expressive as well as receptive, of themselves and others.

About the book

The chapters in this book describe music therapy with a broad spectrum of patients and clients, incorporating diverse ways of thinking about the group process. They have in common, however, an emphasis on a psychodynamically informed approach. Describing the interactions and network of communication and relationships in a group is difficult. How do you put a musical mood into words? Only an approximation can be verbalized after the event or experience has taken place. If music therapy is to reach a wider audience, the need to struggle to articulate the process is ever-pressing. It is in this context that we have asked music therapists to contribute towards this book.

We have taken our subtitle 'Sound Company', from Chapter 2 by David Stewart. It suggests the feeling of music as well as a sense of belonging in a group. His theoretical framework, using the psychoanalytic thinking of Bion, Klein and Winnicott as well as Daniel Stern's ideas on the pre-verbal, musical relationships of infancy, is echoed throughout the book by other contributors. In the spirit of a collaborative approach, the joint writing of chapters has been encouraged. Sometimes this co-operation takes the form of descriptions from co-therapy partnerships, such a Chapter 8 on learning difficulties by Eleanor Richards and Hayley Hind or the work described in Chapter 13 by Doris Knak and Katherine Grogan with children. In Chapter 12, Julie Sutton writes about a joint project which integrates a staff group who act as assistants for music therapy in a school with special needs. In Chapter 11, Ruth Walsh describes the outcomes of working methods with children with autistic spectrum disorder, which involved a collaboration with both a speech therapist and a class teacher.

Music therapy as a diagnostic tool in a child and family unit is presented jointly by Amelia Oldfield and Emma Carter in Chapter 10. They describe how this is a 'valuable addition to other more conventional methods of assessment'. Tessa Watson and Linda Vickers, Chapter 9, present an innovative and joint approach to groups with both music and art. Working in these two media as a combined approach is not often explored in the clinical setting. They describe it as having 'been [an] inspiring and moving experience for both therapists'.

In Chapter 6, Helen Loth puts an argument for a 'single issue' group for clients with eating disorders. She sees the value of an inpatient music therapy group for these clients. In its capacity to recreate the dynamics of family, peer group and the ward community, it allows a look at the ' here and now' through words and music improvisation. In Chapter 5, Rachel Darnley-Smith explores the potential for creative expression and the sense of belonging through music therapy with a group of older adults, an area of music therapy work less often written about.

The challenge of music therapy with young people and their struggle to grow up and take their place in the adult world is the subject of Chapters 14 and 15 by Helen Tyler and Tuulia Nicholls. The latter describes music therapy with severely learning disabled adolescents and how they can use the group to explore 'their roles in groups and thus their social identities'. Helen Tyler's emphasis is upon looking at group work as formulated by Nordoff and Robbins's idea of 'work,' and 'play' in the Winnicottian sense.

Music therapy in neurology, working with clients with head trauma and brain damage, is the subject of Catherine Durham's chapter (7). She describes how a music therapy group helps to develop a quality of life that is communicative and 'every bit as meaningful as a group with articulate individuals'.

In Chapter 4, Helen Odell-Miller focuses on the clinical implications of a long-term approach when working with people with severe mental health problems. She recounts the 'experience over time' of an individual patient within the group and how it parallels his growing network of relationships outside the group. John Glyn discusses music therapy in a forensic setting in Chapter 3. This is a patient group where music therapy is having an increased presence. He explores the internal world of the forensic patient, looking at the music therapy in relation to the dynamics of the institution and the rehabilitation of this particular group of people.

The final part of the book focuses on student groups and supervision. Elaine Streeter in Chapter 17 takes a personal look at music therapy training groups. She shares some of her observations on the themes that 'might affect the work and development' of a group on a training course. Alison Davies and Sue Greenland (Chapter 18) discuss together the use of group analytic theory in working with student training groups and the value of applying this theory to experiential groups for music therapists in training. Alison Davies asks the question: How does the music earn its keep? Esme Towse and Catherine Roberts (Chapter 16) take a look at how the understanding of music therapy groups can be informed by the writing of S.H. Foulkes and, in particular, his idea of the matrix. These ideas are further explored in an account of the supervision of a music therapy group for children with severe learning difficulties.

We hope that this book will be a source of stimulus not only to those within the music therapy profession, but also to anyone with an interest in the arts therapies. As we begin to establish an increasing body of theory born of our clinical experience, so group music therapy can both acknowledge its strong connections with the wider world of therapeutic practice and take its place as a distinctive and serious approach in its own right.

References

Chazan, R. (2001) *The Group as Therapist.* London: Jessica Kingsley Publishers.

Feder, S., Karmel, R.L. and Pollock, G.H. (eds) (1990) *Psychoanalytic Explorations in Music.* New York: IUP.

Feder, S. Karmel, R.L. and Pollock, G.H. (eds) (1993) *Psychoanalytic Explorations in Music.* (Second Series) New York: IUP.

Foulkes, S.H. (1990) 'The group as matrix of the individual's mental life.' In S.H. Foulkes *Selected Papers.* London: Karnac.

Gans, S. (1999) 'Levinas and the question of the group.' In C. Oakley (ed) *What is a Group?* London: Rebus Press.

Jones, E. (1957) *Sigmund Freud: Life and Work.* London: Hogarth Press.

Langer, S. (1942) *Philosophy in a New Key.* Cambridge, Mass: Harvard.

Langer, S. (1953) Feeling and Form. London: Routledge & Keegan Paul.

Leader, D. (2000) *Freud's Footnotes.* London: Faber & Faber.

Phillips, A. (1998) *The Beast in the Nursery.* London: Faber and Faber.

Steiner, G. (1998) *Errata.* London: Phoenix.

Stern, D. (1985) *The Interpersonal World of the Infant.* New York: Basic Books.

CHAPTER 2

Sound Company

Psychodynamic Group Music Therapy as Facilitating Environment, Transformational Object and Therapeutic Playground

David Stewart

Introduction

This chapter presents a theoretical overview of psychodynamic group music therapy primarily from a Winnicottian perspective. The first part outlines a 'developmental object-relations' framework, while the second discusses how this body of theory has helped in better understanding group work processes with people with chronic mental health difficulties. In particular it explores the potential psychodynamic group music therapy affords for (re)experiencing a 'facilitating environment' (Winnicott 1965), 'transformational process' (Bollas 1987) and play (Winnicott 1971). Each of these interrelated areas is essential to early emotional development and primarily concerned with building self-experience and intersubjective relationships. They are viewed as key developmental tasks in work with people with chronic mental health difficulties who are seen as having an impaired sense of self due to a complex interplay of constitutional and environmental factors early in life.

Part 1 Theory

Psychodynamic music therapy: a 'developmental object-relations' model

The broad theoretical stance I have developed over 11 years practice might best be described as 'developmental object-relations'. Both these strands were emphasized in my music therapy training at Roehampton Institute, London (Sobey and Woodcock 1999). A weekly mother–infant observation was coupled with a study of both Stern's (1985) empirical research on mother–infant relationships and the British object-relations school of Klein and Bion. This overall focus emphasized the importance of pre-verbal relationships and their intrinsically musical nature (Stern 1977, 1985, 1991; Trevarthen and Marwick 1986). It also gave a clear model for understanding the nature and function of co-improvised music in the music therapy setting (Stewart 1996b).

Latterly, Winnicottian theory has been to the fore in my thinking. Essentially a developmentalist (Hurry 1998), Winnicott saw the purpose of therapy as restoring natural maturational processes. In looking to the mother–infant relationship as the model for the psychotherapeutic process, Winnicott saw that development could only happen within a relational–interactional context. His much quoted phrase 'there is no such thing as a baby' (Winnicott 1965, p.39) underlines the notion that where there is a baby, there is always someone to care for her. An emphasis on the *quality* of the external caring environment and its impact on development is part of Winnicott's unique contribution to more mainstream object-relations which privileges the role of internal processes.

In acknowledging the legacy of psychodynamic thinking within music therapy, I also believe that music therapy has much to offer in return. Indeed, music therapy's 'moment' may be now, given the current debate within psychoanalytic circles concerning the importance of non-analytic aspects to therapeutic change (Stern *et al.* 1998). A growing body of research proposes that change takes place within the therapeutic relationship itself – the realm of 'implicit relational knowing' (Stern *et al.* 1998, p.905) – rather than through interpretation. This 'knowing' arises out of 'moments of meeting' between therapist and patient. 'Now moments' – particular moments of meeting which become 'lit up subjectively and affectively, pulling one more fully into the present' (p.911) – are seen as instigators in the change process. An essentially interactional, in-the-moment medium, co-improvised music makes a vital contribution towards enabling both the process of 'implicit relational knowing' and the crucial 'now moments'.

Some UK music therapists are uncomfortable with the idea they see as 'borrowing' from external bodies of theory, arguing instead for a more indigenous theory of music therapy (Ansdell 1999; Bunt 1994). As a counter to this, I would state that the integration of psychodynamic theory below is by no means a simple borrowing or imitation. Employing Winnicottian terminology, it is not a mere 'accommodation' of the external but, rather, a process of 'assimilation', resulting in something new and distinctive. It can be a creative, synergistic process from which a new form emerges.

Psychodynamic music therapy: parenting, play and pathology

Parenting: a parallel between therapy and parenting processes

This is key to understanding the overall process within psychodynamic music therapy (Sobey and Woodcock 1999), validated by the experience of mother–infant observation and the notion of music as a universal 'first language' of experience and intersubjectivity. The environmental provision of music therapy can be seen as akin to the 'facilitating environment' (Winnicott 1965) provided by the parent. Perhaps the central parental–therapist task in this environment is what Daniel Stern (1985) terms 'affect attunement': how the parent/therapist 'tunes in' and responds to the infant/patient needs. Indeed, Stern (1991) makes an intrinsic link with music in his description of this pre-verbal process and one that has proved a rich resource for many UK music therapists. Sobey and Woodcock (1999) refer to the music therapist's attunement task as one of 'attentive, empathic accompaniment' (p.144). Attending to countertransference reactions – the feelings evoked in the therapist by the patient – is seen as essential to the attunement task (Steele 1988) and now generally recognized as key to psychodynamic work with verbally impaired people (Sinason 1992).

The importance of emotional 'holding' (Winnicott 1965) over making 'clever' interpretations is a further important idea, linking with music's particular role as an essentially holding medium (de Backer 1993). The focus is more towards form and the experience of a relationship, rather than content and verbal insight. In this sense music therapy work can be seen as enabling the fundamental processes of self-organization and self-definition.

Play: psychodynamic music therapy as a form of playing

Winnicott memorably stated that psychotherapy was about 'two people playing together' (1971, p.38). This points to a central concern in Winnicottian theory: the capacity for play as an indicator of emotional health and as a medium for the developmental process itself. Play is essentially 'a way of being yourself and knowing yourself ... about discovering your part in the wider world ... discovering the 'otherness' of the world and the limits it presents you with' (Stewart 1996a, p.12). Where this capacity is impaired, Winnicott saw the therapist's task as 'bringing the patient from a state of not being able to play into a state of being able to play' (1971, p.38).

Co-improvised music offers a valuable opportunity for play in Winnicott's sense (Bartram 1991). Here the therapist and music medium can act as a new, 'developmental object' for the patient (Hurry 1998). A focus on establishing new, more productive attachments, as opposed to 'working through' past relationships in the transference, marks a fundamental shift in my current practice and one which is echoed in the wider psychoanlytic field (Holmes 1998).

Pathology: a language of 'developmental needs and difficulties' as opposed to 'pathology' and 'abnormality'

One of the more negative aspects in mainstream psychoanalytic thinking is, arguably, its tendency towards pathologizing people's difficulties. Within the kind of developmental model outlined above, this more pejorative framework is turned around. Here there is an emphasis on a germ of development in even extreme difficulty and impairment, in each individual a 'voice of health' and some capacity for development. Working within this principle necessitates an acknowledgement of the dynamic between deficit, disorder and damage (Alvarez 1999) in the functioning of many who make use of music therapy. Working with deficit is a more hopeful concept, one suggestive of growth. Something is not yet in place which, given a developmentally attuned environment, may be nurtured into being. The clinical use of music can prove a powerful developmental tool in helping to establish and strengthen new patterns of communicating and relating.

Psychodynamic group music therapy

The central tenents of Winnicottian theory have been applied to group analytic psychotherapy (Nitsun 1996; Schermer 1994) and group art therapy (Killick and Greenwood 1995); they have also informed my own group practice (Stewart 1996b). The concepts of the 'facilitating environment', 'potential space' and 'play' are of particular significance.

These areas find echoes in Foulkes' group analytic theory. Here a crucial emphasis is on the group as matrix, an 'hypothetical web of communication' that draws on the past, present and future lives of the individual members, conscious and unconscious, verbal and non-verbal, to become the dynamic core of group development' (Nitsun 1996, pp.21–2). Clearly this has resonance for group music therapy which might be seen as enabling a network of musical–emotional relationships. In emphasizing the role of communication within the group matrix, Foulkes (1964) highlighted the use of:

1. Mirroring

2. Exchange

3. Free-floating discussion

4. Resonance

5. Translation (Nitsun 1996).

Important links with group music therapy here are its emphasis on affect attunement (techniques 1, 2 and 4), improvised music making (3 and 4) and verbal reflection (5).

Arguably, however, Foulkes tends towards idealization of the group and its capacity for wholeness. Nitsun's work (1996) on the 'anti-group' provides a helpful balance to this idealism. It also counters the overtly pessimistic strain of Bion's group theory (1961) with its emphasis on primitive anxiety and the basic assumptions of dependence, flight-fight and pairing. Nitsun's belief is in a dialectic approach where actively working with destructive, anti-group forces can generate new and creative solutions. This has been an important framework for understanding the shifts between destructive and creative forces in the group which I will now go on to describe.

Part 2 Applied Theory

Aims of psychodynamic group music therapy with people with chronic mental health difficulties

To begin this section, I will summarize what I see as the key aims of psychodynamic group music therapy with people with chronic mental health difficulties:

- to provide an experience of *consistency, reliability, structure* and *boundary*

- to provide opportunities for primarily *non-verbal communication, play* and *relating*

- to provide an experience of *transformed self* and *self–other relationships* through *shared musical play*

- to help develop an experience of *trust, cohesion* and *belonging*

- to provide an experience of *being listened* and *responded to* and *thought about.*

Introducing the group

The group took place in a therapeutic community setting and ran for two and a half years. It met on a weekly basis for an hour and a quarter with five resident members and one staff member as co-therapist. I wish now to look at how the group has provided opportunities for its members to experience a 'facilitating environment' (Winnicott 1965), to use the music medium as a 'transformational object' (Bollas 1987) and to engage in therapeutic play (Winnicott 1971).

Experiencing a facilitating environment

The facilitating environment is the crucible for the developmental process. It provides the fundamental security that enables the baby to piece the world together, and its part in it, bit by bit. The quality of parental input is crucial here, providing the two cornerstones of *reliability* and *adaptability*. These qualities communicate a sense of *boundary* and *space* for the infant (Davis and Wallbridge 1981). The parent acts as a protecting frame or boundary, keeping external impingements at bay. Within this reliable structure a space can open up for the baby, characterized by relaxed receptivity and active adaptation to her needs. Parents' attunement skills are to the fore here.

Winnicott (1965) describes 'holding' as a central task within this environment. More than just a physical act, holding concerns parents' capacity to imaginatively 'hold together' their baby's feelings, especially anxious ones. Holding concerns the infant's evolving sense of self: the baby that is held will gradually be able to hold its own feelings and thus develop its own identity.

For people with chronic mental health difficulties, this sense of self may be greatly impaired through a complex interplay of environmental, social, relational and constitutional factors (Dallos and McLaughlin 1995). Winnicott (1992) saw psychosis as an 'environmental deficiency disease' (p.246) arising in early life when the infant was maximally dependent on the environment for survival. However, he also recognized the infant's 'inherited potential' in how environments can fail adequately to meet a particular infant's needs. From a Winnicottian perspective, the therapy environment affords a 'second chance' to experience a facilitating environment and to re-establish the self-definition process.

Offering a facilitating environment, however, does not guarantee a capacity to *experience* it as such. Thus, the basic need to enable a sense of inclusion and belonging constitutes a core aspect of this work. An experience of being held in the group is often a tenuous one which can come under threat at times of transition: when a member leaves or joins the group, when there is a holiday, when a new area of experience is being explored. However, as the ebb and flow of the group returns to these fundamental experiences, it has a chance to revisit them and slowly ingest a more stable feeling of inclusion.

Example 1: searching for a facilitating environment

M's case highlights the question posed by patients with the self-deficit underlying much mental disturbance: 'Are you glad to see me?' M has a desperate – though mostly hidden – wish to be 'seen' by the group, to be welcomed and accepted. This is matched only by her capacity to frustrate and confound this wish. Consistently M finds herself appearing 'stupid', 'shamed' or a 'failure: arriving late for sessions and asking if it's OK to come in, not understanding instructions, lifting instruments precariously so they fall from her hands.

A recent example typifies the traps she can set for herself. On arriving M wanted to move her armchair closer into the group circle. She stood behind it and struggled with it until the right side was touching a second chair, the left a table. She tried to get into her chair from behind; of course, she couldn't. She was trapped. Suddenly, filled with rage, she pushed the chair this way and that, eventually returning it to its original position where she sat down. I said, 'M I can see you really wanted to get closer to the group but part of you ended up trapped outside.' 'Mmm,' she grunted, her face flushed and angry.

In working with M it has been vital to hold together these competing aspects: the wish for inclusion and the capacity to destroy links with others. M's music vividly portrays her conflict and she has been able to work with these contradictory impulses through the group music. Initially, it was out of synch with the others, a relentless pounding with her face a tense, fixed stare. Sometimes she played in the shared group tempo, often she was at odds with it. She found it hard even to share a level of musical intensity with the group. Over a period of three to four months M's music began to change. The first development was her playing in triplets with the group pulse, quite a feat of 'musical belonging with built-in ambivalence'! Later, she would play with the straightforward group beat, though it could always slip between this and her more fluid tempo again. Finally, M's music began to assimilate the group pulse more consistently. The quality of her playing changed too, as a softer, more fluid music emerged, especially on the metallophone. Her drumming could also take on a lively, syncopated pattern, sometimes providing a clear lead to others. Occasionally M found herself able to hear others' appreciation of her changing music and even shared in it herself with a smile. In this respect M reminds me of Alvarez's (1992) notion that, in therapy with deprived patients, having a good experience and *enjoying* it proves as challenging as exploring difficult feelings.

Enabling these changes posed a considerable musical, emotional and psychological challenge. In my view this was met through the total provision of the therapy environment, not just its musical aspect. Musically, the co-therapist and/or I would play a syncopated pattern while M was playing in a relentless manner. We heard this as promising life beyond her rigid, adamant pulse. On occasion she took in some of the implicit playfulness of the 'offbeat' to bring a more flexible, alive patterning to her music. Playing out a strong version of the group pulse has also been an important communication when M's playing was at odds with the underlying tempo. I heard this as a firm stating of the boundary of the group pulse, an invitation to make rather than avoid connection.

Verbally, we have had to acknowledge both M's wish to belong and her feeling that all she deserves is to be rejected. Sometimes this involves simply surviving her tests and traps, communicating that she *can* be contained within the group. At others it involves simple verbal statements which try to understand her conflict and predicament. Sometimes we get it right, sometimes not. Contradictory states of mind are avoided by patients such as M where, as Pines (1994) remarks, 'the ego states are vigorously kept apart and the therapist's efforts to bring these contradictions to the patient's attention are strongly resisted' (p.147).

Experiencing the music as a 'transformational object'

Communicating and relating in a non-verbal medium can give access to early modes of feeling of at oneness and fusion. This type of communication featured strongly in the life of the group from about its third month.

Example 2: music as self and group transformation

When in this mode of communication the group would play in an overtly cohesive way. Bound together by a strong shared pulse, members would often imitate each other's exact subdivisions of the beat. In one example the group was playing in a slow tempo using two bass chime bars, a metallophone and a large Chinese drum; I played the piano. The overall effect was one of a rich musical sonority and a steady emotional intensity. At one point T, an otherwise virtually silent community member, initiated a clear crescendo which the others followed. Once it had peaked the group allowed the music to fall back to its earlier dynamic. This instance also saw M make an emotionally engaged contribution on the metallophone, remarkable for its fluidity and carefully shaped phrases returning to a 'home note'.

The opening solo introductions could also highlight the music's transformational function. In the session described above, T took three minutes to 'sign in' on bongo drums. Halfway through he introduced a new method of playing: tapping a basic pulse on the larger head, he began to drag his nails across the smaller one. On remarking to T about this afterwards, he looked directly at me and, smiling, said 'Different'; probably the third word T volunteered in the course of the group!

Similarly, other members took three or four minutes to complete their solos. Afterwards I commented on how lively individuals' playing had been; how I was aware that many group members didn't talk much outside the group; how different it was when given a chance to play and how music could give us a different view of ourselves. M offered a view that the group did most of its 'speaking' in the music. Later, after the group improvisation already described, B and I had this exchange:

B: Isn't it surprising?

DS: What's surprising B?

B: How we can all play together!

DS: Mmm – yes – a *good* surprise.

This particular mode of music has a primitive togetherness reminiscent of Balint's (1968) 'harmonious interpenetrating mix-up' of early mother–infant experience. (Interestingly, one member frequently commented that the group was 'harmonizing' in this type of playing.) It also seems linked to what Winnicottian psychoanalyst Christopher Bollas (1987) calls a 'transformational object' (p.14). He refers to the way a mother acts as a transformer of her infant's experience, how she becomes a process of 'cumulative internal and external transformations' (p.14). As a transformational object, the mother/carer is essentially engaging in a process of aesthetic transformation. Bollas locates this process early in the infant's life, equating it with a merged in form of relating, before separation has been fully established. He believes we seek these experiences out in later life where, say, a holiday or a new job holds out the promise of self-transformation. I feel the everyday listening to music also evokes just such an experience, where a particular music 'hits the spot' by simultaneously mirroring an important element of our experience, but at the same time transcending it.

In terms of the music described, I believe the process of playing and internalizing a harmonious musical cohesion provides a form of self- and group-transformation from which a more solid sense of self can then take shape. I have come to understand these as vital developmental experiences. Their function is to create the sense of basic trust required to move to the next phase of *playing together,* where the task is one of moving away from feelings of at oneness towards greater differentiation of self from other. It has been useful to link this growing awareness to Nitsun's (1996) ideas on group psychotherapy as a transformational process, in particular his thinking on the group as an 'aesthetic object' (p.209). He sees this as key to a transformational group perspective. In his view the opportunity for aesthetic transformation afforded by the group sees the individual 'becoming him or herself by contributing to the group becoming itself' (p.209).

Experiencing play

Play is the medium through which we feel connected with life and the process of living in a personal way. Play allows us to feel alive and real. Play is about communication, relationship and personal meaning. Winnicott again locates the developmental origins of play within the mother–infant relationship. He traces its beginnings to the period when the baby is becoming less dependent on the mother/environment, when they are both beginning to wake up to the world around them. The baby responds to this separating out through play: hence the teddy, blanket or thumb – Winnicott's 'transitional objects' (1971) – which act as soothing alternatives to the parent's presence. Here then is the infant's first creative gesture towards a realization that the world contains both 'me' and 'not-me'.

This play occurs in what Winnnicott (1971) referred to as the 'intermediate' or 'potential space' that opens up as mother and baby separate out from each other. This space allows for the overlap of worlds: inner and outer, mother's and infant's. It is a place between these worlds that affords the playing individuals an experience of exploring the relationship between them. The example that follows illustrates how the music therapy environment can enable the development of this intermediate play space. Again this is a crucial focus with this patient group where an experience of an insufficiently adaptive environment in early life can result in an impaired sense of play and corresponding self-deficit.

Example 3: differentiating a musical 'me' and 'not-me'

B is protagonist in this example. She is the most verbally articulate and socially competent member of the group. Generally, she functions well day to day but is prone to thought hallucinations and periods of psychotic illness during which she is hospitalized. B has a quiet firmness about her. She is a 'conflict avoider'. In the group she is concerned that the music sounds 'harmonious' and connected. In this way B's own feelings can get lost in a desire for harmony. In Winnicott's terminology she is mostly 'compliant', as opposed to 'creative', in her attitude to living (Winnicott 1971). In example 2 above B's playing was particularly compliant, providing a steady quiet drum pulse, very much in the musical background. On listening to an audio recording afterwards I was aware how faint her music sounded. B commented on how she could hear T and M's music. I asked if she could hear herself. 'Oh yes,' she replied. A few moments later however, she said that she thought she'd 'vanished' in the music. We talked about how it was hard to hear the details of her playing although we were aware of her background presence. I wondered to B if that wasn't a bit like her in real life, staying in the background, making sure everything was OK, but not standing out from the crowd, not making her voice stand out. She felt this might be so.

In the second group piece an interesting change occurred as B took to playing two drums, the large Chinese drum from the first piece and a smaller African hand-drum she had not played before. I observed that B sat more upright in this piece as she moved between the two drums. Her playing on the hand-drum was more declamatory than before, more of a statement, letting her musical voice come to the fore.

In the closing verbal reflection I commented on the change in B's playing, to which she replied, 'I was making myself heard.' I said she had brought a new part of herself into the group, a part that could stand up a bit more and let her own voice be heard. This session saw B able to use the therapeutic playground to expand her personal repertoire and to engage with an essential human project, that of managing the interplay between internal and external realities. For B this involved a movement from her state of 'compliance' – 'not-me' – into one of greater personal creativity – 'me'. It was a movement from excessive adaption to external reality to one which could allow momentary interplay between internal and external.

Conclusion

In this chapter I have shared my own developmental journey towards a fuller understanding of psychodynamic group music therapy processes with patients with chronic mental health difficulties. Winnicottian theory has been particularly valuable in mapping this therapeutic territory. This thinking, grounded in a core confidence in the developmental processes, has provided me with a vital line of hope as therapist. Similarly, my central belief in music as a communicative, interactive and transformational medium has provided a necessary holding function to enable me to continue working in this challenging area.

In mapping this journey this chapter has sought to illustrate how psychodynamic group music therapy can offer patients with chronic mental health difficulties a 'facilitating environment' in which to explore, establish and build a more secure sense of self. It is an environment which offers an experience of basic trust and belonging and can help negotiate the difficulties inherent in holding on to this fundamental experience. As a boundaried space which also allows for closeness and intimacy, music therapy offers the opportunity to re-experience early modes of relating and to use them to enable a transformation of the sense of self. It offers a place in which to play, in which to manage the separation of 'me' and 'not me'. Above all I hope it has illustrated how the music therapy environment can become a place to meet up and experience some measure of 'sound company'.

Acknowledgements

I would like to thank Mrs Patricia Druse for her supervision and Mr Michael Kelly for his contributions as co-therapist during the work described in this chapter.

References

Alvarez, A. (1992) *Live Company*. London: Routledge.

Alvarez, A. (1999) 'Addressing the deficit.' In A. Alvarez and S. Reid (eds) *Autism and Personality*. London: Routledge.

Ansdell, G. (1999) 'Challenging premises: a response to Elaine Streeter's "Finding a balance between psychological thinking and musical awareness in music therapy theory – a psychoanalytic perspective".' *British Journal of Music Therapy 13*, 2, 72–76.

Balint, M. (1968) *The Basic Fault: Therapeutic Aspects of Regression*. London: Hogarth.

Bartram, P. (1991) 'Psychodynamic music therapy.' In *Music Therapy and the Individual*. Edinburgh: Scottish Music Therapy Council. Conference proceedings.

Bion, W.R. (1961) *Experiences in Groups.* London: Tavistock.

Bollas, C. (1987) *The Shadow of the Object.* London: Free Association Books.

Bunt, L. (1994) *Music Therapy: An Art beyond Words.* London: Routledge.

Dallos, R. and McLaughlin, E. (1995) 'Mental health.' In R. Dallos and E. McLaughlin (eds) *Social Problems and the Family.* London: Sage.

Davis, M. and Wallbridge, D. (1981) *Boundary and Space: An Introduction to the Work of D.W. Winnicott.* London: Karnac.

De Backer, J. (1993) 'Containment in music therapy.' In T. Wigram and M. Heal (eds) *Music Therapy in Health and Education* London: Jessica Kingsley Publishers.

Foulkes, S.H. (1964) *Therapeutic Group Analysis.* London: Allen and Unwin.

Holmes, J. (1998) 'The changing aims of psychoanalytic psychotherapy: an integrative perspective.' *International Journal of Psychoanalysis 79,* 227–240.

Hurry, A. (ed) (1998) *Psychoanalysis and Developmental Therapy.* London: Karnac.

Killick, K. and Greenwood, H. (1995) 'Research in art therapy with people who have psychotic illnesses.' In A. Gilroy and C. Lee (eds) *Art and Music: Therapy and Research.* London: Routledge.

Nitsun, M. (1996) *The Anti-Group: Destructive Forces in the Group and their Creative Potential.* London: Routledge.

Pines, M. (1994) 'Borderline phenomena in analytic groups.' In V. Schermer and M. Pines (eds) *Ring of Fire: Primitive Affects and Objects Relations in Group Psychotherapy.* London: Routledge.

Schermer, V. (1994) 'Between theory and practice, light and heat: on the use of theory in the "Ring of Fire".' In V. Schermer and M. Pines (eds) *Ring of Fire: Primitive Affects and Objects Relations in Group Psychotherapy.* London: Routledge.

Sinason, V. (1992) *Mental Handicap and the Human Condition.* London: Free Association Books.

Sobey, K. and Woodcock, J. (1999) 'Psychodynamic music therapy: considerations in training'. In A. Cattanach (ed) *Process in the Arts Therapies.* London: Jessica Kingsley Publishers.

Steele, P. (1988) 'Children's use of music therapy.' In *Music Therapy and the Life-cycle.* London: British Society for Music Therapy. Conference proceedings.

Stern, D.N. (1977) *The First Relationship.* New York: Basic Books.

Stern, D.N. (1985) *The Interpersonal World of the Infant.* New York: Basic Books.

Stern, D.N. (1991) *Diary of a Baby.* London: Fontana.

Stern, D.N., Sander, L.W., Nahum, J.P., Harrison, A.M., Lyons-Ruth, K., Morgan, A.C., Bruschweiler-Stern, N. and Tronick, E.Z. (1998) 'Non-interpretive mechanisms in psychoanalytic therapy: the "something more" than interpretation.' *International Journal of Psychoanalysis 79,* 903–921.

Stewart, D. (1996a) 'Boundary, space, play and holding: essential elements in a Winnicottian approach to music therapy.' Unpublished paper.

Stewart, D. (1996b) 'Chaos, noise and a wall of silence.' *Journal of British Music Therapy 10,* 2, 21–33.

Trevarthen, C. and Marwick, H. (1986) 'Signs of motivation for speech in infants and the nature of a mother's support for development of language.' In B. Lindblom and R. Zetterstrom (eds) *Precursors of Early Speech.* Basingstoke: Macmillan.

Winnicott, D.W. (1965) *The Maturational Process and The Facilitating Environment.* London: Hogarth.

Winnicott, D.W. (1971) *Playing and Reality.* London: Routledge.

Winnicott, D.W. (1986) 'Creative living.' In D.W. Winnicott *Home is Where We Start From.* London: Penguin.

Winnicott, D.W. (1992) 'Psychosis and child care.' In D.W. Winnicott *Through Paediatrics to Psychoanalysis.* London: Karnac.

CHAPTER 3

Drummed Out of Mind

A Music Therapy Group
with Forensic Patients

John Glyn

Introduction

This chapter looks at patterns of relationships that occur frequently in music therapy groups in a medium secure forensic psychiatric unit which reveal distinctive characteristics of forensic patients and the institution of which they are a part. It will suggest parallels between the structure of the wider institution and aspects of these patients' internal worlds. I hope that in doing this I can point out ways in which group music therapy can make a contribution both to patients and the overall tasks of the institution.

A brief initial sketch and reference to other relevant sources will enable the reader to focus on the main issues without feeling lost as to the context, and provide a picture of what makes this setting so different from others. Following this I will think about some of the psychodynamic implications of an institution that serves both a custodial and containing function, whilst also offering treatment and rehabilitation. I will refer to ideas I find useful regarding the nature of psychotic illness, and think about these in relation to offending, and usually violent, patients. I will then give clinical examples from my work as a music therapist illustrating these issues, with commentaries linking them to the theoretical ideas outlined previously. My aim throughout is to stay close to questions about the 'forensic' aspects of the work.

My main influences for this chapter come from psychoanalytic texts. There are useful papers on music therapy in the forensic setting (e.g. Loth 1994; Sloboda 1996). However, I have not found literature that draws together the institutional and clinical themes I want to explore. I hope this chapter can contribute to discussions within the profession around these issues.

The setting

Many people assume when told about the nature of the forensic patient group that the institution being described is essentially a prison. The fact that a regional secure unit is a particular kind of psychiatric hospital is difficult to grasp. The misunderstanding illustrates a difficulty not only in the minds of people without experience of this setting, but also in the minds of patients and staff within forensic units. The anxieties aroused by the combination of patients' severe mental illness and the extreme violence of their offences tend to provoke various forms of perceptual and emotional locking away. Staff and patients find themselves enacting roles primarily determined by the institution's ambiguous nature, the existence side by side of its custodial and treatment functions.

For the purposes of this chapter the key aspects of the setting are its tasks of both containing and treating mentally disordered offenders. Throughout this process it aims to assess the current risks each patient presents of reoffending and behaving violently. The majority of patients are held under the most restrictive section of the 1983 Mental Health Act, requiring detention in hospital, often for many years, and extremely well-planned discharge. Offences cover homicide, physical violence against the person, robbery, arson, and sexual offending. The most common diagnosis is paranoid schizophrenia, often accompanied by personality disorder.

Whilst the Home Office is the final arbiter of whether a patient remains detained, the consultant forensic psychiatrist is responsible for his or her immediate care and decision making. Patients are housed in locked wards, but are not confined to them 24 hours a day. According to the level of risk they present, they are allowed various kinds of leave of differing durations. Parole is one type of currency in the constant negotiation that takes place between patients and consultants. The other is medication – a highly charged issue for two main reasons. First, the often unpleasant physical side effects lead to patients resisting it or protesting about their doses. Second, the acceptance of medication implies acceptance that there is a mental illness. Thus resisting medication often goes hand in hand with opposing the diagnosis.

Denial of mental illness may be accompanied by denial of the index offence. But whether or not it is denied as an historical event, its significance is often minimized by the patient. Thus the task of risk assessment usually involves the gathering together of observations and viewpoints from members of the multidisciplinary team (MDT), often with the explicit understanding that these are completely at variance with the patient's own self-assessment. Indeed, the patient's level of 'insight' could be said to be the thing most closely observed.

Psychodynamic implications

In thinking about the holding function of a secure hospital, two conflicting models present themselves. In one it can be felt by patients to be a safe, containing setting for treatment. In the other, it is experienced as harshly punitive and restrictive. The two models have a particularly uneasy alliance, because in order for treatment and assessment to take place, there needs to be a flexible structure and a degree of freedom and permissiveness. No psychiatric patient can be treated if he or she is denied basic comforts and care, and the risks they present cannot be assessed unless they are seen operating in a reasonably relaxed environment. At the same time, the safety and legal aspects of forensic psychiatry demand that the authority structure and boundaries be maintained. Thus patients are constantly reminded that their freedom has been placed in the hands of doctors, staff, the wider social services and the Home Office.

In this sense one can think of the institution as having superego characteristics. In Freud's original conception, the superego was understood to be a part of the mind embodying both prohibiting, censoring and judging functions, but also providing a model of what should be aspired to, an ideal. In his famous phrase 'the superego is heir to the Oedipus complex' (Freud 1923), he sees the formation of the superego as the means of resolving the infant's conflicting sexual wishes towards its parents. The child deals with its incestuous wish for the parent of the opposite sex and murderous wishes toward that of the same sex through identifying with the parent of the same sex. By internalizing that parent's prohibition, the child creates an agency within his own mind that regulates and controls these instinctual impulses. He saw the superego as forming around the age of four or five. In Freud's model, although the superego can have overbearing and rebuking characteristics, it is also seen as a hard-earned but vital agency that can be guiding and encouraging, providing helpful internal figures with whom to identify. The containing model of the secure hospital could be seen as having these kind of functions.

Melanie Klein's writing shows a steady move away from this view of the superego. From the early 1920s she began to see it as present from the early months of life and as having a more primitive character than Freud's 'mature' superego. She moved towards a view that what the child essentially fears are its own oral aggressive impulses towards its own loved maternal object. She saw these impulses as innate and not activated simply in response to external factors such as absence or deprivation. The superego is set up to control the aggression that the infant fears will destroy the loved object. This is essentially done through what she later termed projective identification, whereby the feared impulses are split off and evacuated into external 'objects'. The play of small children revealed them creating cruel and terrifying figures that possessed the same kinds of sadistic qualities which the child feared would interfere with its good relationships (Klein 1929). By attributing severe and punitive characteristics to one set of 'bad' objects, and idealized and perfect qualities to another group, separate constellations are set up with the aim of protecting the ideal. Klein's model of the superego consists of these sets of internal objects fiercely interacting within the child's internal world. The more hostile the original impulses, the more aggressively they need to be opposed by the forces of 'good'. Thus the severity of the internal objects is seen to be in proportion to the innate aggression of the child. In normal emotional development the intensity of these internal relationships becomes moderated, and the superego becomes progressively less harsh. However in disturbed children the need for ever more extreme splitting and projective identification leads to intense terrors of retaliation from the objects into whom the aggression has been projected, and vicious cycles of projection and retaliation are set up.

As Klein's thinking moved forward, the superego as a distinct concept became subsumed into her concept of the depressive position (Klein 1935). In this she saw the task of emotional development in terms of recognizing the object as whole and separate from the self, as opposed to an amalgamation of the parts of the self projected into it. This in turn involves developing the capacity to experience guilt and to repair damage caused to relationships by the kinds of primitive modes of relating described above. She saw all adult life as a constant process of shifting between 'depressive' functioning and the more primitive 'paranoid-schizoid' functioning (Klein 1946) characteristic of small children, but for chronically ill patients the task of achieving any consistent degree of depressive functioning remains impossibly elusive.

The term superego continued to be used by Kleinians but less specifically, to denote harsh and punitive characteristics (ie 'superego-ish'). However some writers, particularly Bion (1959, 1962) and Rosenfeld (1971), continued to develop the concept in ways that linked it particularly to schizophrenia and to the kind of primitive emotional states characteristic of offender patients. Bion described an 'ego-destructive', or 'super' superego, hidden and split off from the rest of the personality and made up of surviving 'archaic' elements of the infant's life, that continues to exert a deadening, anti-creative and anti-communicative presence in adult life. Rosenfeld described in detail the persecutory nature of the superego of an acute schizophrenic patient over the course of a long analysis, and later what he described as an internal 'mafia'-like gang that terrorizes the parts of the personality that are capable of more healthy interactions (Rosenfeld 1971).

These writers have shown that, far from having no superego, the psychotic patient, and especially the forensic patient is likely to suffer from the most murderous superego, Bion's 'ego-destructive' superego. For these patients, the task of dealing with such a superego is felt to threaten the unleashing of terrible forces.

What happens to such an internal structure within an institution that in one of its aspects seems to offer itself as a modified version of the more rigid, intrusive and omnipresent version of the superego? The institution can come to represent parts of these internal relationships, which are unconsciously enacted through a multitude of established forms, systems of confidentiality and security, and the exercise of authority through the ranking of individuals by role and profession. It seems that for patients the external form, the institution, can become a much easier enemy than the internal one, their own severe superegos. The punishment offered by the institution is preferable to that from the superego, which attacks the very right to be a person and to experience emotions such as loss and dependency, and which equates autonomous activity with murderousness. Alternatively, it can become a place that is felt to offer infinite protection and support, an idealized place from which all intrusive and dangerous elements have been banished.

A key question, then, is how is it possible to enable someone to take on more superego functioning, when this is taken on so much by the institution? In terms of rehabilitation this would seem a central task, but one which by its very nature the institution often backs away from. The consequences are evident in the number of patients who either show a high level of compliance and apparent progress whilst inpatients, but who reoffend or collapse once discharged, or who remain locked in conflict with the institution and cannot move forward. In the clinical material presented in this chapter, I try to show how the kinds of internal features described above manifest themselves in a music therapy group. The improvised and unstructured approach gives the interaction an extreme immediacy, making such a group a means of observing primitive non-verbal behaviour often not seen by professionals in more formal encounters. But I also hope to show how becoming more aware of these processes can be helpful for patients in bringing about change.

The group

Palmer Ward is an 18-bed, male-only, medium secure rehabilitation ward. There has been a ward music therapy group for five years. It is run on a slow-open basis, with a maximum of seven places. Generally between five and seven patients attend. Sessions take place in a room just off the ward.

In the middle of the room is a low round table around which are set chairs for the members expected. On it are a variety of small hand-held, mainly percussion instruments. Outside this circle there are larger floor-standing instruments, such as piano, electric keyboard, steel pan, small drum kit and vibraphone. The members assemble round the table and a slit drum is passed round the circle, each patient improvising on it in turn in their own way. Apart from this being repeated at the end of the session, the session is entirely unstructured. In the context of this chapter, the passing round of the drum highlights the issue of how the individual can retain a sense of autonomy and self in the face of intense pressure to surrender to forces generated by the group.

After this opening, patients often stay within the circle for a time, using the smaller, quieter instruments. Some may then gravitate to other places in the room and play larger instruments. As a music therapist, my approach is to join in with the playing, trying to notice and follow different strands, and to comment occasionally on what I think is happening. Sessions move between improvised playing and periods of discussion, with the balance varying from week to week.

What follow are extracts from four sessions. The first two were consecutive and are presented and discussed as a pair. I then present the remaining two, also consecutive sessions, from about five months later, with a commentary on each. The material is chosen because I think it reveals the themes I have been describing. But I also think it shows some progress in the group's capacity to tolerate and look at the anxieties connected with these issues.

The group members

Although some members do not feature prominently in the material, they are all described so as to build a more complete picture of the group.

Harry, a young man, murdered a friend having become convinced that she harboured dangerous intentions towards him. His elaborate delusional system was not known about by his family or the wider services. He is a skilled musician. His manner is polite and friendly, but he is reticent and anxious seeming about disclosing his thoughts and feelings. In the group he seems to withhold his musicality, giving a slight impression of superiority accompanied by painful inhibition.

Laurence, a man in his mid-thirties, has a long history of schizophrenic illness. He assaulted a small girl, believing that she was making a sexual advance towards him. He presents as amiable and friendly, but shows little insight into his underlying psychosis. He brings skills as a drummer and has been attending the group for over six years, tending to see himself as its guardian.

Richard, is in his thirties. His offences involve violent sexual assaults on young girls, and he has a diagnosis of paranoid schizophrenia. He has a range of delusional beliefs, which remain mostly concealed, and he denies having any illness. His can present as irritable, impatient and dominating, but he also has a naive and ingenuous quality. He plays in a self-absorbed way as if trying to refine complex tasks, even though he lacks formal skills on the instruments.

Adam is in his early thirties. His offence was rape. He had many previous admissions, with a range of diagnoses. He has expressed multiple grandiose religious delusions. He appears lost, anxious to please and apologetic, and tends to play in a distant trance-like way. He makes offbeat associations to the music or the instruments which are often unintentionally humorous.

Mathew, in his early thirties, had an index offence of rape and false imprisonment. His mental illness diagnosis is paranoid schizophrenia. He denies his offence and is at an impasse with the MDT. On the ward he paces like a caged animal. In the music therapy group he plays in a rudimentary way, scraping and scratching the surfaces of instruments, poking objects into cavities and trying to prise them open. He is often prepared to speak and express his grievances, and can show warmth at times.

Martin is an elderly man who killed a close relation with whom he had lived for many years in seclusion. He has multiple delusions. He has been extremely withdrawn since coming to the unit. In music therapy his participation is very quiet, appearing to be deep in concentration making tiny sounds on hand-held percussion instruments.

Norman, in his forties, killed a man in a premeditated attack. He has many delusional ideas and denies the offence. His situation in the unit has remained unchanged for several years, as expressed in enormously ritual-istic personal habits. A skilful drummer, he seems to withhold his skills from the group and often plays in a relentlessly repetitive way whilst maintaining a superior and aloof attitude. However, he can be more constructive and animated.

Luke, in his early twenties, was convicted of armed robbery. He was found to be in a delusional mental state, in which he remains, with very little involvement in ward activities.

Clinical examples

The first two excerpts described took place in the sessions immediately before and after a two-week Easter break.

Session (a)

Laurence, Richard, Harry, Adam, Mathew, therapist (JG) and the co-therapist (AM) are present. At the beginning, patients refer to the break.

> *Laurence*: There are two more sessions before the break, aren't there?
>
> *Mathew*: This is the last one.
>
> *Laurence*: Will you put it in the diary for us, tell the ward staff?

The therapists remind the group that a new member will be joining after the break: 'Who's that? Luke? Oh, that'll be good. He's alright, Luke.' The slit drum is passed round, with approving comments made after Harry and JG's turns.

Laurence picks up a shaker, begins playing, and the group members join in, making lively, rhythmically cohesive music.

The therapists also pick up small percussion instruments and support the music by reinforcing and developing what the patients are playing. They try to draw out the more coherent and organized elements whilst noticing and responding to the quieter and more disparate parts.

Richard goes to the keyboard, turns the volume to the maximum level and plays. His playing is untutored and clumsy, but he gives the impression of a virtuoso striving to produce an elusive motif. The others manage to maintain a steady rhythm together, despite being almost inaudible due to Richard's loudness. Richard seems oblivious to the others' music.

JG goes to the piano and tries to connect Richard's keyboard playing with the rest of the group, and for a period the group maintains a tenuous unity. Then Richard returns to the circle, picks up the guitar, and plays with similar detached intensity.

> *Richard:* [to *JG whilst others are still playing*]Where's the other guitar, with the metal strings? [*as if in order to play louder*].

The music dies away. Laurence goes to the drums and Harry, who very rarely moves to another place in the room, goes to the steel pan. A clear piece of music emerges, with melodic and rhythmic interplay, until Richard, who has been carefully arranging the roto drums, crashes in with loud and unrelated rhythms. Harry registers irritation and goes to the keyboard (again, very unusual), where he begins to play a well-known disco melody. He smiles as he plays. The others peter out and listen.

> *Adam:* How do you do that?
>
> *Harry:* I just worked it out. [*Group members are very impressed.*]
>
> *Mathew:* He's got his own instrument. What's it called, Harry?
>
> *Harry:* [names the instrument.]
>
> *Laurence:* It's like a violin.

The music starts again. Richard is very loud on drums.

> *JG:* [*finding the loudness almost unbearable, holds up a hand and the music stops*] People were impressed by Harry's tune on the keyboard. I don't know how it made them feel, that he can play like that.
>
> *Richard:* Jealous. It makes me feel jealous.
>
> *JG:* I think that might be right. And what then?
>
> *Richard:* It makes me want to jump on the bandwagon.

He starts playing the roto-toms again, very loud and chaotic. The group plays in a desultory, futile way. Again JG gestures for the music to pause.

JG: And I wonder what's happening now.

Laurence: [*who has been playing the drum kit*] Richard's hitting the roto-toms too hard.

Richard: [*to Laurence*] You need to *hit* it [i.e. the drum kit] harder. You're just tickling it, Laurence. [*He demonstrates.*]

JG: I think when you say 'jump on the bandwagon', it means obliterate the other sounds, because it's too hard to bear the feeling of jealousy.

Richard: Yes.

JG: There's a feeling that blocking out the other sounds is the only way to deal with it.

Richard: We could all take it in turns.

The music towards the end has a more integrated feel. Mathew tries a variety of new (to him) instruments. Richard is less aggressively loud.

Session (b)

Laurence, Richard, Harry, Adam, Mathew, Luke, Therapist (JG) and Co-Therapist (AM) are present. There is close attention to each person's playing in the passing round of the slit drum, with comments and mock cheering at moments. Luke, the new member, in particular is watched and commented on ('Oh, he's good').

Following this Richard makes his way to the drum kit. Other members silently communicate apprehension. The group begins to play, but immediately Richard starts hitting the drums very hard, his face wearing a look of frowning concentration as if he's trying to work out a difficult problem. His playing shows no awareness of what others are doing and overwhelms the group. In contrast to the previous session, the group, including the therapists, seems unable to confront the problem.

The experience in the room is of something unbearable that has to be endured, a surrender to a force too powerful to be resisted.

JG eventually says he thinks we should pause. There are some muted comments that the music wasn't very 'co-ordinated', and that everyone was 'doing their own thing'. The loudness of the drums is referred to in a circumspect and indirect way. Then Laurence makes the important suggestion that we're not used to playing together because of the break. Almost as soon as this is said, Richard speaks.

> Richard: [*still at the drum kit*] John, how do you tilt this drum? [*the snare drum, on a stand*] Can you help me? I can't hit it cleanly.

He manages to tilt the drum himself and starts banging again, as before. After a further period of music similar to the earlier one, there is a pause. Luke appeals to the therapists to provide something more structured or education based and suggests an exercise. The group now begins to feel very fragmented. Laurence sets off the pre-programmed demonstration pieces on the keyboard. The therapists feel defeated and unable to make any useful contribution. After the session the therapists talk about how extremely incapacitated and battered they felt.

Commentary

I would like to think about these examples in relation to the ideas put forward earlier. One thing that stands out is Richard's behaviour and its impact on the other group members. How can one understand the apparent contradiction between his benign demeanour and behaviour that is experienced by the rest of the group as violent and intrusive? There seems to be no awareness in Richard of what he is doing to the group and he goes about his business in a state of cheerful oblivion. This can be seen as the deadened, nirvana state that results from the assaultative superego extracting any capacity for mindfulness. It can also be understood as an expression of a psychotic system in which there is absolute denial of the index offence and the presence of mental illness.

One can see the offence being re-enacted in the therapeutic setting. Richard is identified fully with the superego characteristics, and he projects into the other members the parts of himself that are being assaulted, which one imagines he also did in his offences. It is the vulnerable parts that the others and the victim are forced to experience. However, it is the more painful aspects of this that are put into the therapists, while for the other members of the group the effect is more one of a temporary disruption. This is especially so for Harry, who puts himself into a superior position through his skills.

It is often surprising to music therapists that the more passive members of a group like this seem so ready to be on the receiving end of these experiences and to return the following week. This can be understood in terms of the distinction mentioned above. On one level the group and the therapists are collectively made into victims, at the mercy of a madly omnipotent figure. However, the hopeless and incapacitated feelings reside in the therapists. It is they who are experiencing the assault and hate, whereas the other group members have used this member to project their own murderous superegos into. In other words they identify unconsciously with Richard. Their lack of surprise at Richard's behaviour reflects their identification with the obliterating superego.

We can see Richard's drumming as a kind of sensory-motor enactment through sound of a set of relationships that in the earlier of the two sessions he appears momentarily able to represent verbally and therefore symbolically ('it makes me feel jealous', etc.). I think this apparent glimmer of insight is illusory, in that whilst there is a part of him that is able to see and acknowledge jealousy in himself, the vital component of the 'K' link (Bion 1959), namely the capacity to experience the emotional consequences of this in himself and others, is entirely absent.

The metaphor of being 'drummed out' can be thought about in several ways. The psychotic 'drums out' elements of the self to avoid what are feared to be intolerable feelings. What are the specific feelings in this material that need to be kept out? As Laurence begins to say, the break may have a bearing on why it is difficult for the group to play together. In his words, 'we're not used to playing with each other'. Richard's way of saying this is to give the therapists a first-hand experience of being drummed out. In this context his jealousy and anger are directed at the group that has not been available and the therapists who have been able to take themselves off for a holiday. Again, it seems that Richard is being the appointed representative of the group that collectively feels abandoned.

Richard's jealousy seems specifically directed towards Harry, who appears less driven to surrender his creativity. Yet Harry's way of dealing with Richard's tyranny is to place himself in a superior position whilst projecting his own authority into the therapists. His extreme passivity and reliance on external figures to control the unruly omnipotent elements reveals something of the pathology expressed in his index offence.

Richard says his jealousy of Harry makes him want to 'jump on the bandwagon'. The intended meaning is that by developing similar skills he will then not feel left out. But wanting to jump on the bandwagon suggests not so much an attempt to learn as greedily getting in on the act, grabbing the position of a 'have' and looking down on the envious 'have nots'. It is a statement that embodies omnipotent denial in that the wish is then acted upon as if the painful process of accepting one's actual level and relying on other people for help can be bypassed. The bandwagon then becomes not one containing a band of people able to play well together, but one producing undifferentiated noise in which creativity and reality are obliterated. Richard's denial of his murderous jealousy and his complete negation of thought brings to mind the 'mafia gang' characteristics of the psychotic superego described by Rosenfeld (1971).

These examples may convey a bleak picture of this kind of work and its potential to bring about change, but I feel the following examples, from several months later, show the group slowly developing some awareness of the issues under discussion.

The group had been joined by two new members, Norman and Martin. In the first session after a long summer break, Harry had confronted Richard's overbearing behaviour much more directly within the music and without placing himself in a superior position. People spoke openly about how Richard's playing had made them feel, and Richard had seemed to show some awareness of what he had been doing.

Session (c)

The following week Richard didn't come for medical reasons. Several comments were made that linked his absence with what had happened in the last session. A long and cohesive piece of music followed in which everyone played sensitively and creatively at consonant levels. Members expressed much satisfaction with the piece. Laurence said the group should make a record and perform to other patients. Some agreed with this, but Norman chuckled dismissively: 'It wasn't *that* good.' Laurence said it was probably because Richard wasn't there: 'He plays too loud.'

The group began playing again. The piece was similar, but lacked the depth of the previous one, as if the good qualities were being clung to self-consciously. As the music was continuing, Laurence turned to me and said, 'Did you think I was staring at you?' The question was repeated. The group members noticed the exchange and stopped playing. I asked Laurence whether he wanted to tell the group what he'd asked, which he then did.

JG: It sounds as if you have an idea of a bad kind of looking.

Laurence. Staring is different from looking.

He said that staff had been telling him he had been staring but he wasn't aware of it. He repeated the question insistently and seemed unable to move forward without a concrete answer.

There was a further piece of music, rather similar to the second. Norman then noticed a CCTV camera mounted on the wall, pointing down into the room (the camera is disconnected).

Norman: [*whilst the music continued*] Is that working?

JG: I think it's like the question Laurence asked.

Norman. It's not like that.

When the music stopped the group returned to what had been said.

Norman. I don't want to be filmed. You're watched all the time here.

JG: I think there is something intrusive and interfering in the idea of staring, and of the group being observed from outside. But the theme is also here in terms of the way we play music together and thoughts about some people dominating and others feeling over-powered.

The group talked about this, with reference to Richard, and the need to listen to each other. We came back to the question of being observed generally in the hospital.

Harry: It's all right. You get used to it.

Others spoke about their own feelings about being observed as patients.

JG: I think there's an idea that here in the group you can get away from the constant observation, and be a bit freer. But you also know that I and CD are members of staff, so that something like that must also be going on here too. Some people seem to think the watching isn't too bad, might even be helpful, but others are saying it doesn't feel good at all.

There was a thoughtful silence for several minutes before the session ended.

Commentary

At the beginning of the session Laurence shows some insight into Richard's absence. He also really wants to know how he is experienced by others. Both can be seen as expressions of Bion's 'K' (1962), the wish to know and understand, and a move towards a more depressive position looking, that is at that moment passed round the room. However, his confusion as to whether he is staring and whether his object is annoyed by this suggests an anxiety that if he is staring he must be doing something bad and destructive. The problem with the kind of superego being discussed is that any kind of looking is seen as cruel. Curiosity all too easily gets assaulted by the superego or hijacked by the cruel part of the self that is then attacked by the superego.

The opening music is vibrant and flowing, but the group finds it hard to sustain. Norman attacks the naive expressions of pleasure in the music, and the group then explains the success of the music by projecting all the destructive impulses into the absent Richard. The music then becomes rather lifeless.

In Richard's absence, Norman becomes the group's elected representative of the overbearing superego. He watches critically over the group ('it wasn't that good'), and later projects this quality into the institution (i.e. the CCTV camera). This leads the therapist to link the themes that seem to be occupying the group, and members express feelings about the institution that represent the two models elaborated in this chapter. For Norman, the institution is felt to be spying and malign, reflecting the presence internally of a superego that ensures he remains fixed, ritualistic and lifeless. Harry expresses the other view, that the looking is tolerable and may even serve the interests of the patient.

Session (d)

The following week Richard came. Norman and Adam were absent. Unusually, Richard stayed in the circle for a long time, playing quietly and in time with the others. The piece was cohesive and satisfying. He then moved to the steel drum and again played it lightly, finding melodic phrases that fitted with the music around him. For a long period the music had a very co-operative and ordered feel. It then became fragmented and disorganized and people withdrew into playing without reference to one another.

> Richard: [as the music is playing] I can't hear myself think.

The group managed to re-establish musical cohesiveness, which then continued to near the end. At that point there was a brief discussion. Members expressed satisfaction with the music.

> Laurence: Richard was playing much quieter. You could hear
> everything that was being played.

> Richard: Quiet? I thought I was loud.

Martin, the newest member, spoke for the first time. He felt it had been better and said one way to deal with the loudness is to play louder yourself. But he carries on playing at the same level in the hope that others will play quieter.

Commentary

Complementary shifts have taken place in Richard and the group as a whole. His less intrusive playing indicates that he has taken in something from recent sessions. But the change is only possible because the group no longer needs him to the same extent as a repository of their cruel superegos. This suggests that the group members are able to experience their own underlying impulses and feelings as more tolerable, with correspondingly less need for these to be projected into Richard. Richard is then freed from his constructed role and his musicality becomes available to the group in a more digestible form. Now, not all looking is bad. Richard is able to look at himself and acknowledge the possibility of himself being loud, and the presence of different perceptions of his behaviour. Martin movingly places himself in relation to the group's development, voicing the group's aspiration that it can look at itself without excessive judgement, and maintain a degree of hope that in doing so positive change can come about.

Concluding remarks

I hope that the clinical material outlined above shows how some of the polarizations within such a group can become modified. However, in an institution such as this only a small fraction of the total amount of patients' time is spent attending the various sessions that make up the treatment programme. The questions that then need to be asked are: what happens when the patients go back to the ward? Do the patients and staff immediately reinstate the kinds of superego roles described at the beginning of this chapter, and that characterize the group in its more primitive stage of functioning. Without a parallel movement taking place on the ward to that which has taken place in the group, there is little chance that any permanent and significant change can come about.

I discussed at the beginning of this chapter two models of the institution that tend to exist in the minds of patients. In one the institution is experienced as all-protecting and all-providing, to which the patient inevitably forms a passive and dependent relationship. In the other it is seen as harshly authoritarian, invasive and restrictive, to which the patient responds rebelliously or fearfully. I tried to show how these models are projections of particular kinds of internal object relationships. In one there is an idealized superego to which the self clings and merges. In the other the superego is felt to be unbearably punitive, faced by which the self becomes squashed into submission or devious and delinquent. One major task for all staff in the institution is to be aware when they fall into the two types of roles corresponding to these two models, of either relating to the patients as just vulnerable and failing to recognize the hidden aggressive sides, or conversely becoming dismissive and superior. Individually much of the care is informed by an awareness of these issues. But as a whole the institution can operate with a near blindness to the fact that the instrument providing the care is more than just the sum of its therapeutic parts. It is the totality of the institution itself. Thus one challenge of the institution is to develop the capacity to recognize and work collectively with the kinds of splitting and projection that are endemic within it. For a music therapist, the task is far wider than simply the running of sessions. The nuances and complexities of the work have to be communicated and thought about with the MDT. The thinking needs to address how in this particular treatment a patient forms relationships that may be in stark contrast to those he or she reveals in the context of other treatments. Furthermore, the insights about patients provided by this kind of data need to be used for self-reflection by the MDT. Specifically staff need to build into their ongoing practice an awareness of the roles that are induced in them by patients and reinforced by the anxieties that work in forensic psychiatry arouses.

References

Bion, W.R. (1959) 'Attacks on linking.' *International Journal of Psychoanalysis 40*, 308–315.

Bion, W.R. (1962) *Learning from Experience.* London: Heinemann.

Freud, S. (1923) *The Ego and the Id. S.E. 19.* pp.3–66. London: Hogarth Press.

Klein, M. (1929) 'Personification in the play of children.' *The Writings of Melanie Klein*, Vol. 1. pp.199–209. London: Hogarth Press.

Klein, M. (1935) 'A contribution to the psychogenesis of manic depressive states.' *The Writings of Melanie Klein*, Vol. 1. pp.262–289. London: Hogarth Press.

Klein, M. (1946) 'Notes on some schizoid mechanisms.' *The Writings of Melanie Klein*, Vol. 3. pp.1–24. London: Hogarth Press.

Loth, H. (1994) 'Music therapy and forensic psychiatry – choice, denial and the law.' *Journal of British Music Therapy 8*, 2, 10–18.

Rosenfeld, H. (1971) 'A clinical approach to the psycho-analytical theory of the life and death instincts: an investigation into the aggressive aspects of narcissism.' *International Journal of Psychoanalysis 52*, 169–178.

Sloboda, A. (1996) 'Music therapy and psychotic violence.' In E. Welldon and C. Van Velson (eds) *A Practical Guide to Forensic Psychotherapy*. London: Jessica Kingsley Publishers.

CHAPTER 4

One Man's Journey and the Importance of Time

Music Therapy in an NHS Mental Health Day Centre

Helen Odell-Miller

The business of the therapist is to hold the meeting at a specific time and place. Within this defined context the patient may explore the space and the limits of its boundaries. (Walshe 1995, p.415)

Introduction

This chapter will explore the music therapy group process for Steve, a man diagnosed with severe depression and anxiety. He attended a music therapy group for people with long-term mental health problems in an NHS mental health day centre. I work within a psychoanalytically informed framework, emphasizing rehabilitation. The long-term nature of the group has led me to consider the significance of time, both during musical improvisations in sessions, and within the lives of the people concerned. Steve attended the group for six years. Consideration of the ending over at least a year was important, owing to his history of difficulty with endings in other relationships in his life. However, I am aware that within the current climate of short-term therapy models such as cognitive analytic therapy (CAT) and cognitive behaviour therapy (CBT) this period seems long. I will describe the therapeutic process for Steve, focusing on issues of time, boundaries and the meaning and benefits of thinking about internal and external space in relation to the group.

What are the apparently simple boundaries needed to enable the 'business' of the group to take place? This is a question for most psycho-therapists, but in my view the 'business' is even more complex for music therapists. In addition to the outer boundaries of the group, there is another internal set of boundaries: the movement in time between words, thinking and music.

An important element that I have developed is the use of time frames for improvisations in the group. Winnicott (1971) discusses the 'transitional space' where internal and external reality meet; we could think about musical sounds and silences as symbolic of the wider picture. In this group, starting an improvisation usually involves a crucial negotiation of boundaries. Members decide when and if they are going to play music during the group. My task is to enable meaning to develop through this process, and to think constantly about what might be happening in the playing, as well as when there is no music. I have found that a time boundary is helpful at the outset of some improvisations. A suggestion near the end of a group, reminding members of the relationship between the internal and external world, can be made in the form of: 'This piece should end by 3.20.' This leaves the group free to end the music any time before this, yet maintains a helpful boundary. At some stages, particularly in the latter stages of the process described here, this might not be so necessary. The general element of timing, however, is central to the work For those with long-term mental health problems, a long period in a group may be significant in reducing, rather than increasing, dependency.

Steve's journey through the group will form the narrative of this chapter and will illustrate these and other considerations, such as the importance of setting and the interface between the therapist, the patient and the multidisciplinary team as discussed elsewhere (Odell-Miller 1991, 1995).

The music therapy group

My approach is not based on one theoretical framework, but has grown from years of clinical practice and supervision. It involves practical music making, using improvisation as the focus. The way clients improvise may reflect their current states and can lead to an understanding of internal and external, intrapersonal and interpersonal changes which may be desirable. A variety of instruments is used, including percussion, violin and piano.

Music therapy provides an experience of the here and now. Interactions are played out within improvisations; the therapist must recognize this and not avoid issues she perceives or hears. The therapist is a musician trained in this way of working, but clients need not have any previous musical skills.

Time boundaries and their meaning

This was a long-term, semi-closed group run weekly at a psychiatric day clinic for 55 minutes. It was important at the outset to set a time scale that was realistic and that would not change . The group was encouraged to explore the use of the time in terms of managing the time boundaries. Talk or improvisations sometimes began almost before the official starting time of the group, and at others continued while the group was officially ending. Musical structures offered a means for these dynamics to be heard musically, rather than through conversation. I listened to rhythmic and harmonic nuance: tempos slowing down, or cadences building up towards a climax. Sometimes the group would discuss these things. In music therapy, some group dynamics, for example, the general mood of the group, who is leading, who supporting and so on, can be heard musically by the therapist and other members.

Summary of the approach

In addition to improvisation, talking, thinking and reflection were also important parts of the process. Members would comment that they heard the music of other group members, or experienced the group's 'piece', in ways that related to a significant aspect of the group or of a particular member. For example, the group explored whether their music was 'together' or not. Sometimes the group could experience a feeling of 'togetherness' more easily through musical expression; at other times feelings of difference and conflict emerged. In general the group might explore the meaning of how these experiences were related to life outside. The group became at various times symbolic of family, friends, home, community, relationships, work and psychiatric services.

Trust, transition and endings were significant issues for the group. Members thought about what an ending might be like and what might be the 'right' time for it; the manner in which improvisations ended was a recurring theme. Both sudden and prepared endings were usually significant for members and acted as a reflection of internal issues which were not always articulated in words. Musically, the group worked at an intense level where insights were opened up as a result of improvising together. Changes were often made or negotiated in terms of the way members related to each other and the musical interactions seemed particularly to help members to consider one another's positions within the group.

Steve

Steve was referred in April 1994. He was 45 years old and suffered from depression and anxiety. The reasons for referral were to build confidence, to contain anxiety and to enable him to express some of his more inaccessible emotions such as anger. He attended the group until April 2000.

Referral and assessment

In his assessment Steve appeared as a quiet, intelligent, careful person who was interested in thinking in depth about his problems. He seemed lost and to be looking for a safe place to be looked after. There were issues of aggression and somatization manifest in acute anxiety and symptoms of colitis and skin problems. He described childhood emotional deprivation, particularly from his mother, whom he experienced as disapproving, and the subsequent severing of relations with family members. He discussed how he would like to get back to his work in the field of art at some point in the future.

Steve had attended a music therapy group on an acute admission ward and found it beneficial. The referral came from the staff nurse, who had been the co-therapist in that group, with the support of the community occupational therapist (OT) and the consultant psychiatrist. Steve had been admitted following an overdose after moving from the north of England to be near friends. This had followed what he felt was an abrupt end to 13 years of individual work with a female psychotherapist, after which he described himself as feeling angry and 'dismayed'. He had trained as a graphic designer and found his work stressful; he had high expectations of himself. He felt isolated and had few friends. In the group on the ward he had used music expressively, at times seeming dominant or controlling. He had some insight into the effect of this on others, however.

Steve mentioned that he had felt symptoms of nausea and anxiety during the group on the ward, but that often these had subsided in the course of a session. He felt this implied that something important was happening: he would be able to work in music therapy. From this and other aspects of the discussion I felt that Steve had some destructive parts of his personality which he was trying to understand, and that he pushed himself hard. He seemed to have a notion that he must experience pain before getting better. He was keen to talk, yet I felt that he was holding back from speaking about himself, and in particular about the childhood emotional deprivation he had alluded to. It was as if he could not easily function as an integrated person relating to the world, but instead had to be totally absorbed or else 'cut off.' I also had a sense that he was frightened of something. After the traumatic ending of his psychotherapy it was important not to encourage a repeat of this pattern, so individual therapy was not offered. Steve was offered a place in the music therapy group:

- to provide a place for him to express himself where words were not the major vehicle, offering the possibility for him to find another way of addressing his underlying destructive and aggressive tendencies

- to provide an opportunity for building relationships in a regular contained setting

- to help him work through some of his traumatic experiences and return to a more healthy lifestyle, psychologically and physically.

The first year

This was a settling in period. Steve became engaged in improvisations, but hardly talked. Through comments and interpretations from me and from group members he gradually developed an insightful awareness of the whole group, which led to him starting to trust the situation more and so to discuss issues more openly. After about three months he started to express, mainly through music, some of his inner chaos and disintegration. He had by this time made an identification with the gato drum. He played in repetitive rhythms, sometimes sounding almost perseverative, reflecting the more obsessive aspects of his personality. At other times he played drums and cymbal loudly and arhythmically without apparently listening to other people's music. He played for long periods on the gato drum but in short bursts of more chaotic music, as if he was not at ease with his more negative feelings. If attention was drawn to this he seemed inhibited, and appeared quietly regressed in the group at times. As a result of recognizing this and the effect it had upon the group, he gradually began discussing his fear of attachments. He said he was afraid to start to attach himself in the group. Improvisation seemed to help, because when improvising he was often closely interacting with others. Eventually he was able to acknowledge his fears of death and abandonment. A particularly significant moment in this first year was when during the last minute of a session he banged the drum in front of me so loudly that it made me jump. His fears were discussed in the group at the beginning of the following session. This seemed an important symbol of what he was trying to contain; the long time scale of the group allowed the time and space to build up relationships of a kind which elsewhere he had not been able to sustain. The musical process enabled this rage to be expressed as if in essence, allowing everyone to hear, but without having to explain the detail. The time boundary was particularly significant on this occasion as his playing took place in the last moments of the group, allowing no space for discussion or musical response. His music was heard and accepted. It is difficult to see how he could have such feelings accepted and understood through words alone; at this stage nearly all his expressions were through music.

Reflections on duration

There are important questions about length of treatment. Steve's previous individual treatment had been very long term, but one might question how effective it had been, particularly in view of his history of maternal deprivation. Could he have developed an addiction to therapy? Whilst I am sure that the length of time in the group was right for Steve, I had to consider these issues. Although he never revealed all the details of his relationship with his family, and with his mother in particular, it appeared that some of his difficulties with attachment arose from these experiences. He described his mother as over-critical and disapproving. He was deeply entrenched in some of these ideas, and so I thought it necessary for him to take his time in the group, whilst recognizing the possible difficulties of over-dependency. The group was taking place within a well-established culture of long-term therapy.

The second year

At this point Steve revealed that he had often 'dreaded' the group because it raised painful feelings, physical and emotional, not only when improvising, but also just before starting to play music. He said he now felt more excited about the group and looked forward to it, which surprised him. I noticed that he started to relate more directly to others in the group and to express thoughts and feelings to them about himself, and about what they were experiencing. He said that this group was the only place where he could feel accepted and close to others, and that he felt this particularly in the music. He thought this was partly due to a release of tension followed by exhilaration. I made several comments about this over the weeks in terms of what he seemed to be voicing for the group. In summary, the destructive, painful, 'real' feeling world that the group found hard to address seemed to be the central issue here, represented musically by loud cacophonous playing. Steve also seemed to be voicing the ambivalence in the group about making close relationships, and to be actually trusting that the group might be a safe place for all kinds of issues to be expressed and explored. In the middle of this stage Steve went through a period of feeling 'unwell'. He started to miss sessions and we looked at what he might be avoiding in terms of the pain and fear of possible rejection or abandonment. Here the internal and external representations of the group, both musically and otherwise, were important and it was essential to draw him into the process. The fact that the group functioned when he was absent and, indeed, that others thought about him and played music for him in his absence, was significant throughout the long period of time.

Towards the end of this year he became more vociferous and was really beginning to work in the group. He worried about how he could integrate his emotions, often saying that he could be at one extreme or another – placid or angry – but never integrated. I shared with the group my sense that he represented to and for the group the split off, emotional world that perhaps had never been fully nurtured earlier on for him and others. Could the group repair any of this? Allowing that would mean coming to terms with conflicts in the group and differences between members. At this stage Steve often acted as a catalyst for acknowledging conflict, but the group was perhaps not ready to be able to work at this level. The group acknowledged that expressing feelings through music might be safer than articulating them verbally. Steve was able to discuss his fear of affection, and behind this his fear of his own destructiveness. At this point perhaps some of the work Steve might have done in the group was curtailed by people joining or leaving (which we were able to look at later as connected with the group itself, rather than just as 'accidental'). Steve often became paired with a new young female member of the group with whom he made endless very tribal sounding music, but with whom he was never able to speak other than in polite pleasantries. Membership changes in the group raised his anxieties and he retreated into himself. He was able to express his sadness after the female member left the group, but not in the period up to her departure. In terms of the internal and external use of space, this was markedly different to the final year in which at last he became able to address issues musically and verbally with members of the group in their presence.

The third year

Steve seemed to go through a period of 'resistance', and acknowledgement of this led to a powerful working through of some of his destructive tendencies in relationships. He played these out in the group by improvising extremely loud music, particularly on the piano, often drowning out others' music and sounding omnipotent and angry. He would later feel ambivalent about this and was able, with help from the group, to look at what it represented for him in relation to his life both in the group and outside it. He wanted to have the final say and often seemed unable to take others into account, whereas previously he had been prepared to help others at the expense of mentioning his own needs. This is where the time elements of the musical improvisations were most crucial. There were musical 'battles' between group members over how to end the pieces and over who was leading or setting the pace for the cadence points. Steve needed to know that the group could survive his destructive loud piano playing, and eventually others were able to risk sharing this role at a point when the group reached its most potent level of tolerating open conflict rather than hiding from it. Particularly important in this were exchanges between Steve and another male member who was sharing his childhood memories of abuse, and close interactions with an older long-standing female member of the group, which at times felt like an established 'marriage'. Steve seemed to move forward both inside and outside the group. He began to work again in his field and joined a specialist Eastern music group. He felt sustained and encouraged by knowing the therapy group was there as his support.

The fourth year

Starting work raised enormous anxieties for Steve. He worked full time for a few months, building attendance at the group into his timetable. Precipitated by difficulties with work colleagues, Steve explored openly and in depth his real difficulties with trusting in relationships. Later, prompted by the powerfully annihilating music, I suggested he was also afraid of the 'murderous' things he might want to do to people who might hurt or abandon him, an indication of the enormously painful anger which he felt towards his parents. These feelings were towards his mother in particular, whom he felt had abandoned and rejected him and for whom he was never 'good enough'. Musically he started to take risks and to explore chordal progressions on the piano. He said he felt it was a relief to have some of these things understood and admitted that he usually compromised himself in relationships to avoid confrontation and then ended up feeling resentful. He related his dominant music to allowing himself to 'misbehave'; not playing nicely and supportively in the group allowed him to be anarchic whilst still maintaining some social responsibility as he became able to start to think about the effect of this on others. So at this point he allowed himself to be in touch with his most primitive destructive feelings, which was frightening, yet brought him some relief. This was a turning point: disagreement and conflict, as well as challenge to the therapist and her role, became possible.

This exploration brought some very difficult periods for Steve which later led to him moving on and coming to terms with his difficulties. At the time, however, it was a painful process. He developed colitis and was unable to go to work. He managed to attend the group regularly, none-theless, and brought with him an 'oppressive' presence. He acknowl-edged that the child part of him always wanted desperately to be helped, but owing to his abusive earlier experiences, he often felt in the role of victim and could not believe help would be forthcoming. He was striving to be an adult, which he understood as being able to recognize others on an equal footing. He was very reflective at this stage and at the end of the period he also started to address the issue of leaving the group. He was terrified at the thought, but knew he would have to face it at some point. He was silent throughout the whole of one session at this time and needed the group to accept him as he was, even when he felt at his most vulnerable. Here the boundaries between the internal and external space of the group were particularly important because Steve was allowing different aspects of himself to emerge within the safety of the group. This enabled him to feel held outside the group and to accept aspects of himself even if his work environment, for example, was difficult.

The fifth year

During this period Steve really began to work on his painful difficulties. He showed musically how he 'cut off' from people if they came too close; after improvisations he spoke of the fears underlying this. I felt most of all that the group offered the safe, containing, nurturing space that he desperately needed. He spoke of the conflicts he felt within relationships because of his destructive feelings, manifested sometimes in stabbing, discordant music. There was a sense that his music was 'breaking down' and that he was afraid of 'breaking down' himself.

In one sense he did 'break down', but owing to the support of his care co-ordinator, the music therapy group, his GP and one particular set of friends, he managed not to be hospitalized, although he was extremely depressed. He felt a failure owing to losing his job (which he eventually managed to go back to the following year). Dependency and trust became big topics for Steve and the group, together with the establishment of the group as a caring family rather than the frightening one which it had represented during the previous year. Gradually he returned to work.

Steve discussed how he could hide behind his music and how at the same time it had been the very vehicle that allowed him to come to terms with his destructiveness. He worried about whether he was too dependent on the group and so started to think once more about the prospect of leaving, this time working on it more and feeling more ready. He showed his ambivalence about being assertive in relationships and taking risks, but admitted that he had never thought he would have to make an ending. He thought that one day I (the therapist) would leave and that would be the end. He would not have to face up to doing the leaving. We acknowledged that leaving was going to be one of the most significant times in the therapy for him and the group as a whole. He gradually became more able to integrate his good and bad feelings.

The sixth year

Steve spent much of the final weeks exploring his relationship with the group, and in particular exploring his feelings about me. Had he become too dependent? What were the group and I feeling about him in terms of approval or disapproval? He now felt he wanted to go off and 'be an adult'. He discussed how affected he was by different people in the group and how he had taken risks in expressing competitive feelings towards some members, caring ones to others and confrontational ones at other times. He had survived all this, which seemed both a relief and a surprise to him. He had resumed his job and began to speak of starting to live his life. I reflected to him that following such a long therapy this was now going to be the best outcome: to live his life without therapy. He grappled with how he had always avoided endings or had them 'done to him' and wondered whether he had continued so long in the group owing to habit, fear of change, or fear of making an ending. In the past he had felt that in making an ending destructive parts of his personality had always taken over his whole life and not just the part of his life he was leaving (he feared 'breaking down' during this leaving process). He was extremely insightful at the very end of the group and the last few weeks were very poignant. He said he had bought a self-help CBT book. We discussed how this could be a way of helping to manage the ending and to give him a sense of a continuity. Perhaps he was now 'becoming his own therapist'; on the other hand, perhaps in order to end properly he had to undermine (or destroy) this form of music therapy by suggesting another, as an aspect of his destructive tendency. As a result he was able to voice some extremely sad emotions surrounding the ending and expressed these musically and verbally.

In the penultimate group there was a very intense atmosphere and he was healthily grappling with some angry feelings and struggling to keep the balance between his capacity for integration and his tendency to split off parts of himself. He discussed his contempt for some members and his feelings of envy and omnipotence. A very important earlier stage had been concerned with helping him recognize that the group would go on and survive without him. He admitted that leaving was like leaving a family. After so much work and preparation, in the final group he managed the whole session and made an appropriate, almost celebratory ending with all the members. He later followed this up with a letter indicating how important the group had been, although very hard work, and that after one week 'so far so good'. He was given the chance for a six-month, follow-up appointment which in fact took place after a year (at the time of preparing to write this chapter), as he had not initiated it previously.

Conclusion: the significance of time

Ending in this music therapy group came at the right time for Steve. As his time to leave approached I took a more proactive role. At the beginning he had seemed isolated, disabled and unable to make relationships. By the end he had a network of friends, work and other activities outside the group (including musically related ones, the latter being an important 'by-product' of the group). At the beginning he had suffered acute anxiety about going out and putting himself in the external arena. Physical difficulties had also seemed very disabling; by the end these were no longer significant 'symptoms'.

Another way of looking at the length of treatment involves taking account of the fact that a music therapy group necessarily involves the act of making music and that this way of relating through improvisation is unique to each patient's life. It is not the usual way of conversing or relating to others, but in this group it was a means that Steve found beneficial.

Thinking about discharge from the group involved stopping the action and the idea of relating through music in a way which was understood and accepted, whatever the external sounds produced. This unconditional aspect of the relationship sometimes accounts for the length of treatment. Attachment theory is central to an understanding of this process. Major aspects of the group, such as the consistency of membership and reliability of the therapist, needed time to reveal themselves, especially as Steve's experience of relationships had been that they were not consistent enough and that his family did not have his best interests at heart. The fact that he needed this long time to be convinced of this and for it to become a reality might call into question the benefits of his years of individual therapy. Perhaps something very different was happening in this group for him to allow himself to become involved in another long attachment and the risk of eventual separation that it involved. Other people were present who represented different elements for him in his life, to whom he became very committed and with whom he could relate on a musical, non-verbal and verbal level. This in turn enabled him to express strong emotions in a way that was not acceptable or possible in the external world. This process needed time to unfold and develop meaning.

Acknowledgement

I would like to thank Steve for allowing me to write about his experience in the group, and from whom in turn I learned so much. I would also like to acknowledge other group members and colleagues who have contributed indirectly to this process, and in particular Peter Berry, whose insights were invaluable during the last year of Steve's membership of the group.

References

Odell-Miller, H. (1991) 'The experience of one man with schizophrenia.' In K. Bruscia (ed) *Case Studies in Music Therapy.* Pennsylvania: Barcelona Publishers.

Odell-Miller, H. (1995) 'Why provide music therapy in the community for adults with mental health problems?' *British Journal of Music Therapy 9,* 1, 4–10.

Odell-Miller, H. (2001) 'Music therapy and its relationship to psychoanalysis.' In Y. Seale and I. Streng *Where Analysis Meets the Arts.* London: Karnac.

Walshe, J. (1995) 'The external space in group work' *Group Analysis 28,* 413–427.

Winnicott, D.W. (1971) *Playing and Reality.* London: Tavistock.

CHAPTER 5

Music Therapy with Elderly Adults

Rachel Darnley-Smith

I want to present some thoughts in this chapter about group music therapy with elderly adults. I shall be describing the work very much from a practitioner's point of view, presenting my own process of trying to understand the client's responses to the different forms of music making which are possible within group music therapy. As many readers will be aware, the practice of music therapy in the UK is based upon live music making, at the heart of which is free improvisation. We work with a basic assumption that in encouraging the client or clients to make whatever sounds they like, we are inviting them to present themselves as human beings through the medium of sound. The therapist facilitates the emergence of the client's self through music by also playing, and thereby developing an interactive therapeutic relationship so that the musical sounds become central to the client and therapist's encounter with each other. Many music therapists in the UK also work with an assumption that to encourage the client to make any sounds they like, is to encourage all music that emerges or seems relevant, ranging from free improvisation to music which is pre-composed.

However, particularly with elderly adults, such freedom can create intense anxieties in both the client and therapist. It is not always a simple matter within a group setting to find a musical place where group members and therapist can be together and come to know each other. Why might this be so? The relationship between the elderly client and the therapist, who is often younger, brings particular dynamics and anxieties to the therapeutic process which I suggest frequently become manifest in the music making. Porter (1991) writes of the 'fear of failure in the presence of the older figure' (Stern and Lovestone 2000, p.501). Martindale (1998) writes of the potential clash in the unconscious needs of the elderly person and their younger carers. The elderly person may project their need for care from an idealized daughter or son onto their younger carer, whereas the younger carer may be at a time in their life when they are psychically engaged with individuating from their own parents. In music therapy such a psychodynamic process of transference and countertransference can involve the therapist feeling trapped in the role of being the idealized 'all-good music lady or man', the only 'real' musician in the room and therefore the only person capable of contributing to sessions.

The main question which has arisen from my own day-to-day clinical practice has been how to work with such intense transference relationships, and how to incorporate all kinds of music making, as seems appropriate in any one moment. In particular how to move between singing pre-composed songs, which elderly clients frequently expect from a music therapy session, and free improvisation, towards which they often express much bemusement and anxiety. Through either form of music making, interpersonal relating can happen at an exploratory and meaningful level. For some groups, however, either form of music making can feel 'wrong' to the music therapist in any given moment, even if it is being actively wanted by clients, leaving the therapist feeling anxious and wondering what to do next. Furthermore, combining songs and improvisation can feel an unsatisfactory way to work, as it sometimes means an awkward shift between facilitating patients to 'play what you like' and playing a particular piece where notions of 'right' and 'wrong' cannot be avoided.

I am going to describe part of the process of facilitating a music therapy group (Darnley-Smith 1996) for elderly adult patients who all experienced short-term memory loss resulting from the early stages of senile dementia. They were attending a day hospital for assessment of their needs and psychological support. They were between 70 and 90 years of age.

Clinical vignette

The group had been meeting for almost 12 months. The group members as usual have been invited to play whatever they want. Michael begins from the guitar, gently letting his thumb catch each string as he drops his hand across the instrument. This has the effect of a repeated pattern of six notes, starting on a highest string and ending on the lowest. In response the therapist plays a low E on the piano and the co-therapist, a nurse, taps the gato drum at the same speed as Michael.

At the same time, beginning just after Michael, Brian plays the bass drum, playing faster and faster beats which turn into a galloping type rhythm before settling into a knocking sound, where some notes are emphasized but not in time with Michael's guitar playing.

Kathryn plays scales on the metallaphone at approximately the same tempo as Michael, although this may not have been deliberately in time with him. The therapist roughly matches the pace of the two patients, gradually incorporating the knocking beats of Brian, as Daisy begins to pluck at the individual notes of the auto harp.

Each member has an individual musical 'cell' of an idea, which they play repeatedly, mostly in isolation, but for fleeting moments there appears to be some meeting. The therapist listens to their playing and tries to connect with some of their sounds whilst holding a bass note as a pedal note.

This was typical of the music making in sessions at this time, and the sense of disconnection which I felt between group members and myself was extremely uncomfortable. I tried to introduce structures which might help to make sessions feel more manageable and create a clearer sense of stopping and starting. I introduced a hello song and also suggested songs, or encouraged suggestions from group members. However, the shift from free improvisation into structured music making within a session felt too sudden and somehow like an imposition, rather than freely arising out of what was already happening. Furthermore the group members regularly expressed their doubts about musical skill, worrying that their music was not 'real music', 'just noise'. A number of writers comment upon this issue, some doubting the suitability of working with free improvisation at all with this client group. Esmé Towse (1995, p.328), in her discussion of music therapy techniques with elderly people, writes of the difficulty that the lay person may have with free improvisation, which 'produces sounds which are often atonal and generally unmelodic ... and can sound like random noise'. Towse questions the relevance for an elderly person of creating 'atonal' music if, as is usual, it has not been part of their lifelong musical experience and they can see no reason for doing so. Bright (1997, p.137) raises a similar concern 'that we must not perceive impro-vised music therapy as the only "real" music therapy [and] that we do not add to the confusion by playing music which is unknown and strange'. Clair (2000, p.82) comments on the 'struggle to establish a non-threatening environment that encourages singing and dispels indi-viduals fears and anxieties of retribution for inadequate musical products' which she sees as a 'prerequisite to the development of therapeutic outcomes with singing as the medium of intervention'.

However, I began to think about the anxieties of these particular group members concerning musical skill as reflecting part of a wider anxiety they were experiencing in their lives in general. I began to feel less need to structure sessions and more open to what individuals might be trying to express. With this group, improvised music was the way in which they gradually used the sessions, as they became more trusting of the group space. Through what they talked about and how they played, they frequently conveyed and pinpointed anxieties and feelings of depression. They and the music therapist related their feelings not only to a growing realization that they were losing mental capabilities, but also to other life events, mostly losses which reflected their stage of life.

Daisy's sister died during her time in the group and she was losing her hearing. Brian's wife became very ill and was in hospital with little time to live, and he was told that his children wanted him to live in a home out of London, away from his home of 50 years. Kathryn had more severe dementia, was consistently anxious and could never settle. Six months later, Kathryn had left the group, and Bert had recently joined. He was an inpatient in the hospital waiting for a place in an old people's home and had sung in a church choir as a child. At first he had been openly scornful of the music therapy sessions. By now he had begun to find a way of improvising music that seemed to suit him. The music had completely changed over this period. These group members became far more assured in their use of the music as a way of being themselves and being together, although verbally they continued to express grave doubts as regards their musical skills. Here is a description of an improvisation which took place at this time. Michael was absent from the session.

> The therapist is playing a progression of repeated major and minor chords, with added sixths and sevenths on the piano in a repeated quaver pattern, reminiscent of a minimalist style of composition. The pace is fast and the therapist is matched in an even rhythm by her co-worker on the gato drum. Daisy plays the maracas and Brian plays the small drum in the same repeated quaver pattern, playing with vigour. Bert plays the cymbal adding a triplet rhythm to the music. The overall feel is one of integration. The therapist decides to change what she is playing and 'breaks out' into an ascending melody in octaves climbing up into higher pitches, and signifying some kind of ending to the improvisation. The group members stop briefly but then continue. Bert plays two long notes on the cymbal. Daisy responds to him as if in dialogue by shaking the maracas. He answers her with quicker sounds at a similar tempo. Brian joins in with a firm beat on the drum, introducing a new pattern. This dialogue continues for three or four minutes, listened to by the two therapists.

This improvisation, in particular, could be said to reflect the dynamic of group sessions, expressing feelings the group members have towards each other. They seemed pleased to see each other each week, although apparently they rarely spoke outside the sessions in other parts of the day hospital. The two men were actively sympathetic towards Daisy at the time of her sister's death, expressing concern and sadness for her. This three-way relationship began to develop through a weekly routine whereby Daisy would both musically and verbally encourage the two men to compete for her attention in a flirtatious and playful manner. This they did, joining in with 'the game' and making us all laugh. As the group came to an end, all the group members were able to express their attachment to each other quite explicitly through the quality of interaction in their music making, which had now become more spontaneous and relaxed.

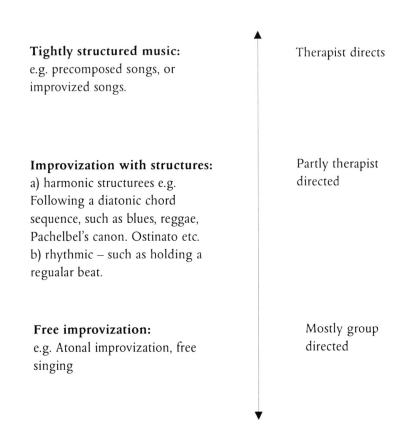

Tightly structured music:
e.g. precomposed songs, or
improvized songs.

Therapist directs

Improvization with structures:
a) harmonic structurees e.g.
Following a diatonic chord
sequence, such as blues, reggae,
Pachelbel's canon. Ostinato etc.
b) rhythmic – such as holding a
regualar beat.

Partly therapist
directed

Free improvization:
e.g. Atonal improvization, free
singing

Mostly group
directed

Figure 5.1 Continuum of musical structures to be found in music therapy

I have written elsewhere (Darnley-Smith 1993, Darnley-Smith and Patey, in press) describing a continuum relating freely improvised music and pre-composed music (see Figure 5.1). Using this idea I have considered the amount of musical structure a music therapist provides or does not provide. Along this continuum the music therapist can freely follow or lead the client as intuitively seems right. The psychoanalytic technique of free association (Rycroft 1979, p.54), so closely akin to musical free improvisation, is particularly helpful in supporting a belief that if we follow our clients' music wherever it takes us, we will be engaging with them in authentic self-expression. Averil Williams (2001), music therapist and Jungian analyst, has described the potential for free improvisation to be a kind of 'acoustic dreaming' deriving from our unconscious. Indeed, like our dreaming in sleep, freely improvised music often finds its own form as it goes along. By definition its content, outcome, or length cannot be predicted. It may end gradually or suddenly, it may feel full of life and feeling, or it may feel empty and flat. I have found it helpful to begin to include pre-composed material in a group session with the analogy of dreaming in mind. Where pre-composed songs are allowed to occur freely in a group, either through the suggestion of the therapist or patient or just by being spontaneously sung, together with free improvisation, they too could be understood as part of a dynamic process of 'acoustic dreaming'. I want to advocate that this process of moving between musical structures in improvised music therapy again is in itself an improvisation, involving the facilitation of spontaneous choices which might allow unconscious material to emerge, whether through improvised sound or a pre-composed song.

Clinical vignette

I am now going to describe a sustained piece of music therapy work with a patient whom I shall call Harry (Darnley-Smith, in Press). During a two-year period of music therapy, after his assessment he felt unable to improvise and preferred to sing songs. Harry was a 78-year-old Jewish man who had grown up in Glasgow. He had a diagnosis of mild dementia, mostly manifested through short-term memory loss, when he was referred to a mental health elderly day hospital music therapy group. He presented as a very articulate man, but partly due to his memory impairment, there were large gaps in his history. Six months previously he had been found wandering lost in the streets and was taken into hostel accommodation by a charity organization for the homeless. The day hospital was working with the charity organization to help to find him long-term accommodation and also to assess his other needs. His referral to the music therapy group was based upon his expressed enthusiasm for music and his often dismissive attitude to the talking and activity groups.

Harry came to two individual assessment sessions and sang with unusual gusto whilst I played the piano. He spoke nostalgically of having played the harmonica a long time ago but felt unable to do this any more. Together we played the percussion instruments on this first occasion and generally improvised musical sounds. He improvised vocally with great ease and feeling around melodies either of tunes that he knew or in a style he was familiar with (e.g. blues). I realized in the first session what a strong attachment he had to music. In his first 'group' session he obviously found the experience of having to share my attention extremely difficult and for the first time I had a sense of his emotional fragility. He rejected any offers of music making and expressed no interest in the other members of the group. He began to talk with some tearful distress about his wife's death and the subsequent conflict and estrangement from his children. Having gained the attention of myself and the group, he began spontaneously to sing a medley of songs: 'Night and Day', 'Let's Face the Music and Dance', 'The Lady is a Tramp', 'It was a Fine Romance but now It's Over', 'You Are So Easy to Love', etc. The rest of the group and I joined in the best we could by playing along or, where we knew the tunes and words, by singing.

Soon after this beginning, as it was summer I went on annual leave and the group had a break for three weeks. When I returned I discovered that Harry had been expressing strong feelings about me to other members of the day hospital staff. It was as though he had needed to keep me alive during my absence by professing his wish to others to marry me. During the first music therapy session after the break, he seemed extremely distressed. He didn't want to sing or play and just kept asking me personal questions about my life and 'holiday'. I felt some guilt that in engaging him in music therapy I had invited him to connect with an emotional part of himself that was vulnerable, intensely lonely and in need of contact with another human being. He made me feel extremely powerful but at the same time rather overpowered, as I felt unsure how to respond and indeed felt flattered by his attentiveness and praise for my musical abilities.

The sessions continued into the autumn, during which a pattern emerged. Harry would attend sessions regularly, sitting in the same chair each week and rejecting instruments which were offered to him. Sessions always contained a mixture of pre-composed and freely improvised music, sometimes including special music to begin and end sessions. The contents were never planned, always in themselves improvised. Where there were pauses, Harry would always fill them saying, 'Come on, let's sing something', or he would simply start singing. He had a wide repertoire of mostly British and American romantic songs from the 1940s, which he would sing in the form of a medley, 'leaping' from one song into the next. If I tried to encourage him to join us in playing the instruments to improvise, he would usually refuse, saying, 'I'm no good with my hands, I keep telling you.' If I tried to ask him how he felt about his participation in the group, his relationship to me, or his relationship to others, he would retort 'talk, talk, talk', as though we were embroiled in a lover's row and he was needing to defend himself. He became stuck in a pattern of interrupting other group members with his songs and dominating the sessions. At the same time I kept trying to find a way of responding to his need for special contact with me and the powerful sense of loss and rejection he continued to convey when talking about life experiences. I tried to understand the guilt I felt in not agreeing to his demands. That is to say, as I worked hard to process feelings of flattery and of being seduced, I felt unconfident in my attempts to set boundaries around his domination of group sessions.

Other group members had by now begun to contribute songs such as 'What Shall We Do with the Drunken Sailor', 'Autumn Leaves', 'Amazing Grace', 'La Vie en Rose', 'Danny Boy', 'Summertime', etc. As if in response, Harry's music no longer felt alive with energy and feeling, but instead like angry demands for individual attention which in turn made me feel angry with him. It felt as though when he was singing in the group nothing else could happen and the other group members simply had to wait. Everything was on his terms; the relationship was one way. This impasse lasted with varying degrees of intensity for about eight months, during which time he moved into a residential home which was permanent accommodation. The following autumn a series of events leading up to his discharge from the day hospital and the music therapy group affected the relationship, allowing me to provide more containment for him and to be more consciously therapeutic, less caught up. He began to suggest different songs, sometimes sung in different languages and sometimes in response to the nationalities and first languages of other members of the group. There was a German song that he began to sing one day which seemed to prompt him to talk about his terrifying experiences during the war of watching people he counted as friends being blown up in front of him and of running for his life: 'I had ten seconds to get out' he would frequently say. He would speak of the nightmares he still had. It was as though he was becoming more trusting of the group space. This also coincided with a series of concerts being organized in his home, from which he brought the programmes to show me and which prompted some discussion in the group.

About the same time, during one session I suddenly found a new way to respond to his regular medley of songs, which in retrospect was reminiscent of our joint music making in the first assessment session. Instead of simply trying to sing with him, I now improvised around the melodies; instead of just singing the tune I improvised harmonies and counter-melodies, whilst he continued with the original. This was a move that he accepted readily and joined in actively and which also had the effect of involving other group members at the same time. It seemed remarkable that through this music making we were beginning to be able to link together as a group at last. I felt that I had found the musical meeting ground where he could be creative in relationship to me and the rest of the group, and at the same time feel some attention and nourishment. Three months later we set a discharge date for him from the day hospital. He was now settled in his new home, having been there a year, and seemed more secure in himself having made some contacts amongst staff and residents. In his last two sessions we sang through much of his medley which now had regained its expressive quality, but this time had a feel of a much firmer relationship that was being bade farewell.

The painful dilemmas I experienced with this man and his disruption of the group over a long period of time prompted once again the question posed at the beginning of this chapter. A group in which there was a mixture of improvised music and pre-composed music had often felt awkward and unspontaneous. How was it possible to move from freely improvised music into singing songs which required prior knowledge, not just in terms of melody, but also technical matters such as words and harmonies?

During the same period in this music therapy group with Harry there was an Irish patient called Annie. Annie had mild dementia but severe dysphasia, which meant that she had great difficulty verbally expressing herself. I realized from her few words and her musical responses to playing and singing music that she had grown up making music in this free way, moving from singing to playing back to singing again. With Annie, in addition to conceptualizing the facilitation of a group as a process of 'acoustic dreaming' or free association, I was reminded of how a similar process of music making can happen outside music therapy settings.

During a holiday in the Republic of Ireland I spent a lot of time listening to traditional folk music in pubs and bars. I noticed in places where the musicians were less commercially aware of tourists such as myself there was a type of freefloating process occurring. The musicians would move through a repertoire apparently effortlessly, without a planned programme or having to remember what was next, each one taking turn to suggest the next item, or one item simply merging into another. Sometimes they would sing songs or play jigs and reels. One musician might go to the bar and order more drinks and whilst this was happening another item would start without him or her. Occasionally one of the audience would request a song or be invited to contribute a song, encouraged with the words, 'Come on, it doesn't matter what, just sing something.' Over the course of an evening a rich variety of moods and energies would be conveyed through the music making.

How does this link with music therapy? The music appeared to happen with great spontaneity, as though with little conscious planning. The sequence of what happened appeared to be the song or piece that came to mind. This music bonded people together in the moment. To me even as an outsider, and a British one at that, there was a kind of non-verbal welcome. The bonding was personal because it appeared to be spontaneous and in response to the musicians playing together in a particular place at a particular time with a particular audience.

Conclusion

In this chapter I have shown how music therapy can facilitate a creative process of music making and relating in groups of elderly adults; how reference to dynamics of transference and countertransference between elderly adults and younger therapists can inform some of the musical tensions to be found in group music therapy. I have also shown how the musical contents of a session can emerge through a process of free association which has here been characterized as 'acoustic dreaming'. This 'dreaming' process can take place whether the music which emerges is freely improvised or highly structured as with pre-composed song. Through case examples I have tried to show that such a process is highly relevant to elderly patients, particularly where they are experiencing cognitive impairment. Free improvisation alone might feel too unstructured and the planned or conscious use of songs alone might not address unconscious needs of those patients taking part. A freely improvised use of music can enable the spontaneous building of a group culture, and facilitate an unconscious process of 'acoustic dreaming', through which emotional expression and interaction may occur. Finally similar musical processes may take place in other settings where traditional folk music is performed.

Note

An earlier version of this chapter was given as a paper presentation 'Group Music Therapy for Older Adults with Memory Loss: Reflections upon Meaning and Purpose.' European Conference of Music Therapy, Naples 2001.

References

Bright, R. (1997) *Wholeness in Later Life*. London: Jessica Kingsley Publishers.

Clair, A. A. (2000) 'The importance of singing with elderly patients.' In D. Aldridge (ed) *Music Therapy in Dementia Care*. London: Jessica Kingsley Publishers.

Darnley-Smith, R. (1993) 'The music therapist as group leader: a proposal for a practical model.' Unpublished paper presented at the Seventh World Congress of Music Therapy, Vittoria-Gastiez, Spain.

Darnley-Smith, R. (1996) 'Experiencing senile dementia as bereavement – using music therapy as a response.' *Music Therapy in the Third Age*. London: British Society for Music Therapy. Conference proceedings.

Darnley-Smith, R. (in press) 'Psychodynamic music therapy in the care of older adults.' In S. Evans and J. Garner (eds) *Talking Over the Years: A Handbook of Psychodynamic Psychotherapy with Older People.* London: Routledge.

Darnley-Smith, R. and Patey, H.M. (in press) *Music Therapy.* London: Sage.

Martindale, B. (1998) 'On ageing, dying, death and eternal life.' *Psychoanalytic Psychotherapy 12,* 3, 259–270.

Porter, R. (1991) 'The elderly.' In J. Holmes (ed) *Textbook of Psychotherapy in Psychiatric Practice.* Edinburgh: Churchill Livingstone.

Rycroft, C. (1979) *A Critical Dictionary of Psychoanalysis.* Harmondsworth: Penguin Books Ltd.

Stern, J. and Lovestone, S. (2000) 'Therapy with the elderly: introducing psychodynamic psychotherapy to the multi-disciplinary team.' *International Journal of Geriatric Psychiatry 15,* 500–505.

Towse, E. (1995) 'Listening and accepting.' In T. Wigram, B. Saperston and R. West (eds) *The Art and Science of Music Therapy.* Amsterdam: Harwood.

Williams, A. (2001) Personal communication.

CHAPTER 6

'There's No Getting Away From Anything in Here'

A Music Therapy Group within an Inpatient Programme for Adults with Eating Disorders

Helen Loth

There is something extraordinarily challenging and powerful about working in a group setting with people with eating disorders. At times, such is the strength of feeling evoked in me of despondency and emptiness, of being uncreative and deskilled, that I have questioned both my practice and the appropriateness of music therapy with this client group. At other times, I am convinced that the qualities of shared musical improvisation can powerfully address many of the difficulties faced by these clients. In seeking to understand this contrast, I have become more aware of how the experience of music therapy can be a very disturbing one for people with eating disorders. Put simply, if all your energies are directed towards remaining unaware of your feelings and emotions, then to hear them expressed in sound for everyone to hear can be terrifying. The person who makes this happen, the therapist, is a persecuting bully for putting them through it. She is 'making' them be aware of and think about things they do not wish to know about. She can 'see' things they want to hide. Hence the comment from a young anorexic man in his first group session: 'There's no getting away from anything in here.' In this chapter, I am going to explore what it is that makes music therapy such a challenging medium for these clients and also what makes it so effective.

Some thoughts on the pathology of eating disorders

There are many theories as to why and how a person develops an eating disorder and the reasons will be different for each person. Of the several psychodynamic theories, I will describe briefly those that I find most useful and relevant in my thinking about the music therapy group.

Eating disorders are frequently thought about in psychodynamic terms as defences. There has often been a disturbance in the early mother–infant relationship. Whether because of a real or a perceived failure of environment or lack of a containing maternal figure, patients experience need and dependency as intolerable and develop defences against them. In Kleinian terms they do not successfully negotiate the paranoid-schizoid position and carry into adult life the use of splitting and projection as their way of relating to the world (Klein 1946).

The eating disorder can sometimes be understood in the context of the family experience of the sufferer. Families may be enmeshed, there may be little differentiation between family members, or the child may have had difficulties separating from a parent or vice versa. In some instances the child may be caught in an unaware enactment of the parents' inner worlds, or something unacknowledged that is taking place in their relationship. Psychic pain is transmuted into physical symptoms. A refusal of food may be a child's concrete way of refusing to take in the mother's pain.

Much of the psychopathology of eating disorders can be characterized by what psychotherapist Gianna Williams describes as 'impairments in taking from another'. She describes a subgroup of patients who develop a particular type of defence which she names the 'no entry' system of defence (1997a). This is a reversal of the 'container/contained' relationship in which the parent receives the infant's projections, contains and metabolizes them and returns them in a more manageable form. One way that this relationship can break down is when the parent is unable to receive or contain these projections and returns them in their raw form, which the infant experiences as an attack. However, in the 'no entry' system the roles are reversed and the infant has been used as a 'receptacle' of the *parents'* projections of their anxieties which have not been metabolized or digested by the parent. The child is not able to digest these projections and so experiences them as 'persecutory foreign bodies'. The 'no entry' system therefore functions to block access to 'any input experienced as potentially intrusive and persecutory' (Williams 1997a, p.121). Other children, Williams proposes, remain 'porous' to the parental projections and their eating disorder manifests predominantly as bulimia. This theory goes some way to explain the extraordinary depth of feeling which the therapist can experience in the countertransference, which I alluded to earlier. As Williams says (1997b, p.928): 'I have often noticed in my countertransference that "no entry" patients can break and enter into me with powerful projections of an intensity that parallels their dread of being invaded.'

In the treatment setting, people with eating disorders arouse strong feelings in staff, just as they do within the family. This is put succinctly by Land (2000) in describing anorexia as 'a destructive triumph over the hungry/dependent infant self and over the mother (or nurse or therapist), who is feared and hated but also despised, and whose food (care, concern, therapeutic effort) is summarily rejected'.

Whatever the aetiology of the eating disorder, there are some common symptoms in addition to those that are food related. These include a lack of sense of self, extremely low self-esteem, difficulties in forming and maintaining relationships and an inability to tolerate and express feelings and emotions. How these are manifested in the music therapy group will be described later in the chapter.

Eating disorders and group work

Some eating disorders units are run purely on a group therapy programme as it is felt this is the most effective way of addressing the problems of this client group: 'Groups have therapeutic possibilities that are in addition to, and quite distinct from, those found in individual work' (MacKenzie and Harper-Guiffre 1992, p.29). Difficulties with families, siblings, parent figures and peer groups can all be re-enacted and potentially addressed within the group therapy setting in a way that is not possible in individual work.

Group composition

Whilst in group psychotherapy the model of a mixed rather than homogeneous group is generally favoured, it has been argued that people with eating disorders do not do as well because their psychopathology is often more hidden and they are only too able to appear socially capable and in control. The group may not be able to challenge or address this (MacKenzie and Harper-Guiffre, 1992). When working with eating disorders groups, it has in the past been recommended that anorexics and bulimics should not be mixed, but provided for separately. It is felt that anorexics who purely restrict and control their intake can have very different personalities and problems from clients with bulimia who are overwhelmed by their impulses and lack of control. However, many clients have a mixed anorexic/bulimic picture and these issues, including the rivalry and disparagement each group feels towards the other, can be usefully worked with together, as is now more often the case.

The music therapy group

There is a growing body of literature and research to support the case for music therapy as meaningful intervention for children and adults who have eating disorders. The majority of this concerns individual work, (Frederiksen 1999; Robarts 1994; Robarts 2000; Robarts and Sloboda 1994; Sloboda 1993, 1994, Smeijsters 1996; Smeijsters and van den Hurk 1993), but little has been written about working with these clients in a group.

The existing literature on groups describes work within eating disorders programmes, often for inpatients. Justice (1994) uses interventions including music reinforced relaxation techniques, structured group techniques and music and imagery techniques. Goiricelaya (1988) uses activities including improvisation in addition to exploring issues through discussion of song lyrics, song writing and stress management. Nolan (1989) describes work with groups of bulimic patients in which musical improvisation functions as a Winnicottian transitional object, which facilitates the interruption of the binge–purge cycle. He views improvisation as useful in helping bring about an awareness of feelings and emotions in the moment.

Individual work may be favoured because of the difficulties in addressing individuals' problems within a group. The nature of their defences or resistances can produce enormous feelings of hostility towards the therapist and a corresponding powerlessness in the therapist. Frank-Schwebel (2001) talks of her difficulties running a music therapy group with these clients and identifies the group's hostility as being the cause of 'the stomach ache I would develop regularly on the eve of the group meeting and my acute feelings of not wanting to go to work'. Frank-Schwebel describes how she overcame the problems and came to focus on her understanding of the sound-object in the group and on sound as a transformational experience. She uses a variety of musical mediums, including bringing favourite pieces, listening to classical and popular music, lying on mattresses, dance and live improvisations. Whilst I too have searched for ways to work with these clients as a group, I have tried to retain the basic model of music therapy that I use. This is a broadly based psychodynamic approach using improvisation and discussion. I have attempted to make sense of the group dynamics through thinking about the nature of the pathology of eating disorders and how these are reflected in the music and in the way the group play together.

The setting of the group

The group takes place within a specialist inpatient programme for adults suffering from severe eating disorders. These include patients with anorexia nervosa, whose weight is critically low or has been very low for a long time and who have not responded to outpatient work and patients with severe bulimia nervosa who need a period of symptom interruption in order to try and regain some control over their eating pattern. The aim of the unit is to help with the eating difficulties, to try to establish a healthy eating pattern and increase weight if appropriate, whilst also beginning to address the underlying issues associated with the eating disorder.

The unit has a large treatment team providing medical, nursing and dietary care, psychotherapeutic, educational and practical group activities and weekly individual therapy.

Treatment philosophy

The unit uses the concept of splitting in its model of treatment (Klein, 1946). It is understood that these clients are often using paranoid-schizoid mechanisms. The treatment team provides fertile ground for the projection of split-off aspects of themselves. It is accepted therefore that in contact with different people and different sorts of therapies and activities, patients will behave differently. All these different aspects are brought together at the weekly team meetings, at which each patient is discussed. Each team member who has had significant contact with that patient will report back and then we will think together about her. The idea that the team tries to help the patient 'put herself together', that is move towards the depressive position (Klein, 1935), is an underlying assumption of the team, but one which can be difficult to hold on to in practice, and the team can find itself acting out the patient's internal conflicts. It is within this context that the music therapy group has its place.

Group composition

Just as in the group work described earlier, I have found that the music therapy group works best when there is a mix of patients with anorexia and bulimia. The music of a group of restricting anorexics can be starved and impoverished. There can be a great resistance to playing, the instruments are toyed with and tiny sounds made, and no one wants to be heard to make more sound than anyone else. This echoes the situation in the dining room when the need to eat is in conflict with rivalry to eat the least and intense anger at those who manage it (not eating) better. The addition of more impulsive bulimics to the group adds noise and liveliness to the music. The anorexics can be envious of the sounds the bulimics are able to make and they have more freedom to play themselves as they can 'hide' beneath the levels of the 'bulimic' music, as well as compete with them. The group has a slow-open structure with a maximum of seven members.

Purpose of the group

Perhaps the most important aspect of the group is that through music the patients have the possibility of experiencing themselves, and themselves in relation to others, in a different way. The work of the group changes and relates to the individual journey each patient is taking as they progress through the programme. Material may be brought or emerge during the session related to understanding the eating disorder and what lies behind it, patterns of communication with others, family and sibling problems and issues arising from being on the unit. Patients may also find a way of experiencing and expressing emotions that have been repressed for a long time, as well as those aroused by the pressures of the treatment programme. In thinking about what is happening in the group and in the music, I need to be able to move flexibly between group and individual meaning. We will at times focus on an individual and at others think of an individual's contributions as an expression of something for the whole group. Talking about a patient holding or expressing something on behalf of the others can be a less invasive and threatening experience for these patients, and allow them not to feel persecuted by being singled out.

Therapeutic alliance

I have found it necessary to establish some form of connection between the patient, myself and the instruments before they join the group; something I do not necessarily do with other client groups. When faced with the music therapy group, the feelings of inadequacy, embarrassment and humiliation may be so overwhelming that defences such as hostility, mockery and devaluing are evoked very powerfully. It can become almost impossible for them to accept anything from the group or me and they are only able to participate from a position of contemptuous superiority, from which it is hard to move without the feeling of 'losing face'. There have occasionally been times when the group has been effectively destroyed and rendered unable to function by this.

Before a patient joins the group therefore, I take her into the music room and explain what happens in the group and what music therapy is about. I ask about her previous experience of music and her relationship to it now. I then encourage her to try out all the instruments, explaining the range of sounds available and the potential musical 'vocabulary'. This does something to lessen the potency of her fear in the group so that she does not have to act entirely from a position of defence, but can allow herself to engage with the group a little. The situation is analogous to a mother bringing a child into a family meal in which a huge array of new and exotic food is presented from which she has to fill her plate, whilst everyone is tucking in or sitting staring at their own empty plate. The child reacts with panic. By taking her alone into the dining room before-hand and encouraging her to have a little taste of everything first, she can come to the table with a little more confidence in her ability to join the meal.

Group attendance

It can be difficult to establish a therapeutic alliance when attendance of the group is compulsory. In the unit, all groups are compulsory. When there is a choice about attendance, patients can find it hard to say 'yes' as this would be seen as acknowledging desire or need and openly accepting help. Patients often feel in a dilemma when given the opportunity to refuse. This is a key dynamic in eating disorders and is shown in its extreme form by patients who ask to be fed by nasogastric tube. They say that they want to eat and do not want to die, but they are unable to feed themselves. In this case, patients may prefer to be given no option, as that is the only way they can allow themselves to have something.

Aspects of eating disorders addressed in the music therapy group

There are several aspects to the pathology of eating disorders and the way they are experienced which are particularly evoked by the music therapy group setting.

Experiencing emotions

A common feature of people with eating disorders is an inability to experience and process painful or difficult emotions. The eating disorder can function to stop these feelings intruding. By controlling need and appetite, they are able to control their feelings and exist in a state of indifference to pain. The effects of starvation can also include a light-headedness, a high, which is like an anaesthetized state. As the patients increase their intake of food on the unit, so the feelings and thoughts which they have been trying to keep out return. This can be quite unbearable and they do not know what to do with them. Reactions may include outbursts of temper and anger, self-injurious behaviour such as cutting and burning, as well as the eating disorder associated mechanisms of vomiting and over-exercising. Music therapy can be a place to bring these feelings. Group members can use the instruments, sometimes in a cathartic way, not only to release tensions, but also to express and experience these feelings in a new way through the music. This can be a containing experience, allowing patients to process their feelings and ultimately reintegrate them. It is very striking how group members' music changes over time in the group, as their eating disorder improves or deteriorates. The following example illustrates how one group managed to go beyond the cathartic experience of playing and discover other possibilities.

> This group had been meeting for a few sessions together. The group began by playing 'what they came in with'. This started out as rather random sounds, building into somewhat chaotic loud playing, with little interaction between group members. People seemed to be focusing on their own needs. Felicity in particular struck various drums as hard as she could and shook the maracas forcefully. The players moved around various instruments restlessly. I remained at one of the pianos, picking up on the searching restless quality of the playing. After about ten minutes the sound began to die down, but instead of finishing then as it usually did, the group fell into a slow beat that was shared by all. Felicity, on the tympani, maintained this beat, varying her drum and cymbal. On the piano, I was able to play slow chords that were tonally matched by Millie on the second piano. Within this we interwove simple motifs and melodies. What was striking was the sense of space in the playing. It was very slow with an open texture and I found

myself feeling very moved by it. Eventually the music began to grow quieter and came to an end. Following a comfortable silence the group members made some comments on the piece. They acknowledged how different it felt, that they were really playing together and that this had felt very satisfying. Felicity said that she had been thinking about my words of the previous week, when I had wondered aloud what might happen if the group were to go beyond the need to bang out their frustrations in order to gain relief. She said she had carried on playing after she had done this and was very surprised at what had happened, that she had been able to rest and listen and had become aware of the others. She found that she liked sharing in the music with them.

This was an example of how the group was able to use the music not only to express something of the anorexic state and to gain some relief through the playing, but also to experience letting go of this and finding a new way to relate and interact with each other.

One of the things which makes this client group difficult to be in is the rawness of the unprocessed, undigested painful emotions which are 'poured out' into the music. Frank-Schwebel (2001) uses the 'music-as-food' metaphor in her description of the group work. She suggests it is possible to think of a music therapy session as 'a pre-cooked meal, a buffet or an opportunity for a binge' and that the group's responses can parallel their attitudes to food. They could 'accept, reject, hesitate over or even "vomit" the sound-food served and would then "cook" something else'.

The music can be used as a defence. Some groups make a huge amount of noise, which rather than being an expression of feelings which allows thought and reflection, is an expelling of feelings which are undigested and allow no interaction with other group members or the therapist.

Another form of defence is the denial of meaning. If I comment on how something sounded – 'sad, hesitant' for example – the response might be 'that's because we don't know how to play the instruments'. My comments can be easily heard as a criticism or attack, which have to be defended against.

Control

The issue of control has been well documented in the study of eating disorders, as well as in the music therapy literature. Patients' attempts to control their musical output for fear of doing it wrong or unintentionally letting something out are common features. In the group setting, the person, even if able to control his or her own output, cannot control that of the others and cannot control their *input*, that is, what they hear. It is easy to see how for patients whose anorexia functions as a 'no entry' defence system, as described earlier, music therapy can be experienced as a persecutory attempt to breach their barriers and in this case to penetrate through their ears.

> Leila, a young woman with severe anorexic and bulimic symptoms, would with reluctance regularly attend the group. On entering the room she would go to the same chair, sit on it and tuck her feet on the chair, hug her knees and drop her head onto them. When the music began, she would cover her face with her hair, shut her eyes, and often block her ears with her hands. She could at times be seen to be shaking or sobbing. Occasionally she would look up panic stricken at the door, but never ran out. When able to talk in the group she said she could not bear to hear the emotions in the music, because it expressed what she was feeling but did not want to feel. She therefore tried to stop any of the experience entering her body. Leila had been the recipient of many unwanted sexual experiences, which she had felt powerless to prevent. In the music therapy group, she could not prevent these 'unwanted' emotional experiences by leaving the room, but sat in the middle of them, and tried to 'not hear'. Leila was using a 'no entry' defence system, and was experiencing the musical sounds as 'persecutory foreign bodies' as described by Williams (1997a). I think there was also a wish and a hope in Leila that things could be different. She did, over time, become a little more able to listen to the sounds, and began to participate in the playing in a very tentative manner as the

time of her discharge approached, and she was beginning to engage more with the outside world.

Sharing and competition

One of the striking features of the music in the group is how unconnected each person's playing can be from the others. The anorexic's ability to freeze out everyone else and not notice what is going on around her is carried into the music. Bulimics often cut right across everyone with their loud surges and uncontrolled outbursts of playing. In their list of 'musical symptoms' of anorexics in individual work Robarts and Sloboda (1994) include 'difficulty in empathic interaction with the therapist' (p.9). The difficulties in interaction are exacerbated by the group setting, bringing the possibility of addressing them very directly. Issues of competition and envy, characteristics of patients from high-achieving families frequently arise.

Sense of self

The lack of a sense of self can be compensated for by an eating disorder, which gives the sufferer an identity. As the eating disorder is challenged, these feelings re-emerge. Patients frequently say that they do not know who they are without their illness. This sense of fragility was graphically illustrated by Toni, who began to break down quite seriously during her stay of many months.

> Toni was very keen to attend the group, and felt that it was very important to her and her treatment, although she was not sure exactly why. In her first few months of attendance she would engage fully in the playing, and give thoughtful comments on this and the group in discussions. As her symptoms improved, she began to withdraw. In the discussion she began to say that she found the music very difficult to listen to because everyone else was playing her feelings. She felt as if the things she was experiencing inside her head were known to others because she could hear them in their music. Toni often felt that I was 'mocking' her in my playing. This happened when I picked up some aspect of her

metallophone playing, a harmonic motif, interval or rhythmic fragment, and incorporated it in my piano playing in some way. It was as if Toni had no boundaries between herself and others, she was unable to regulate her experience with the external world.

Some patients have a terror of merging and subsequent loss of self, related to an unsuccessful transition from symbiosis with mother to separation. This can be enacted in the music. Patients can use the group to help develop a sense of self, to find a way of distinguishing who they are and how they are different from others. How to maintain your identity whilst being in contact with others is an issue which is often addressed in the group. The question frequently asked is: 'How can we play what we feel together when we all feel different things?' It is as if each person's sense of self is so fragile that by allowing it to mingle with others in the form of sounds, to adapt a little and change in order to form something shared, she will lose it all together. She will be obliterated, subsumed or merged. This illuminates something of the anorexic/bulimic experience.

Robarts (1994) writes in depth of how the use of clinically orientated improvisation in individual music therapy with children suffering from early onset anorexia can help them to develop their sense of self. She proposes that the 'paradoxical phenomena of early self and self-in-relation experiences can be expressed in musical dynamic forms, symbolically akin to those of the mother–infant relationship' (p.243).

Defences

It should be acknowledged that defences can serve a very important function for people in helping them deal with the world and should not be seen as something to break down. Frederiksen (1999) studied the elements of resistance in her work with an anorexic teenager. She argues that in psychotherapeutic work with psychiatric clients resistance should be understood as 'an essential protection of the client against a terrifying emptiness and chaos' (p.212). The resistance is seen as a resource, rather than as something purely to be interpreted and analysed. She suggests that music therapist 'soften' this resistance through the way they play music with the client, meeting their expression cautiously and with respect, but also challenging them a little.

Transference issues

Remaining alert to countertransference feelings is particularly necessary with these clients who project so much of their own state outwards. I often feel I am being experienced as the mother, who is trying to feed them the music that they are rejecting, the one who 'makes' them play. In some groups when there is such a painful feeling of resistance that no one is able to play, I have played alone, reflecting on the piano my sense of the emotions in the room. When this is not responded to I can feel rejected and humiliated. I compare this to the experience of the mother, who having gone to great lengths to prepare something small and appetizing for her starving child, is left eating alone at the table, barely able to swallow, opposite her stony faced, closed mouthed child. This may also be something of the experience of the child, or the patient in the music therapy room, who also feels rejected and humiliated. The desperate sense of emptiness which the anorexic or bulimic patient achieves through their lack of food, but also tries not to feel, can be projected onto me as therapist, leaving me feeling deskilled and useless.

Summary

My experience with people with eating disorders has shown me that whilst they may find the music therapy group challenging, threatening to their defence systems and sometimes persecutory, they can also find ways of experiencing themselves, their feelings and their difficulties that can be liberating. It is the task of the music therapist to help them through their defences in order to find the creative possibilities of the music and the group.

References

Frank-Schwebel, A. (2001) 'The sound-object in anorexia nervosa.' Paper given at Fifth European Music Therapy Congress.

Frederiksen, B.V. (1999) 'Analysis of musical improvisations to understand and work with elements of resistance in a client with anorexia nervosa.' In T. Wigram and J. de Backer (eds) *Clinical Applications of Music Therapy in Psychiatry.* London: Jessica Kingsley Publishers.

Goiricelaya, F. (1988) 'The role of music therapy in the eating disorders programme at St Mary's Hill Psychiatric Hospital.' *Australian Music Therapy Association Conference Proceedings.*

Justice, R.W. (1994) 'Music therapy interventions for people with eating disorders in an inpatient setting.' *Music Therapy Perspectives 12*, 2, 104–110.

Klein, M. (1935) 'A contribution to the psychogenesis of manic depressive states.' In J. Mitchell (ed) *The Selected Melanie Klein.* Harmondsworth: Penguin.

Klein, M. (1946) 'Notes on some schizoid mechanisms.' In J. Mitchell (ed) *The Selected Melanie Klein.* Harmondsworth: Penguin.

Land, P. (2000) Unpublished paper.

MacKenzie, K.R. and Harper-Guiffre, H. (1992) 'Introduction to group concepts'. In H. Harper-Guiffre and K. MacKenzie (eds) *Group Psychotherapy for Eating Disorders.* Washington: American Psychiatric Press.

Nolan, P. (1989) 'Music therapy improvisation techniques with bulimic patients.' In L.M. Hornyak and E.K. Baker (eds) *Experiential Therapies for Eating Disorders.* New York: Guilford Press.

Robarts, J.Z. (1994) 'Towards autonomy and a sense of self. Music therapy and the individuation process in relation to children and adolescents with early onset anorexia nervosa.' In D. Dokter (ed) *Arts Therapies and Clients with Eating Disorders.* London: Jessica Kingsley Publishers.

Robarts, J.Z. (2000) 'Music therapy and adolescents with anorexia nervosa.' *Nordic Journal of Music Therapy 9*, 1, 3–12.

Robarts, J.Z. and Sloboda, A. (1994) 'Perspectives on music therapy with people suffering from anorexia nervosa.' *Journal of British Music Therapy 8*, 1, 7–14.

Sloboda, A. (1993) 'Individual therapy with a man who has an eating disorder'. In M. Heal and T. Wigram (eds) *Music Therapy in Health and Education.* London: Jessica Kingsley Publishers.

Sloboda, A. (1994) 'Individual music therapy with anorexic and bulimic patients.' In D. Dokter (ed) *Arts Therapies and Clients with Eating Disorders.* London: Jessica Kingsley Publishers.

Smeijsters, H. (1996) 'Music therapy with anorexia nervosa: an integrative theoretical and methodological perspective.' *British Journal of Music Therapy 10*, 2, 3–13.

Smeijsters, H. and van den Hurk, J. (1993) 'Research in practice in the music therapeutic treatment of a client with symptoms of anorexia nervosa.' In M. Heal and T. Wigram (eds) *Music Therapy in Health and Education.* London: Jessica Kingsley Publishers.

Williams, G. (1997a) *Internal Landscapes and Foreign Bodies.* London: Duckworth.

Williams, G. (1997b) 'Reflections on some dynamics of eating disorders: "no entry" defences and foreign bodies.' *International Journal of Psychoanalysis 78*, 927–941.

CHAPTER 7

A Music Therapy Group in a Neurological Rehabilitation Ward

Catherine Durham

Introduction

Four people sit immobile in large wheelchairs facing inwards in square formation. Their heads are held by headstraps. A music therapist sits between two people and improvises vocally, playing a guitar. Suddenly there is movement from one person's foot and windchimes positioned near the floor are activated into a peal of sound. Immediately another man shakes an elbow, creating a juddering noise on a keyboard held there by a therapist. A third man laughs and a fourth groans with the effort of moving a beater on a cymbal, his arm being supported by a third therapist. The beater produces a tiny sound. Five people are making group music together.

Background

When someone is referred to group music therapy, the referrer expects that the person may derive therapeutic benefit from group music making. By implication there may be some social and emotional benefits above and beyond the individual musical relationship that one-to-one therapy offers. But where a person is so severely disabled that it is difficult to tell how conscious they are, the prospect of group therapy seems ambitious.

Several years ago I worked on a neurological rehabilitation ward where patients had head trauma rendering them profoundly brain injured. A number of them participated in a music therapy group that ran for over two years with myself and two therapists from the multidisciplinary team. Not all group members attended for the full duration that the group lasted as they were moved to other wards or out of the hospital. However, a core group of four was maintained through-out the period. Each member showed that there were ways of making contact with others through music which were unexpected or not imme-diately detectable even to the careful listener.

The primary focus of this chapter is to explore the feelings that were worked with in the music of this group, and the differences between members. First, however, we explore the practicalities of setting up such a group.

Dynamic administration

In group analysis, 'dynamic administration' refers to the work related to the setting up of groups. The potential membership of groups requires detailed preparation (Stock Whitaker 1985, pp.63–4). This may mean thinking about the balance of personalities, differences, experiences and needs of each member. The size of group, time of the session and length of the input are also factors to be weighed carefully. In the case of the rehabilitation group many complex factors needed to be taken into account. Some people on the unit were there for assessment only whilst others stayed for over a year. Therefore I concluded that the groups could run as slow-open groups (Woodcock 1987), allowing new members to join when there was an appropriate space for them. The typical length of stay on the unit meant that it was possible to maintain a core membership.

Timing

Some people had disrupted sleep-wake cycles as a result of their head injury. As there were ward 'quiet' hours, family visits and rehabilitation timetables, very few slots in the day were likely to result in full and alert attendance at the group. However, once a time and routine was established, relatives organized their visits to avoid clashes.

Set-up of the room

Most potential group members had visual problems such as difficulties co-ordinating eye movements. Some could not make sense of what they saw – visual agnosia is described in detail by Sacks (1985, pp.7–21) – whilst others had neglect on one side (Sacks 1985, pp.73–5) or were blind. Nearly all group members were in wheelchairs, with the others in bed. This had implications for space, the number of people in the group and positioning of instruments. At one point there were five people in the group. However, the number was more usually four.

Part of the preparation involved measuring room dimensions and drawing positioning diagrams. Because of the size of the wheelchairs, I ended up sitting on a high stool. Was this a preoccupation with the practicalities? At the time I thought this was because of an influence from occupational therapists. Later I realized that providing a meaningful environment which allowed the fullest independence for the participants was an important way of providing containment for them.

Balancing different people's needs was important. I soon discovered the difficulties of containing a group where one person responded very impulsively to anything that happened, whereas his neighbour took thirty seconds to respond. A person's speed became a factor in determining the group composition.

The Group

As the group was based on a slow-open framework, membership changed when someone was discharged. Typically there was only a week or two of notice given before someone left, leaving little preparation time for departure within the therapeutic process. The two other therapists involved were a speech and language therapist and an occupational therapist. They contributed to administration, running and evaluation of the group. It was clear however that this was a music therapy group and the focus was on clinical improvisation and pre-composed songs. The criteria for entry was that each member had already had some established form of communication. In effect, the group was offered to people where the referrers felt there was a chance that people would be able to communicate choices. The group provided opportunities for encouraging awareness of other people in the room, and offered some motivation for making movements. The primary aim of the group remained the same throughout the two years: the forming of relationships through music with a clear emphasis on emotional expression.

Assessment

I spent several individual sessions with each person before deciding whether a group was appropriate. We had a chance to get to know one another and I was also able to think about the balance of the group and to gain an understanding of each individual personality and needs.

Being present in the group

All group members were physically unable to move their own wheelchairs. Some were able to indicate yes/no by the use of electronic buzzers. One buzz was for 'no', two buzzes for 'yes', making it physically easier to refuse than consent. People would use these to say if they wanted to attend, but some no clear informed consent could be given. Therefore, during every session, the question 'do you want to be here?' was present. In this group it was a question the therapists constantly held in mind. Leaving by refusing to communicate or falling asleep was easier than physically going. This led to a dilemma. Was a person falling asleep in the group because they were fatigued by the effort needed to participate or was it because something had happened in the group that had aroused despairing feelings? What we tried to do was to say 'You've pushed the drum away – maybe you don't want it now', for example, which explained our interpretation. The danger is that therapists' anxieties feed into interpretations. I needed to work hard in supervision and in evaluations with the co-therapists in order to maintain openness to the various meanings inherent in the group members' behaviour.

The therapist's perspective
Working with feelings in the music

As I began to relate more to the group members through the music, I felt it became possible to know when someone was avoiding contact. I paid attention to how I was feeling in the music. There was sometimes a mismatch between the feelings aroused by what I saw or heard. One man might put immense effort into producing a sound resulting in my own feelings of frustration. However, the sound produced might be brief and quiet, arousing different feelings when heard on audiotape. I learned to listen to the beginning of the sound, so that a quiet harshness at the beginning of a note took on greater significance. I began to accept that the sound world of the group was within a narrow 'bandwidth' of volume. Tiny changes were deeply expressive. Sometimes it was helpful to close my eyes during the music. Once this began to happen, the flow of my own music became less interrupted and I felt more able to support. Often it was important to provide pulse, which was one thing that was difficult for group members to generate. Pulse relates to the body, giving continuity and a future to the music. I believe that pulse can create a sense of physical well being for people with severe physical disabilities. Most interesting was the way in which each individual found his own methods of expressing himself and then how the group music itself evolved.

John, Mark, Sean and Dermot

John was in his early thirties and had been in a head-on car collision. He had held a demanding job. Now he communicated words only with a high-pitched buzzer. He could also vocalize within a very restricted pitch range. Epitomizing vulnerability because of his physical weakness, the emotional nature of his communication was heightened. He would jab at the buzzer as if in a fury of frustration.

Mark, the same age, had fallen downstairs for his head injury. He seemed disorientated most of the time. He was able to move his right arm at times to explore objects. He appeared to be able to see. However, he did not combine looking with reaching out. Although unemployed before his accident, he had been a musician in a band.

Sean communicated using a buzzer. He was blind in one eye and his movements were dyspraxic. He was completely silent. His severe physical disabilities were caused in a motorbike accident. Aged 24, he seemed withdrawn and depressed. The team members felt his mood was an indication of some insight into his situation.

Dermot was 19 and had been a pedestrian in an accident. He could only move his head. Most of the time his head was supported by a headstrap. If another person held his head lightly at the base of his skull he was able to move more freely. He laughed much of the time he had any contact with others. This was labelled 'emotional lability' by the team; that is, an excessive or inappropriate emotional reaction to any situation, caused by cognitive damage. But Dermot's laughter had musical shape to it, so that different emotions seemed to be expressed, including distress. At times Dermot's laughter seemed to be an expression in response to the music or feelings expressed by others.

Feelings

All four men seemed traumatized by their accidents. All four seemed to be experiencing extreme frustration when trying to communicate and had a tendency to withdraw due to repeated failures. It was important to offer plenty of space for them to respond in any way they needed to. I had protective feelings for these fragile men. At times I experienced emotions which swung between fury and despair. I explored the possibility that I may have been experiencing extreme countertransference feelings. With supervision I began to learn to survive these feelings and bring them into the music.

The group music

The group music initially contained a considerable amount of tension. None of the men appeared to have the control to be able to time their sounds meaningfully and at first the music was more about whether someone made a sound at all within the space. Musical beginnings were unclear. It took some time for each man to choose an instrument and for it to be set up. As soon as John had an instrument he began to play it, not waiting for others; possibly not aware of them. Dermot was only able to play the windchimes and tired after just a minute. Mark was keen to play a drum but had difficulty getting his hand to it. The music was rhythmically chaotic and many attempts at sounds resulted in silence. The music did not always represent the energy that had been put into it.

I introduced individual songs for each man supported by guitar accompaniment. I sat by the individual whose name was sung. In this way, his music took place in his space. This also helped group members to identify where others were sitting. One co-therapist sat by Dermot as he needed constant physical support, but the other moved around to support each man as he indicated some desire to play. When each individual song was sung at the beginning of the session, each man had several minutes to find the instrument and get physical movements started. After this a group improvisation usually tended to develop. I soon found that sitting in one place and allowing the sounds of other group members to emerge on their own seemed most containing. Listening to tapes of the sessions, effectively 'blinding' myself from any visual impact of the session, I started to discern what seemed to be patterns of musical relating and interactions between the group members. This did not necessarily relate to my own rhythmic framework. For example, Mark's drum playing alternated with Sean's on the electronic keyboard. If Sean's bursts of sound came later than expected, Mark appeared to wait for him.

Whilst holding the group at the beginning of each session I found it difficult to listen. The effort of containing, orientating and observing sapped my strength to do other things. Also the strong counter-transference feelings and guilt I was experiencing served only to muddy the waters. Sometimes I was more disabled than the clients. I learned to do less in the group so that others could do more. The group members found ways of suggesting a pulse or beginning the improvisation with a particular sound, and soon even John waited for others to start.

Thoughts on disability

During evaluation we acknowledged our own frustrations at the physical limits of the group members, especially Sean's dyspraxia. We often became caught up in the desire to will the movement for him. We did not always accept his disabilities. The remit of a rehabilitation unit is to encourage change and improvement and in this group these pressures became only too apparent. By simply allowing the group members to be and not devise tasks for them was a departure from the structured therapy offered in other therapy sessions. The expectation to perform could be imprisoning for all concerned at times.

We also struggled with personal guilt of being non-disabled. In my own therapy I needed to explore the grief that was aroused by the group members. At times I had dreams about them. In one dream a man who usually only moved an index finger got out of his wheelchair, shouting at me and saying how I was always controlling him. I was delighted that he could walk and talk, expressing his feelings. To me the dream showed me that I had a 'yearning' for him to return to how he was before. Second, it showed me my anger. After taking this to therapy it became possible to work with his anger in the music therapy session.

A co-therapist said that she had 'recognized' a patient on the ward walking down the street, only to discover that it was someone different. The disabled academic Michael Oliver (1996) writes of the 'personal tragedy theory' of disability. He argues that in the UK disabled people are thought of as tragic cases that prevent them from being seen as the people they really are. As a member of staff on the unit I was very taken by the shocking histories of each group member. Over time I realized that feeling pity and fascination with what had happened to them was quite removed from the 'here and now' experience of the group. People wanted to get angry, to relate, to refuse, to experience power over us and to express a sense of humour.

Humour

Humour was most easily expressed in the music. John was keen to play his chosen instrument, except when it was his 'turn'. Then he abjectly refused to play and would smile. As soon as I moved on and sang another's name, he would play. As well as being amusing, it was his opportunity to gain some control over the artificial structure I had introduced. Another time Sean played the demo button on the keyboard and suddenly in the middle of very minimal and disjointed improvisation a rich funky

Latin-American dance was synthesized. The absurdity of this man transforming our simple group music into one of sexy sophistication seemed shocking but hilarious. We laughed because of relief from the painful process of making tiny sounds, but also because of our own perceptions of Sean's disabilities. I suspect Sean laughed because he had so powerfully challenged the environment. It seemed as if there had been a brief respite from the gulf between therapists and group members. For the rest of the session Sean continued to search for the demo button.

Thoughts on difference

One new group member, Simon, had so little controlled movement that we could not find him an instrument. He was unable to vocalize and was blind. The fact that he understood most of what was said was not discovered for 18 months after his accident; even his family believed that he was in the 'vegetative state' (Boyle 1995; Durham 1995). With an electronic buzzer held to his fist he could reliably indicate 'yes' and 'no'. At that time we did not have access to instruments that could be operated with such a sensitive switch, although he was a candidate for a specially modified electronic instrument. Every week I asked him if he wanted to attend the group. Every week he buzzed 'yes'. We failed to provide any means by which he could be actively involved, which made him different from the other group members. However, just being there seemed to be important to him. I found the concept of 'active listening' helpful, and also Christopher Small's definition of 'musicking' (1998, p.9).

Difference in the group was mainly defined by the instruments chosen, how they were played and when. Music itself provided most of the opportunities for difference. I have found that in other music therapy groups difference between group members is often difficult to acknowledge and members tend to focus on similarities. As the group becomes more established, differences become introduced and the group finds ways to tolerate them. The importance of difference in groups is explored in more detail by Barnes, Ernst and Hyde (1999, pp.125–44).

Group knowledge

In the ward group each member had a severe head injury. However, I never named this similarity in the group. Perhaps this was an omission. In a music therapy group for bereaved children I decided to introduce the first group by saying to the members 'this is a group for children where someone close to them has died'. This seemed to allow them to talk to each other in the way they chose, as death had already been introduced.

What information should be imparted to people in a group when they can't ask for information? Do people have a right to know what has happened to others? In the case of the group we are concerned with here, several members had poor memories. Orientating people who continually forgot where they were or why was quite an important part of my role in this situation.

If others cannot indicate whether they want details about themselves to be given it seems impossible to make that decision for them. The fact that everyone in the group has a severe head injury was something that seemed too difficult to address. With this client group, so much was uncertain about what people knew that many areas became taboo. In a group of adults with previously normal language the therapist's knowledge of their circumstances becomes more loaded. There is a danger of infantilizing patients because therapists withhold knowledge and patients' rights to that knowledge are not always considered.

Thoughts on gender: difference and exclusion

Carol was a new group member and she was the first woman to join the group. Women were in the minority on the ward. Normally in groups one may try to balance the gender representation and be aware of the tendency for gender subgrouping (Elliot 1986), but in this case we felt the benefits to Carol may outweigh the possible problems of gender imbalance.

Carol had bouts of uncontrollable crying. Once she started crying she seemed to find it impossible to stop. The question was whether this was for neurological reasons or because she was overwhelmed with grief. The cries were so piercing that she could be heard across the hospital. Carol cried every day for much of the day. In individual music therapy often her crying would abate during the session and for some time afterwards. Eventually I asked group members if she could join. No one communicated that it was a problem although it was unclear whether everyone knew who she was.

When Carol joined the group, she was able to stay without crying for the first ten minutes and then she began. At this point, other group members indicated such distress that I said to her that she would have to leave unless she could stop. Her crying immediately sounded more angry. I felt as if I was denying her the chance to express what was real despair. The truth was that it was not tolerable to other established group members, who started grimacing, moaning and refusing to participate. One even began an epileptic seizure. It felt as though the group was rejecting her. Each week she joined the group and each week she was rejected by other members' reactions and ejected by a therapist wheeling her out. However, she always chose to come. None of the male members of the group cried at all, although some expressed anger. Yet there were two women on the ward who continually cried. Was this a difference because of gender or was it as straightforward as the crying being too loud and unbearable? Carol was furious when she was ejected from the group. The group allowed her a chance to be included for a time and for her feelings to be heard. The group members were showing her that they could not stand her crying, which meant that there was some communication about the situation. I tried to explain what I thought was happening, even that there was a danger of Carol being made into a scapegoat. Group members appeared to listen to this. Carol cried as soon as I said that her crying was upsetting people. Maybe people couldn't bear her sadness. Her crying refused to abate and at this point she asked to leave by electronic communication.

We resolved the next week to try just one more time to involve her and, if the same thing happened, to talk to her about whether she would continue in the group. However the following week she stayed for 20 minutes before crying and then only cried quietly. The group members allowed her to stay in. From that time she was more fully accepted although she did continue to cry in some sessions. As she had some conscious control over this, it became more possible to negotiate with her that if she did cry we would withdraw her until she was ready to return.

She seemed to stop trying to punish the group by crying and became less of a scapegoat as a result (Taylor and Rey 1987). She began to use her voice to sing and this added to the quality of the songs and improvisations.

Co-working

There were challenges in working together with two staff from other professions in the session, but it was also invaluable. Davies and Richards (1998) have written about the value of co-working as music therapists. I found that the knowledge of a specialist occupational therapist and speech and language therapist combined to make both communication and instrument positioning possible and the group members were enabled by this expertise. The half hour spent evaluating the group afterwards provided an opportunity for us to pool observations and feelings. Together we tried to make sense of our experiences. So often one of us influenced the perspectives of the others. The supportiveness of this group was enough to allow us to run the group for over two and a half years with no staff change. In some ways we used the evaluation time for our own peer supervision. Although the group was acknowledged as a music therapy group, it would not have been possible to run it without my colleagues for whom I developed a great deal of respect.

The therapeutic process

The group moved through a complex process that included sessions which were creative and others where boredom and lack of feelings predominated. The general shape of the musical journey throughout this time was from a structured and contrived group to one which had more spontaneous flow. Various group members began to listen more carefully. I learned new ways of holding the group members in music and new ways of listening. Even group members who had very little short-term memory showed a sense of recognition when in the group and reacted to familiar preferred instruments. Relationships between individuals became apparent in the music and changed as time went on. Group members came and went, and were missed. However, the sense of process was at its most keen when we approached the ending of the group.

Ending

I was to leave my job and the group in its present form could not continue. It is always difficult to predict how patients may react to the ending of therapy. Even if they do not understand words, something of the essence of ending can get through (Pavlicevic 1999). With this group I wondered what impact the ending would have. For two of the present group members the news that the group would be finishing in ten weeks appeared to have little impact. Others did react. The countdown was carefully presented at the beginning of each session as the group members had difficulties with short-term memory. John, who had attended weekly for over two years, suddenly became the 'model client'. Instead of choosing to withdraw in parts of the session as usual, he tried new instruments and ways of playing. Having an end in sight, it was as though he was trying to cover as much ground as possible. The therapists were overwhelmed with sadness. John had become close to all of us and his personality had always made a strong mark on the group. Acknowledging this sadness in music and words became an important part of the ending process.

Simon, who had been in the group for eight months, appeared angry and refused to communicate for several sessions. Once he refused to come into the group and communicated 'fuck off' by pressing the buzzer three times in a row. He rejoined the group for the last four weeks, a little more accepting of the ending now his feelings had been expressed. John noticed when Simon was not there and would gesticulate at Simon's place. We told Simon that John wanted him in the group and missed him. This may have been another factor that brought Simon back.

The music in the final group was low in energy compared to the previous weeks. Emotions of anger and regret had been expressed.

I found that the final evaluation was helpful in bringing the process to an end for me. Detailed reports and an overview of the process helped the therapists realize what had been achieved. Many of the emotional issues that the group members faced were related to loss, so careful preparation for the ending and space for expression of particularly uncomfortable feelings had been important.

Conclusion

Throughout the time that the group ran, I became convinced that a group of severely disabled people could develop the dynamics of a group similar to one of articulate individuals. The incidence of scapegoating, forming of alliances, avoidance and initiating of conflict are all characteristic of other types of group. Within this group relationships were formed, negotiated and developed within the music. The three therapists, from different training cultures, increasingly found common ground due to the generosity of the other therapists acceptance that the heart of the group was in the music. Both therapists developed beautiful singing voices and we were able to sing some songs in three-part harmony.

Overall, the group provided ways of reducing isolation between members through the music. This, I believe, was the reason why the group remained running for a sustained period of time. The work discussed in this chapter is described after a break of seven years. The names of all patients and colleagues have been changed. This is a personal account and those mentioned will have different perspectives of the events.

References

Barnes, B., Ernst, E. and Hyde, K. (1999) *An Introduction to Groupwork – A Group-Analytic Perspective.* London: Macmillan.

Boyle, M.E. (1995) 'On the vegetative state: music and coma arousal interventions.' In C. Lee (ed) *Lonely Waters: Proceedings of the International Conference Music Therapy in Palliative Care.* Oxford: Sobell.

Davies, A. and Richards, E. (1998) 'Music therapy in acute psychiatry: our experience of working as co-therapists with a group for patients from two neighbouring wards.' *British Journal of Music Therapy 12,* 2, 53–60.

Durham, C. (1995) 'Music therapy with severely head-injured clients.' In C. Lee (ed) *Lonely Waters: Proceedings of the International Conference Music Therapy in Palliative Care.* Oxford: Sobell.

Elliott, B. (1986) 'Gender identity in group-analytic psychotherapy.' *Group Analysis 19,* 195–206.

Oliver, M. (1996) *Understanding Disability: from Theory to Practice.* London: Macmillan.

Pavlicevic, M. (1999) 'Shireen.' In M. Pavlicevic *Intimate Notes.* London: Jessica Kingsley Publishers.

Sacks, O. (1985) *The Man who Mistook his Wife for a Hat.* London: Picador.

Small, C. (1998) *Musicking.* New England: Wesleyan University Press.

Stock Whitaker, D. (1985) *Using Groups to Help People.* London: Routledge.

Taylor, F.K. and Rey, J.H. (1987) 'The scapegoat motif in society and its manifestations in a therapeutic group'. *International Journal of Psychoanalysis 53*, 3, 1–12.

Woodcock, J. (1987) 'Towards group analytic music therapy.' *Journal of British Music Therapy 1*, 1, 16–21.

CHAPTER 8

Finding a Space to Play

A Music Therapy Group for Adults with Learning Disabilities

Eleanor Richards and Hayley Hind

This chapter examines events in the life of a music therapy group in which we were co-therapists. The group ran for two years. Music therapy is well established in the learning disabilities service in Cambridge, with a strong tradition of group work. In general, however, such groups have been offered to clients with observably severe impairments and corresponding difficulties in social functioning. These people present immediate evidence of the severity and intractability of handicap; not surprisingly, perhaps, they attract frequent referrals to many different disciplines.

There is another group of clients, among them those who appear in this chapter, who are usually the object of much less clinical attention. Their disabilities are, at least in formal diagnostic terms, 'mild'. They may be verbally fluent and socially adept. They have some cognitive limitations, however, and will have used learning disabilities services all their lives. For such people life is difficult in quite particular ways. They occupy an awkward middle ground. They are often not visibly or recognizably handicapped, but nor are they able to live independently.

Our thinking about this group has been informed particularly by the work of Foulkes, Winnicott and Bowlby. Perhaps the most significant piece of common ground for all three rests in their thinking about the formation and nature of the self. Foulkes proposed that the notion of the individual, separate self is meaningless. For him, our existence is given meaning by our part in a pattern of interconnection:

> In a community which stresses individual property and competition, a configuration has arisen which created the idea of an individual person as if existing in isolation ... Yet one of the surest observations one can make is that the individual is preconditioned to the core by his community even before he is born, and imprinted vitally by the group which brings him up. (Foulkes, 1983, p.23)

Bowlby, meanwhile, described attachment theory as 'a way of conceptualising the propensity of human beings to make strong affectional bonds to others and of explaining the many forms of emotional distress ... to which unwilling separation and loss give rise' (Bowlby 1977 p.127). He saw this impulse towards 'affectional bonds' not merely as a spin off from the struggle to gratify instinctual needs, but rather as a primary motivational force. He suggests that we internalize our early experience of relating to make what he termed 'internal working models', which then form the basis of our notions, conscious and unconscious, about ourselves, about others and about our relations with those others and with our environment. The earliest models are formed in infancy, but they may be reshaped in later life and more models added in the light of accumulating experience:

> Each individual builds working models of the world and of himself in it, with the aid of which he perceives events, forecasts the future, and constructs his plans. In the working model of the world that anyone builds, a key feature is his notion of who his attachment figures are, where they may be found, and how they may be expected to respond. Similarly, in the working model of the self that anyone builds, a key feature is his notion of how acceptable or unacceptable he himself is in the eyes of his attachment figures. (Bowlby 1973, p.203)

So each person brings to the group, as to any encounter with others, his or her existing model of relating. In a group where free exchange can take place, our models, with their assumptions and fantasies about others and ourselves, can become more apparent and thus open to modification. Foulkes suggests that the overriding priority for each of us is to be in touch with others, and thus to communicate. We want not only to know, but also to be known. He has tremendous faith in the possibilities of the group, suggesting that the desire to find and sustain meaningful contact (or good attachments) is paramount.

The proposal for this group arose initially through discussions in the multi- disciplinary team. Clinicians were regularly working with certain clients to address particular areas of difficulty (relaxation, social skills), but at the same time there was an awareness that the lifelong, pervasive concerns which might underlie immediate problems were not being addressed. All the members of this group attended a local day centre. When we raised the possibility of the group with staff there, the idea was readily taken up and names were suggested. We were met with apparent warm support, but equally with an underlying scepticism. The recurring 'joke' amongst the staff was that they were the people who really needed some time and some instruments to 'work off the frustrations'. These expressions of envy, with their associated need to diminish the clients' capacities to make use of what therapy might offer, were sharp reminders of the framework of assumptions and ambivalence within which people with learning disabilities may live. In particular, there may be doubts about the learning disabled person's capacity for an active emotional life. Valerie Sinason puts it like this:

> However crippled someone's external functional intelligence might be, there still can be intact a complex emotional structure and capacity. To reach and explore this emotional intelligence a great deal of guilt must be dealt with, guilt of the patient for his handicap and guilt of the worker for being normal. (Sinason 1992, p.74)

We met potential group members individually before starting. Each person was both anxious and compliant. No one had any experience of therapy. They responded positively to our invitation to come to the group, but talked of their expectations of it in such terms as 'it will be good to chat' or 'the music will be nice'.

Sarah was in her early fifties and had lived all her life with her mother. She hoped to leave home to share a house with other day-centre users. Janet also lived with her elderly parents. She was in her late twenties, but her dress and behaviour suggested someone older. She placed great value on her role in helping her mother to care for her frail father. Mary was in her forties. When the group began she had lived for two years with her sister and family after her mother's death. She had a slight visual impairment, but nonetheless laid great stress on her contribution to running the household. Vicky was in her forties and lived with her mother and uncle. She had attended the day centre since leaving school.

The early sessions were explosive and chaotic and quickly revealed facets of the group members very different from those they ordinarily presented to the world. At the start of session three, the group arrived a few minutes early. The level of talk in the waiting room quickly rose from ordinary exchanges to loud, excitable conversation and laughter, mostly from Sarah, Mary and Janet. Vicky sat a little apart. The talk continued without pause when they came into the group room and music began almost at once. Sarah, Mary and Janet hurried from one instrument to another, playing apparently randomly and with little sense of apparent connection. Vicky played a steady beat on a large drum. The music was very loud. People sometimes called out comments or questions to the therapists, but did not wait for a reply. As therapists, we tried to find music of our own that might contain all this, but we were mostly inaudible. It seemed more useful simply to listen. We were being asked to witness and tolerate the group's experience and its expression. It seemed that the responsible, well-regulated aspects of themselves that they mostly presented at the centre and elsewhere had been lifted away to reveal turbulence, anxiety and aggression. Some of the same qualities were present in the group's talk: there were interruptions, the topic flitted from one thing to another and the tone was argumentative. Any contributions from the therapists were dismissed or ignored. Our prevailing sensation was that thought and skill were being attacked.

Jon Stokes's (1987) thoughts about secondary handicap come to mind here. He suggests that in certain circumstances it may be necessary for the disabled person to protect herself by exaggerating her handicap. If she can appear too 'stupid' to be able to reflect on her experience and its meaning, the world will assume that she is incapable of it. She will then be able to avoid acknowledging the reality of painful feelings or taking the risk of being isolated and misunderstood. This generated some powerful countertransferential feelings in us. On the one hand we felt overwhelmed and 'slow' – our own capacity for thought felt handicapped. On the other hand, we were aware of the unexpressed feelings in the room of frustration and anxiety. We felt painfully ignored, much as the group members had ignored one another. We experienced that as an indicator of the sense of isolation and mistrust of attachment that may underlie so much of our clients' apparent 'cheerfulness' and sociability. The music felt 'mad' at times, as though both consciously and unconsciously there was no expectation that anyone might hear, understand or respond to anyone else, or hope to be heard herself. Instead, things felt fragmented and apparently meaningless.

This painful pattern prevailed for the first few weeks. Gradually it became clearer that what was most daunting for the group was silence and potential inactivity. People spoke in terms that implied an assumption that they must be energetic and 'productive'. If the underlying fear is that one does not have the worth to justify one's existence in the eyes of others, what defences must one turn to in order to fight off that thought? Provision for people with learning disabilities often has its basis in organized activity and a clear timetable. Whilst some of that may be to do with organizational matters and a sense of people's needs for consistency, we might also see it as an institutional defence against the pain of handicap itself. When life is busy there is little time for reflection and when people are being encouraged to 'do as well as they can' the frustrations of handicap can be minimized. After some of these big improvisations, group members would look anxiously around and say 'We've played a lot today' or 'We've kept busy', as if to reassure themselves and us that they had done something worthwhile.

After about four months there was a break, during which the community team moved to a new clinical base and the venue for the sessions therefore changed. There was also change within the group. The noisiness and confusion of the early weeks were replaced by something strikingly different, which was apparent in both the music and the talk. People began to arrive with a 'topic' to open the session, often an account of something that had happened during the week. Others would greet this with politeness, appropriate questions and perhaps comparable experiences of their own. These conversations usually concerned events outside the group. Exchanges were beginning to take place between group members, rather than everything being addressed to the therapists, but the tone was cautious. The potential for outburst or spontaneous expression had been covered with a layer of social acceptability. There was a sense that any feelings of envy or exclusion that such exchanges might arouse were far too powerful to risk expression.

This new, careful style seemed in sharp contrast to the wild experiences of the early days before the break. When the therapists remarked upon the difference in atmosphere and wondered what might be behind it, we were greeted with something approaching denial of the reality of the early weeks. The prevailing feeling was that they must be treated as some sort of aberration and that they had no important meaning. The outraged, chaotic feelings had been put back in their place and the effort was redoubled to split them off from everyday experience. As therapists, we felt that we were being asked to hold the knowledge of the much more disturbing material which, at that stage, seemed too difficult to own.

This new 'politeness' also manifested itself in the music. The group developed a style of playing that seemed, outwardly at least, more coherent. It was often based on the steady rhythm of Vicky's drumming. Above that Janet played a high soprano glockenspiel and Mary a hand drum. Sarah played slow phrases on a bass metallophone. The music varied little in pace or intensity and, although Vicky and Mary sometimes looked round the group, and especially at the therapists, the overriding feeling was of a set of sounds moving along in parallel lines, with little interaction or mutual influence. Each person's playing was repetitive, so the music had a slow, steady tread that nonetheless got nowhere. Janet's face looked blank and Sarah sometimes stared out of the window as she played. The music felt timeless, as if there was no reason why it should ever stop. If we brought something contrasting into the music there might be a momentary pause or hesitation, but then it continued as before. If one of us developed a duet within the texture with a particular group member, she was able to engage briefly, but then returned to her place in the overall sameness of things. Surprise, change and difference were things to be avoided.

What could be learned from people's ways of being in the group about their underlying assumptions or models of attachment? Janet found opportunities to act in ways that reflected her life with her family.

During a session when one of the therapists was absent she was especially 'helpful', perhaps feeling that she had to help keep the group together in a way that was reminiscent of her role at home. She comforted another group member who was crying, meanwhile looking round to see if the rest of us were aware of what she was doing. At other times she made sure people had the right chairs, or reminded everyone not to leave anything behind at the end. She brought into the group her feeling that nothing could be left to chance and that what might make her 'worth having' was her usefulness in caring for others.

Mary often spoke of her experience in her family. She had lived all her life with her mother until two years earlier, when she died after a long illness. Since then she had lived with her sister and niece. She recalled life with her mother in very idealized terms, implying that they spent much of their time together in a close understanding. She implied that her present life with her sister was also contented and that she was a valued member of the household. Gradually it emerged that her family was much more ambivalent about her. She needed to talk about her relatives with warmth, however, and could always find good reasons for the more difficult aspects of their dealings with her. This was reflected in her behaviour in the group. She always said she was glad to have come and warmly asked others how they were. When someone else spoke of diffi-culties she was full of expressions of sympathy, but quickly added that one must 'make the best of things'. Often she turned the conversation to something easier. Outwardly, everything about her suggested a warm and responsive way of being with others, but it became increasingly clear that this was in the service of a desperate need to avoid any real encounter with feelings of grief or discontent. She seemed to represent a position of needing to deny difficult experience or angry feelings in the overriding interest of remaining connected, something also characteristic of the group as a whole. The first real challenge to her position came in the music.

During an improvisation towards the end of the first year, Vicky made a much more immediate communication to Mary. She began drumming as she often did, but turned to stare at Mary as she played. The stare became more intense and hostile and her drumming grew louder and faster. As Mary grew more aware of it her own playing faltered and soon afterwards the whole improvisation petered out. Vicky seemed satisfied. Mary was unable to say in her usual way that the music had been 'great'. Instead, she was ill at ease and at a loss for the social liveliness she so depended on. The session ended soon afterwards and Mary was for the first time eager to leave the room.

Vicky had found a way to communicate to Mary some of the frustration she felt in their exchanges. She had brought something to the group that was in sharp contrast to Mary's smiling tolerance. Until this point she had not been able confront Mary directly, but instead had taken to following some piece of Mary's 'good news' with information of a very different order. She described alarming events that had happened in her village, including a road accident and a house fire. She seemed to want to bring danger and issues of life and death into the exchanges. We took this as a mark of her frustration at Mary's determinedly sunny view of the world and an expression of her need both to remind the group of some much darker side of experience and to make an envious attack on Mary's apparent contentment. Vicky was the group member least flexible in her use of words. In the event, she turned to musical means to find a way to cut across Mary's scheme of things. The effect was both to give Mary a quite direct communication and to bring the music as a whole to a stop. One of the group's prevailing patterns had been disrupted.

The following week the three other group members arrived without Mary. When we asked about her, they seemed surprised and said they had no idea where she was. Because of her visual impairment Mary always needed to walk with some one else; this time the others had left her at the entrance to the building. One of the therapists went and found Mary sitting motionless in the reception area, unable to set off on her own or to ask for assistance. When she came into the group the others greeted her effusively. We wondered aloud about what had happened and we were met with quick assurances that it had all been a mistake and each had thought another was accompanying Mary. We continued to seek ways to suggest to the group that perhaps other things had been going on. Mary had become the focus of very basic feelings about disability. Vicky's musical attack the previous week on her defensive optimism had made some uncomfortable things much more apparent to the group. Not only had Mary's music been challenged, but the whole group had found itself unable to keep going. The abandonment of Mary and the subsequent need for each person to say that they had thought she was 'with someone else' implied an attempt to throw off the reality of handicap and to attack it in Mary.

In the following sessions both the verbal material and the music fluctuated. The music became uncertain and fragmented. Some implicit group 'agreement' seemed to have broken down. They could no longer depend upon their shared capacity to sustain a bland, unchanging atmosphere. Mary's humiliation and abandonment had been an attempt to project onto her the group's hatred of handicap. It was clear that at first the other group members had expected disapproval from the therapists of what had happened. Their responses to us were full of explanations and apologies. In subsequent weeks, however, a stronger sense emerged that the group might let go of assumptions about blame and move towards thinking about the meaning of things. Mary had survived both Vicky's challenge and the experience of being left downstairs. By implication, the group itself had survived these events. As we returned more easily to wondering what Mary might have felt like, others began to be able to acknowledge more of their own experiences.

After that discussion the group improvised. Vicky started with the drum, but she played more delicately and thoughtfully than in the past. Mary played a tambourine quietly, occasionally stopping to feel the metal discs round the edge, and Janet turned the rainstick over and over. Sarah returned to the slow ringing sounds of the metallophone. This more gentle handling of the instruments and a growing preoccupation with their tactile qualities continued. In the early days of the group, instruments were sometimes pushed about or knocked over as they were hastily moved round the room. Now, by contrast, instruments began to be chosen more carefully and group members began to comment on their feel and sound. This sense of 'looking after' the instruments emerged alongside a growing capacity to speak about the life of the group. There were more open reactions to breaks and lateness and more concern was expressed about such things as the layout of the room, or whether we might be interrupted or overheard. Whatever was represented at this stage by the instruments and the organizational boundaries began to be experienced as a more reliable and necessary container for what might take place. Perhaps the capacity of the instruments to withstand the violent energy of the first few weeks had been recognized and made use of. The therapists too had survived, held the boundaries and kept thinking.

This newer way of relating to the instruments also had, for the first time, a feeling of playfulness. The instruments became available as objects with which people could form more idiosyncratic individual relation-ships and try out new things. Furthermore, they became a means by which people could more consciously make connections with others. Things had changed from the time when the group anxiously said 'We've kept busy today' to a sense of something less urgent and more spacious, where events could unfold at their own pace and it might be safer to reflect upon experience.

The word 'play', with its multiple meanings, is a familiar one in the vocabulary of music therapy. In this group the instruments had been 'played upon' from the start, but with little feeling of the possibilities of 'playfulness'. Winnicott (1971) remarks that what is important is not in the first instance the content of play, but rather playing itself: 'Playing facilitates growth and therefore health; playing leads into group relation-ships; playing can be a form of communication in psychotherapy.'

As this new quality emerged, the nature of the music itself began to change, becoming more transparent and allowing more variety. Vicky started one improvisation with a quiet pulse on a hand drum. Mary and Janet joined in on tambourine and glockenspiel, mostly playing together but also taking turns. Sarah joined in on the gong. Unexpectedly Vicky dropped out, leaving the three metallic instruments on their own in a rich but less rhythmically defined texture. They gradually grew softer, leading towards a shared, rather mysterious fading out. Vicky marked the end of the piece with a single stroke on the cymbal. This was undoubtedly group music, but it was made up of discernibly individual strands. Instead of the unchanging pace, volume and style of the group's earlier music, this music had a confidence which allowed it to be much more subtle. Players were able to pause without fear of being forgotten and to re-engage without fear of being intrusive. Individually and collectively people took actions that changed the nature of the music. It seemed that the group could accommodate the experience of a process and allow new events to emerge. In this context, at least, group members seemed able to act more autonomously, yet to respond to one another and to recognize their inter-dependence.

Winnicott regards creativity as something fundamental. If the child does not feel that her experience can be seen and contained, then her innate potential for creative playfulness can quickly be superseded by the demand for compliance and pseudo-integration in order to stay in touch with those around her. For many people with learning disabilities, in par-ticular, doubts about one's entitlement to a place in the world override any pleasure in moment by moment living. At this stage the work of therapy is not to organize experience or to offer interpretations. It is rather to offer a space in which play feels possible: 'The significant moment is that at which the *child surprises himself or herself.* It is not the moment of my clever interpretation that is significant' (Winnicott 1971, p.51).

The more careful, concerned treatment of the instruments led to the beginnings of that concern being extended to other people in the group. Group members had always been able to ask one another questions, but the spirit of the enquiries began to change. So far they had been polite and appropriate, but without active curiosity. Now there was a greater sense of the possibilities of recognizing and identifying with another's experience. In *The Beast in the Nursery*, Adam Phillips thinks about curiosity and appetite:

> People come for psychoanalysis when they are feeling undernour-ished; and this is either ... because what they have been given wasn't good enough, so they couldn't do enough with it; or because there is something wrong with their capacity for transformation. (Phillips 1998, p.11)

He goes on to suggest that therapy 'aims to restore the artist in the patient, the part of the person that makes interest despite, or whatever, the early environment' (Phillips, 1998, p.12). If one's world exists mainly within the institutions of day centres and learning disability services and life outside those structures feels unavailable, why wonder or be curious? 'It is both ordinary ... and wishful, in the best sense, to take interest for granted. Every depression, every act of psychic deadening, bears witness to the risk of interest and curiosity' (Phillips 1998, p.14). So how can 'interest' be generated? How can the artist be restored in the patient? The group's primary need was, in Bowlby's words, for a 'secure base'. Then they could begin to make discoveries on their own terms.

From the beginning, this group had played music and the therapists both took part in much of the music and talked about it. This had something of the quality of adult – infant exchanges. What seemed to matter was not the detail of what was said after an improvisation, but rather its tone and the sense that our responses were the outcome of listening and thought. The model of the mother's fascination and preoccupation with her baby's every gesture comes very much to mind here. In her reverie she seeks to find meaning and to make sense of each moment of exchange. For the group and for its individual members this was an unfamiliar experience. In many sessions, after the initial chaotic weeks had passed, there was a sense that individuals were desperately trying to work out what would keep us satisfied and therefore interested. There was an assumption that coming to the group must be a nuisance for us, summed up in someone's comment before a summer break of 'You'll be glad to see the last of us for a while'. Our response that the break might matter to all of us and that it was difficult to find a way to say so was greeted with awkward laughter. The sense that anything that took place could be attended to or thought about felt very fragile. People apologized for strong feelings, 'silliness' or uncharacteristic behaviour.

Conclusion

What contributed to the movement in the life of this group? One factor may be simply that it was possible for group members to allow themselves to become attached, not only to one another and to the therapists, but also to the event of the group itself. The regularity of the sessions and the clear attention to such things as boundaries, breaks and absences offered a 'secure base' within which change and new experiences might be available.

It was in the music that new ways of relating were first tried out, whether in Vicky's confrontation of Mary or the new sensitivity to the instruments. Gradually this was paralleled by more flexible verbal exchanges, as people began to be able to move from trading of anecdotes towards moments that implied greater emotional imagination about another's experience. The members of this group all had verbal skills and had always been encouraged in their use of language. While this meant that people were able to communicate competently, it was also a source of great anxiety. People were very cautious (safer to say something you have said many times before than to risk anything new that might not 'make sense') and verbal exchanges could easily become repetitive and stereo-typed. After the confusion of the first few weeks, the instruments were approached at first with equal caution. It was through the instruments, however, that the possibility that there need not be a 'right way' to do things was first explored. Music making offered a transitional space in which to 'play', where new kinds of activity and experience could be tried out. As therapists we felt no great need to 'translate' the music by means of some kind of verbal interpretation. Often it was enough for us simply to be involved in it, whether as players or listeners, and to find a means to acknowledge its importance. The music provided an invitation to intuitive, rather than cognitive engagement: 'Musical understanding is not hampered by the possession of an active intellect, nor even by that love of pure reason which is known as rationalism or intellectualism' (Langer 1942, p.101). It was through the music that unspoken (and perhaps unspeakable) things could first come to awareness.

References

Bowlby, J. (1973) *Attachment and Loss. Vol. 2: Separation.* London: Hogarth Press.

Bowlby, J. (1977) *The Making and Breaking of Affectional Bonds.* London: Routledge.

Foulkes, S.H. (1983) *Introduction to Group Analytic Psychotherapy.* London: Karnac.

Langer, S. (1942) *Philosophy in a New Key.* London: Harvard University Press.

Phillips, A. (1998) *The Beast in the Nursery.* London: Faber.

Sinason, V. (1992) *Mental Handicap and the Human Condition.* London: Free Association Books.

Stokes, J. (1987) 'Secondary handicap and its relation to trauma.' Paper delivered to the Royal Society of Medicine.

Winnicott, D.W. (1971) *Playing and Reality.* London: Routledge.

CHAPTER 9

A Music and Art Therapy Group for People with Learning Disabilities

Tessa Watson and Linda Vickers

This chapter describes some of our work with clients with mild to moderate learning disabilities, who were referred to or sought help from an arts therapist for difficulties they were experiencing in their lives. Both therapists work within a community team for people with learning disabilities in London. The aim of arts therapies work in this team is to 'enable people with learning disabilities to lead full and purposeful lives in their communities and develop a range of activities including leisure interests, friendships and relationships' (DOH 2001, p.7) and to help clients achieve their potential (DOH 2001). Therapy aims to address difficulties that prevent clients engaging in a full and purposeful life. This is undertaken through the use of individual and group therapy. The two therapists have worked jointly on a number of different combined art and music therapy groups provided in response to referrals from clients, carers and other professionals. These groups have been inspiring and moving experiences for both therapists.

The groups were run for a set number of weeks, usually comprising 12 sessions of music therapy, and 12 sessions of art therapy. In between the two periods of therapy, a visit to Tate Britain was offered to clients to view artwork around the topic of their group. Each series of groups had a different focus or theme, such as anger, loss or communication, according to the needs of the clients and the information received on referral.

Working together

The therapists were both present at each group. On occasion, other members of staff were present by agreement with the group when it was considered that a client's engagement with the therapy would be significantly increased by their support. The two therapists discussed at length the ways to work together to provide the optimum environment for the group. In the event, we found that in our own modality we naturally took a dynamic therapeutic role whilst the other therapist had a more continuous containing presence. Clients identified strongly with our experience of 'not knowing' about the other arts medium.

Introduction to the group

Following referral to the group, one or both therapists met with each client and carers or parents when appropriate to introduce themselves, talk about the group and discuss whether it could provide help with the client's current difficulties. Following this meeting, clients were offered a place in the group if appropriate. Initial appointments were set up in the weeks preceding the group, to give clients and carers the opportunity to find their way to the group venue, see the room and ask any further questions about the group. Group dates were set well in advance and sent to clients and carers. The groups ran for one hour, with strict boundaries of place and time. The therapists maintained contact with carers and other professionals to advise them of work undertaken in the group. Issues were communicated in general terms and details remained confidential.

In each group there an identifiable process which can be described by the following phases:

- Who are we?
- Why are we here?
- How can we be together, how can we be different?

- How can we work together in the group to help each other?

Music therapy group

Music therapy was the first arts therapy offered to the group. When setting up the groups, the therapists had discussed the different ways in which the arts media could be used. Would both modalities be used in the same session, or would they be kept separate – and which should come first? For the first group we decided to keep the modalities separate, with 12 sessions of music therapy and art therapy to follow. Our experience in the first group showed us that this order was helpful for clients and in subsequent groups we followed the same structure. Music therapy allowed a direct emotional engagement with the group through the music made together. Within a couple of weeks, most clients who found engagement with groups difficult were able to feel part of the group and began to participate. Another benefit of this structure was the way in which the group's music, which was often taped, could be listened to in art therapy to provide a further reflection on the work of the group.

Engagement in the group

P, a lady who had moderate learning disabilities, attended a group for people who struggled to manage their anger. She could not tolerate group situations in her day centre and was presenting increasingly challenging behaviour. She had attended an initial appointment with her support worker and had been anxious. She came for the first group but once she saw the other group members and therapists in the room, stopped in the doorway, and shouted with anxiety at the group. She warned us that the instruments were dangerous, and that someone could get hurt if they were hit with a drum or a beater. The therapist said that she was worried about coming into the group in case it was dangerous. P said yes but would not come in. She was encouraged to think what would make it safer for her to come into the group for this first session and identified the presence of her support worker. She was able to come into the group with her support worker and began gradually to feel it was safe to use the instruments, and to identify her own dangerous and angry feelings.

How can we be together?

In the first few weeks, the therapists used a warm and encouraging approach to help clients feel welcome and to identify their feelings about starting in the group. Some structures were used, such as a beginning exercise of passing an instrument around the group, or a semi-organized improvisation. In the beginning weeks the group frequently shared common feelings, with a sense of relief:

> In a group that focused on loneliness and isolation, W kept looking at her watch, worried that the therapists would forget the time. The therapist said that perhaps it was difficult to stay in a new situation, and W agreed. The therapist thought perhaps other people might share that feeling; this produced laughter and nods. L said that it wasn't like work where he knew people, and C said that it was a long way to come. All agreed that it felt strange, and the group played some urgent, fast music that captured the anxieties of a new situation.

Emerging themes

As the group began to form, the therapists began to speak directly about the reasons for the group. This enabled the group music and talk to directly address the group topic, and clients began to share and compare their experiences. This sharing increased the group feeling and seemed to bring hopefulness to the group (Vinogradov and Yalom 1989):

> In a group focusing on loneliness and isolation, O demonstrated behaviour that made it hard for him to function in a group (thus his difficulties at college). He became verbally aggressive, stamping his feet and swearing. He did not want others to play the instruments and when the therapist commented on this, O said that he could not play and that he was scared of the instru-

ments. Others in the group showed him how to use some instruments and he moved from a position of isolation to feeling included and helped.

Managing anger

Along with these explorations can come a realization of the impact of feelings on others:

> F played loudly and angrily on the piano. Some of the group joined him, others were quiet. The next week, T did not come to the group. F was worried – why had she not come, was it because of his music? This led to thoughts about the impact and consequences of anger, and of when and how it is OK to be angry.

The recognition of roles also played an important part in the groups. The therapists began to help the group to see the different roles that could be explored and adopted:

> E displayed aggressive behaviour that isolated him from social situations. In the group he frequently took an aggressive role. He found it hard to know how to be different in the music or talk of the group. One week, during the group's music, E began to play very loudly, gesticulating towards C and appearing threatening. During the music this behaviour, and C's musical response, was contained by the therapist's music, and at the end of the piece C was able to ask E what he had been doing. E said to the therapist that he wanted to make friends. The group helped E to find another way of doing this; by sharing an instrument, and saying 'what's up, C?' E was greatly impressed by the positive response to this different way of being.

How can we help each other?

As the group members became familiar with the setting, each other and the therapists, a sense of warmth and safety emerged. There was a feeling of hopeful expectation at the start of each session. The opportunity for difficult experiences or feelings to be identified and shared was an extremely important part of the group. This process is sometimes not available to clients in their everyday life, but is one that enables change and the development of insight for clients and the staff supporting them:

> K, a lady whose mother had died suddenly, attended the group every week. Though obviously interested in the group, she found it hard to bring her own feelings to the group. One of the group members noticed this and asked her to play something, but she said no. She felt miserable and sad. The group wanted to help. The therapist asked if the group could play for her, and K agreed. The group began to play, quietly. The music was beautiful and very sad, and as several of the group began to sing, the music took on the quality of mourning. Following this K was tearful, but in subsequent sessions she became lively and was able to engage more actively with the group. The group had helped K to share a sad feeling that she found it hard to express directly.

As the weeks were counted down to the end of music therapy, the group were encouraged to think how their trip into the community, to the gallery, might bring up some of the problems that had been thought about in the group. The fact that any incidents or feelings that were experienced on the gallery trip could be thought about in the art therapy group gave a sense of containment and encouraged group members to attend the trip. On occasion these discussions led to clients feeling that they could not come to the gallery. Once the group came together again for art therapy this could also be addressed.

The gallery visit

The visit to the art gallery (arranged at the juncture between the music therapy and art therapy sessions) was introduced with a view to sharing new artistic possibilities with the group. It was hoped that looking at a range of artwork would encourage the group members to begin to realize their potential for self-directed and individualistic art making, and also to begin to identify themselves as artists with a voice within the community. This extension of group work into the community was a fairly unorthodox approach in the context of therapeutic work and the therapists felt that the project was both a positive development of clinical work and a risky venture. The White Paper stresses the need for people with learning disabilities to be 'part of the mainstream' (DOH 2001, p.24) and whilst this is certainly important, it is essential that appropriate specialist therapy is also offered when needed. In the authors' experience, therapy can enable clients to move on and access more mainstream experiences.

Getting there

We were aware of a raised level of anxiety with the imminent trip into the community. Issues already raised in music therapy took on a renewed significance. Difficulties in managing and expressing anger, sadness, loneliness and contact with others had been explored and expressed within the group. How would these issues be managed in the community?

> A group for socially anxious service users travels by underground to the gallery. This involves meeting at our starting point, staying together as we board the tube, and changing lines at a busy central station. R appears frightened as we wait on the platform and is visibly relieved when he is seated with the group for the final stage of the journey. R wonders what would happen if he got lost. Animated discussion ensues as each person imagines this scenario, and the group joke with one another with increasing humour about such a predicament. R's expressed fear has resonated within the group. In vocalizing his feeling, anxiety is transformed by humour.

For some service users, a trip into the community triggers feelings of vulnerability. Most group members have experienced a sense of otherness, of living life outside of mainstream, and have a heightened sensitivity to this:

S, a woman with mild learning disabilities, was referred to a group for socially isolated service users. As our group is being guided around, gallery visitors stop to listen to our guide. S is unable to tolerate the attention that is being drawn to our space, and shouts out, 'Stop staring at me!' Our guide is able to contain her anxiety. She acknowledges S's fear, but also explains that people often stop and look and listen when she is guiding a party around as they are interested in what she is saying about the paintings. S and J are able to have a dialogue about social difficulties. Instead of employing her usual coping mechanism of running away from the situation, S is able to remain with the group for the rest of the visit.

The focus of each group was transferred to the gallery visits with our guide introducing themes that echo those in the group. This will often enrich the experience of the group members in realizing that their difficulties are part of human experience:

O, a man who lives alone and is sometimes agoraphobic, is drawn to a painting entitled *The Lonely City*. Our guide notices his interest in this picture and listens to his responses. She tells him about the artist, who felt lonely and frightened. O remembers this image and reflects upon it in subsequent art therapy sessions.

J, an angry woman who had extreme difficulty in valuing her own contributions to the group and her wider life, questions the value of each piece of artwork. In one gallery, there are samples of canvas and brushes that show the materials used. J says they must be worth a lot of money, and, unaware that she is observed, slips one piece into her pocket. She seems to be trying to hold on to something of value. The discreet intervention of Linda enables the material to be returned, and some of the meaning of the gesture to be understood. Later, in art therapy, J struggles to keep any of her artwork, scribbling over most pieces by the end of the session. With support from the co-therapist she is able to paint a messy and frightening picture and leave this valuable image in the studio.

Art therapy group

Having experienced being together in the music therapy group and visiting the art gallery, the group members were presented with a new space and medium. Sessions took place in a different room – the art therapy studio. Tables and materials were arranged in the room so that there would be an option to work together as a group and/or individually at smaller tables around the room. As sessions progressed and confidence grew, group members showed minimal interest in contributing to a group artwork, showing a preference for working on their individual work. Each session was structured with a space at the beginning for the group to talk with each other before engaging in artmaking and with time at the end to be together and to share artwork with the others.

Images created individually were sometimes discussed between individuals as they worked together around the large group table. This mode of working was the favoured one and seemed to provide group members with the opportunity to develop their creative process in the presence of others (Winnicott 1971). Clients were afforded the opportunity to be individuals within the group, where differences and commonalities could be tolerated:

> P had been referred to a group for help in managing his anger. He could be aggressive in his interactions with others which often led to his feeling alienated and rejected. K, another group member, is confident in producing a bright felt pen drawing of a band emblem – his favourite band. P, who likes a different band, is initially hostile to K's image, making derogatory remarks. Linda suggests that P use the materials to describe something about his band. He paints the name of his band which he then shares with K. The quality of interaction between P and K becomes more jocular and bantering in tone. K is less fearful of P, and P discovers that it is possible to share differences in a creative and friendly way.

Sometimes group members are more explicit with regard to their difficulty, and do not require intervention from the therapist:

> A, a man with mild learning difficulties, attended a group for people who were socially isolated. He was living alone in a flat and

missed his mother who had recently died. In recent months he had become depressed and was unable to manage taking care of himself. He was waiting to be placed in a supported group home. He produced a series of drawings over the course of sessions and was keen to share them with the group. They were self portraits of A with others – some are people he has met in the group – in a variety of landscapes such as parks and the countryside. Others are views of his flat with A being the only figure present. A produces these images with fervour and is self-absorbed as he draws them. He shows them to the group at the end of each session, telling them of the loneliness he has been experiencing and of his need for friends. Over the course of sessions A becomes increasingly animated in his interactions with his peers and begins to overcome his fear of travelling to and from the sessions alone by public transport.

Individuals were often referred due to their difficulties in relating with others and were able to explore, in a containing space, the limits of what could be tolerated within the group. It is often possible to translate the therapeutic experience in relationship to the outside world. What do we do with our difficult feelings? What is acceptable in this social context? How might this relate to the outside world?

B attended a group for help with managing his anger. He was anxious about attending the group, unable to contain his own anger, and fearful of the anger of others. How might the group take an expression of anger? He had been able to express his anger in his use of the musical instruments, but was anxious in the unfamiliar setting and medium of the art therapy group. He arrives late to the first session and tells us that he has been bothered by the noise of his neighbours. Sometimes he gets so angry about it that he smashes things in his home. Linda asks the group if they ever get angry? There is a group discussion about being angry. What does it feel like? What do you do? B spots a sculpture of a volcano on a shelf – the artwork from another group – and remembers the painting of a volcano we were shown at the gallery. He tells us he feels like exploding – like a volcano. In the ensuing sessions he produces bold paintings of fireworks and volcanoes, which appear to provide him with containment and are symbols of his anger that he is able to share with the group.

Some difficult feelings are harder to contain in the group without more help. In these instances the presence of two therapists allows for one to hold the group together whilst the other provides one to one intervention when necessary:

> C has been having difficulty at his workplace. He is often sexually inappropriate in his interactions with women and is jeopardizing his place at the work centre. C insists on sitting next to Linda when he arrives to the first art therapy group, and is aggressively sexual in his interactions with her. Linda talks to C, saying that it is difficult to help him if he speaks to her in this way. The group appears attentive to this interaction but remains silent for some time. G, another group member, breaks the silence by asking if he can begin painting. The others follow. C asks Tessa if she will help him with his artwork, and they work at an easel. He is reluctant to begin mark-making. He whispers to Tessa that Linda has 'sexy legs'. Tessa draws an image that she calls 'sexy legs'. In discussion with the group about the artwork produced, C begins to talk about an imaginary girlfriend and in subsequent sessions is able to express his wish for a girlfriend. His descriptions are less sexualized and he speaks of his wish for an emotional contact. Thus he begins to address his many anxieties.

However, even in their absence, individuals are kept in mind by the group, and the feelings of loss that are experienced are expressed and acted upon:

> N, a woman with mild learning difficulties referred to a bereavement group, was not able to attend any of the art therapy sessions (due to transport problems at her group home). Her chair remained empty at every session and the group commented on her absence at

every session. Eventually the group has the idea of making and sending N a card. A card is made and sent to N's home. By acting upon something that they felt, the group were able to take control of their experience and thus engender a sense of empowerment for themselves.

How do we end?

Common to many therapy groups is negotiation of the transition of ending and the accompanying (positive and negative) feelings in response to this. The way in which group members dealt with their attachments to the music (instruments and tape recordings) and the art objects was often a gauge of how they had incorporated their experiences. All artwork was stored in the art room for the duration of the sessions in order to provide containment and continuity. Upon ending group members were faced with choices as to what was to be done with their work. Clients could leave some or all of their work in storage and/or were able to take pieces of work home with them (this included a tape of the group music). As the art therapy sessions reached a close, Linda offered the group the opportunity to review their work in their penultimate session and to think about what they would like to do with their images. The range of responses indicates the multilayered meanings of the artwork to each group member:

> A [mentioned above] had very positive associations with his drawings which symbolized hope. He chose one image that he was particularly happy with and spent some time in his last session framing this piece. He was also very keen to take away other images. A had valued the social contact that the group had been able to offer him, and was more confident of his ability to make friends when he moved on.

> In contrast, E had great difficulty in looking at his folder of work. Many of his images had expressed his anxieties and fears. His use of artmaking had been more process as opposed to product oriented, and had been one in which he expressed his 'devils' and

'monsters'. In producing them, he had given the therapists a powerful visual communication of his inner world which enabled us to begin to address his fears. E decided that he would like to leave his folder of work with us for safekeeping. Interestingly, in later weeks he requested, through his keyworker, permission to return to the art room, explaining that he had left behind valuable objects. Fearful though the images were, they had been valuable in enabling E to express his distress. Notably, after attending the group E became more settled at college and was able to engage more easily with his peers and work.

In the process of ending, each group also reflects on the music therapy and often chooses to listen to the group tape again. The group is given the opportunity to discuss the music therapy. They remember favourite instruments and the way that they and their fellow group members played. Listening to the tape allows experiences to be recalled and there is often surprise from the group members as they remember how difficult it was to be together in the beginning. It is clear that each group has moved along in their journey. The group members are given the opportunity to take away a tape of some of the group music and most wish to do this:

> One year later, Tessa bumps into K as she attends a meeting. Both are pleased to see each other. K speaks with warmth of the group, describing clear memories, and he wonders how the other group members are. He is working in a training work placement; he has made friends and is pleased with his life. Through colleagues, the therapists follow the progress of group members after they leave the group. All group members are invited to contact the therapists should they feel they need further help.

Clients with distressing difficulties that have prevented them from accessing full and satisfying lives have been able to use these therapy groups to feel, express and share painful and frightening feelings. They have worked powerfully in their groups to develop their abilities to manage and overcome their problems.

References

DOH (2001) *Valuing People: A New Strategy for Learning Disability for the 21st Century.* London: The Stationery Office.

Vinogradov, S. and Yalom, I. (1989) *A Concise Guide to Group Psychotherapy.* Washington, DC: American Psychiatric Press.

Winnicott, D.W. (1971) *Playing and Reality.* London: Routledge.

Further reading

DOH (2001) *London Learning Disabilities.* London: The Stationery Office.

Moore, E., Adams, R., Elsworth, J. and Lewis, J. (1997) 'An anger management group for people with a learning disability.' *British Journal of Learning Disabilities 25*, 2, 53–57.

Nitsun, M. (1996) *The Anti-Group: Destructive Forces in the Group and their Creative Potential.* London: Routledge.

Part 2

Music Therapy Groups with Children

A Music Therapy Group to Assist Clinical Diagnoses in Child and Family Psychiatry

Emma Carter and Amelia Oldfield

Introduction

A music therapy treatment group has been run by Amelia Oldfield at the Croft Unit for Child and Family Psychiatry since September 1987. From 1995 the Croft began to focus on assessment work rather than long-term treatment. The music therapy group has reflected these changes by developing an approach aimed at using the group to assist the team in their diagnostic process. Since September 2000, Emma Carter has taken over this diagnostic group, keeping some of the established structures and activities but also adding ideas of her own.

Although a number of music therapists such as Hibben (1991), Tyler (2001), Oldfield (2001) and Molyneux (2002) have written about music therapy groups with children, none of this literature describes work which is specifically to aid diagnosis. It was therefore felt that it would be useful to describe this new approach to group work with children.

The Croft Children's Unit

The Croft Children's Unit is a psychiatric assessment centre for children up to the age of 12 and their families. There are usually no more than eight children attending The Croft at any one time. In recent years the most common diagnoses of children seen at the unit have been: attention deficit disorder (with or without hyperactivity), autistic spectrum disorders including autism and Asperger's syndrome, Tourette syndrome, developmental delay, attachment disorders, specific language disorders and conduct disorders. Although some families are admitted residentially, other children attend on a daily basis and regular meetings are arranged with the parents. Children are generally only admitted if their parents agree to work closely with staff on the unit. Assessments may last from two to six weeks. Occasionally, some children will attend for a longer specific piece of work that might last from 12 weeks to six months. During the day the children attend a unit school in the morning. In the afternoon they attend various groups, such as social skills, art and recreation groups, which are run by unit staff.

Staff on the unit include: psychiatrists, specialist nurses, a teacher, classroom assistants, health-care assistants, clinical psychologists and two music therapists. Social workers, health visitors and the teachers involved with the children outside the unit work closely with staff on the unit.

General organization of the music therapy group

The group takes place every week at the same time and lasts one hour. It is an open group in that all the children who are on the unit are expected to take part. However, occasionally children may be unable to tolerate being in groups at all or find a whole hour in a group too long. If a child is experiencing particular difficulties remaining in the group, this is discussed with the child prior to the group and a strategy is worked out. This may involve letting an adult know that they need to leave the room, or positioning them near the door and agreeing that if they are finding it difficult to manage, they may leave quietly, with the knowledge that a member of staff will be outside to support them.

The group is run by the music therapist in conjunction with a member of the Croft nursing team. This person chooses to work with this group on a regular basis and his or her shifts are worked out accordingly. In addition, there is a named 'back-up' person in case the regular co-worker is unavailable or it is felt that an additional member of staff is necessary.

The music therapist and the co-worker meet before every session to plan the group and after every session to review the session.

The group is held in the music room at the Croft. This room is well equipped with a piano, an electric organ and a wide variety of simple percussion and wind instruments as well as some instruments from different countries. The children are brought to the room by the co-worker and another member of the nursing team. The music therapist sets up the right number of chairs and welcomes the group into the room. At the end of the session, the music therapist and the co-worker take the children back to the 'living area' of the Croft where they get ready to have their lunch. Most of the children who attend the group will also have individual music therapy assessments with the music therapist. This does sometimes affect the work that goes on in the group. When necessary, this issue will be addressed either in the individual or group sessions.

Group philosophy

The group music therapy session at the Croft aims to provide another forum in which the children's strengths and difficulties can be assessed. The children vary in age from five to twelve and will all have a wide variety of skills. Some children will be new to the group and the Croft, others will know the unit and will have very clear expectations. At all times, the therapist has to keep the individual needs of each child in mind as well as being conscious of the needs of the group as a whole. This can be a great challenge and it is essential that the music therapist liaises closely with both the group co-worker and other members of the Croft team in order to be aware of new abilities or difficulties that have emerged since the previous week's session. It is also important for the music therapist to be aware of the group 'climate' at the Croft. There might be, for example, particular rivalries that have developed amongst the children or a generally low or very excited feeling in the group.

Many of the children on the unit lack confidence and have very low self-esteem. The music therapist running the group always makes a point of emphasizing positive aspects of the children's behaviour in the group and tries to avoid focusing on difficult behaviours. If children behave in ways that are dangerous to themselves, to other people or to the equipment in the room, then it is sometimes necessary to exclude them. Nevertheless, an effort is always made to reintegrate the children into the group in as positive a way as possible.

Occasionally the music therapist and the co-worker might disagree on the 'correct' way of dealing with one of the children's behaviours. The way a disciplinary problem is dealt within the group may be different from the way that the same problem is dealt with in other situations on the unit. When this occurs, it is essential that the issue is discussed among staff and a compromise may have to be agreed on, in the best interest of each particular child. For example, some children will be able to manage different rules in different groups, whereas others will find this too confusing. The important issue is that the children are aware that staff talk to one another and are all attempting to understand and help as much as they can.

The dynamic structure of our group is as follows. The music therapist is clearly in charge, suggesting activities and outlining group rules for different types of music making. However, the music therapist will also listen carefully to musical and verbal suggestions made by the children and will constantly pick up ideas and suggestions from them. It is essential that the children in the group feel listened to. When possible the music therapist will involve the children in choices and decisions regarding the musical activities. At times the music therapist and the co-worker will make a point of discussing a contentious group issue openly within the group setting, showing that these issues are considered carefully and not the sole responsibility of one adult. When boundaries have to be set, the music therapist and co-worker will try to explain why these limitations are being imposed. At times it might be useful to involve the children in discussion about why adults set boundaries.

The music therapist and the co-worker will often demonstrate and model activities rather than giving lengthy verbal explanations. The children will usually be 'drawn into' music making in a playful way rather than through a reflective analytic process. Nevertheless, the sessions will always be reviewed very thoroughly and it is at this point that the children's interactions may be examined in a more thoughtful and sometimes analytical way.

Rationale for the group

The reasons for including this music therapy assessment group in the children's weekly programme are similar to the rationale for individual music therapy assessments outlined previously by Oldfield (2000), but the situation is slightly different because the children are seen in a group rather than individually. These reasons include:

- motivation
- music making as a non-verbal way of communicating through sound
- music making as an opportunity to explore issues of control
- the music therapy assessment group is structured, predictable and 'safe'.

Motivation

In general, the children are very motivated to play the instruments and be part of the music-making process. The children want to be part of the music group and it is partly because of the children's high levels of motivation that this group provides the staff taking part in the session with an excellent additional opportunity to evaluate the children's strengths and difficulties. Many children will be excited by playing as a group and easily drawn into group crescendi and accellerandi. Sometimes children will lack confidence to play on their own but will be happy to play as part of a group, where the particular sound they are making blends into the whole and does not stand out.

Music making as a non-verbal way of communicating through sound

Some children with language difficulties will enjoy and feel at ease with the fact that music making allows them to make sounds and express themselves without the need to use language. Spontaneous musical turn taking and exchanging can be satisfying and yet simple to understand and follow. Children who lack confidence to play individually may be happy to play as part of a group. When leading a group improvisation, the music therapist can include all the children in the group equally, even if some children are playing at a more sophisticated level than others.

Music making as an opportunity to explore issues of control

Although the music therapist will very clearly lead and organize the group, the musical control can very subtly be shifted from the music therapist to individual children or to the group as a whole. This allows the music therapist to give individual children varying amounts of control, which may be very challenging for some children and very rewarding for others. Children can be observed in a leading and a following role and the music therapist can 'push' or 'reassure' children, depending on individual strengths.

The music therapy assessment group is structured, predictable and 'safe'

The fact that music happens in time and that songs have a clear beginning and end mean that music making can be reassuring for children who are constantly seeking for reassuring structures in their lives. Of course, much of the music played in these groups is unpredictable and improvised. Nevertheless it is not without form and the music therapists usually make sure pieces have clear, well-defined endings. It is also possible to experiment with musical structures and see how 'free' the children can be in their playing. However, it is always possible for the music therapist to return to a leitmotif or a familiar tune if she feels that a particular child needs to be reassured.

Group structure

In this part of the chapter we will describe different sections of the group and then explain how each activity helps us to assess the children's strengths and difficulties. It must also be noted that, in addition to the diagnostic considerations, the music therapist must be aware of balancing the needs of individual children with the needs of the group as a whole. Thus an activity may be chosen to reassure a child with obvious low self-esteem, for example, rather than purely for diagnostic purposes.

Another consideration will be the contrast and balance of one activity with another. For instance, an activity which involves free movement around the room may be suggested after an activity which involved intense concentration. This can provide the children with an opportunity to 'let off steam'. The purpose here is to structure activities in such a way as to maintain the children's interest. Obviously the diagnostic process will be enhanced if the children remain engaged, so it is important to keep this factor in mind, as well as considering which type of activities will allow the most effective observation of the children's strengths and weaknesses.

It is also important to remember that although the structure of the session and the activities suggested are central to the organization of the group, these activities are only vehicles through which the adults assess the children's strengths and difficulties. The music therapist's approach to the running of the group is flexible, according to the particular needs of the children, and may involve introducing ideas in a very spontaneous way.

Verbal introduction

DESCRIPTION

The music therapist explains that this is the music group and that it lasts one hour and happens at the same time each week. It is also explained that there are two rules in the music room: first, that the instruments are not to be damaged; second, that people must not hurt each other or themselves. Sometimes these rules will be mentioned at the start of the session, but at other times they will be implied rather than stated. For some children with conduct disorders 'laying down rules' at the beginning of a session could be seen as a challenge to attempt to contravene them and might actually encourage children to exhibit challenging behaviours. For other children it will be important to have these rules clearly stated so that a safe and reassuring environment is created.

The music therapist also explains that all the children will have the opportunity to have a free choice at the end of the session, which means that they will be able to choose any instrument and play it to the rest of the group. This is usually something that the children look forward to and can act as a motivator to manage difficult moments during the session.

PURPOSE

The verbal introduction helps to give the group an identity of its own and inform the children that they will have a chance to choose an instrument at some point in the session. 'Old' group members can be given responsibility, which may help them to welcome 'new' children to the group. The 'old' children's enthusiasm for the group will also reassure new children about its value. By encouraging the children to help each other during the session, the music therapist allows them some responsibility for the running of the session. This gives the children a chance to feel that it is 'their' group, rather than just another occasion where they are expected to do as the adults say.

Introduction and hello song

DESCRIPTION

The group always begins with a hello song. Sometimes 'old' group members will be invited to tell newcomers how this initial activity works. The music therapist sings the hello song, accompanying herself with the tambourine, and then passes the tambourine to one of the children in the group. During the singing the rest of the group are encouraged to copy the rhythm of the song, which will vary and change in order to ensure that the children are watching and listening. The child who receives the tambourine then plays it and sings or 'says' the song. Then this child will be copied by the rest of the group and may enjoy trying to 'catch out' other group members by playing in unexpected ways. The tambourine will then be passed on to the next child.

PURPOSE

This is a clear way to start and helps the children to settle and to understand that this is now the beginning of the music group. It is also a way of learning each other's names and of introducing each other musically rather than verbally, which some children find easier. However, some children will struggle to make eye contact with their peers and show little facial expression.

From this simple activity it is possible to observe whether a child can make choices, whether the music engages them and holds their attention and whether they are able to wait, listen and take turns. Sometimes children are reluctant to say their own names and will just beat, or even just hold the tambourine. Other children will refuse to have a turn at all. This could be indicative that a child lacks confidence or has little sense of self. Some children will be reluctant to follow their peers beat and feel a need to be constantly in control. Emotionally 'needy' children might always choose adults to pass the tambourine on to and may generally be very attention seeking.

Passing the tambourine around in a variety of ways

DESCRIPTION

After the hello song the music therapist might suggest that the tambourine is passed around in a variety of different ways, e.g. pretending it is very hot, sticky, heavy or asleep, which would mean that it had to be passed around quietly so that it does not 'wake up'. Sometimes the music therapist will ask the children for their ideas.

PURPOSE

This activity easily involves the children and makes them feel that they have some input into the group, yet at the same time they know that the adults are in control, which is an important feeling for many of the children at the Croft. From this activity the adults in the group can observe whether a child is able to use their imagination and play this game and also see whether they express any positive responses if they are praised for being especially imaginative.

Choosing musical instruments

DESCRIPTION

There is a variety of ways in which the instruments can be chosen. The following is an example of a system that seems to be quite successful. One child is invited to go to the instrument cupboard and choose instruments for each of the children in the group and place them under the children's chairs. Meanwhile the other children are asked to close their eyes so that their instrument will be a surprise. Care is taken to ensure that a different child is chosen each week. Sometimes the job is offered as an incentive to a child who is finding the beginning of the group difficult to manage or to make a child's last group special.

PURPOSE

This activity allows the adults to observe whether children are able to close their eyes, wait and remain in their seat. It is also possible to see whether there is any excitement at the prospect at having something chosen for them and also whether they are able to tolerate it if an instrument has been chosen that is not to their liking. For the child who is choosing instruments, we can see if they are able to risk making their own decisions and taking responsibility. It is also interesting to observe what instruments they choose, both for each group member and for themselves, as this can be an indicator of how they perceive themselves and others within the group or how they would like to be perceived. For example, in a recent group a child chose very small instruments (Indian bells, castanets and a thumb piano) for the other children, but chose bongo drums for herself. It may be interesting to note that she was the only girl in a group of four boys.

Group playing

DESCRIPTION

Once each child has an instrument ready under their chair the music therapist explains how the group playing will proceed. When the music therapist starts playing the piano, the children should pick up their instrument and play freely. When the piano playing stops, they must place their instrument carefully under their chair and put their arms up before moving round to the chair on their left. The music therapist explains that the adults will be looking carefully for the first person who successfully does this. Sometimes the music therapist will insert well-known tunes into her piano playing and encourage children to identify what tunes have been played before moving around to the next seat.

At times, this activity has become increasingly competitive with children insisting they have 'won' and others finding this difficult to accept. Children may have to be encouraged to accept the fact that they cannot always 'win' but that they may have a chance next time.

PURPOSE

It is interesting to observe whether children can tolerate not winning. Often children seem the most unable to accept this during their first few groups, but as they become more familiar with the structure of the activities they appear to relax and allow themselves to accept encouragement from the adults to move on.

Inserting familiar tunes allows the therapist to introduce reassuring structures at the same time as picking up and following different children's style of playing. It will be possible to observe whether a child is embarrassed by hearing nursery rhymes that are usually associated with younger children or whether they do not appear concerned by this issue. Some children obviously love having a chance to be 'little', whereas others dismiss such songs as 'babyish'.

The group playing provides a forum for assessing how engaged and motivated the children are in playing their instrument with others, whether they play in an isolated way or whether they appear aware of what the rest of the group (including the therapist at the piano) is doing. It is also possible to observe whether children can listen to and carry out instructions and therefore what their level of comprehension is.

The activities explained so far are used in every group. Sometimes children take a long time over these activities and there is only enough time left for the 'free choice' and the 'closing activity' described at the end of this section. At other times, the children need to move quickly from one thing to another and a choice is then made as to the most appropriate activities to use next. This depends very much on the children and the types of difficulties they are experiencing. Thought is also given to making them gender, culturally and age appropriate. Some of these activities are chosen or adapted from *Pied Piper: Musical Activities to Develop Basic Skills* (Bean and Oldfield 2001). Sometimes children will have their own suggestions and ideas for an activity. Care is taken to incorporate these into the group whenever possible.

Free choice

DESCRIPTION

As was discussed earlier, the children are almost always offered a 'free choice' towards the end of the group session. For many children this is a strong incentive to manage the rest of the group. The music therapist may refer to the 'free choice' at various points throughout the group to encourage and motivate children to manage their behaviour. Each child chooses an instrument and 'performs' to the rest of the group. Occasionally the music therapist might support and accompany a child on the piano, but only if this has been requested by the child. Sometimes children choose an electronic keyboard with a built-in rhythm section and will improvise dance music. Some groups of children like to dance and move to this music. This is encouraged only if the 'performer' agrees.

PURPOSE

The children's free choices allow us to see whether children can respect each other's opinions and wishes, listen to each other and express praise as well as receiving it. For the 'performer' it is an opportunity to play freely and to be briefly in control of the group. Issues of self-esteem and self-confidence can also be observed in this activity. Will a child play at all? How do they play? How long? What is their body language express-ing? Are they uncomfortable at being in the limelight or do they have a need to be in it and cannot tolerate others taking over? Do they enjoy playing or are they very inhibited?

Closing activity

DESCRIPTION

The activity used to bring the session to a close varies. The music therapist may involve the children in a discussion and ask each child what their favourite and least favourite aspect of the group was. Alternatively, a goodbye song similar to the hello song at the beginning of the session may be used. The music therapist could also use another imaginative activity involving passing a 'clap' around the circle in cupped hands. On other occasions the music therapist might sing a goodbye song incorporating the children's names. Sometimes the children will offer their own ideas as to how the group should end.

PURPOSE

At the end of the session, the music therapist aims to bring the group together in a reassuring way. The children who have been experimenting with issues of control will feel safe when the music therapist is clearly leading the group again for this closing activity. For some groups it may be useful to bring out and remind the children of important moments in the session.

Another important aspect of the closing activity is that the music therapist must say goodbye to the children who are leaving the unit before the next music group. This could be a sensitive issue and might need to be briefly acknowledged without being dwelt on at length. However, in other cases, particularly if a child has been on the unit a long time, it might be important to spend more time thinking about a child's last music group at the Croft. Sometimes the music therapist will ask the other children to consider what music or musical activities will help them to remember the children who are leaving.

The 'closing activity' can also prepare the children for the next part of their day. If the group has been very active and energetic, for example, the music therapist will choose the most appropriate activity to calm everyone down and prepare them for going back to the dining room.

Endings and transitions are difficult moments for many of the children at the Croft and the ways in which the children deal with both the ending of the group and the comings and goings of the children from the unit will be observed and noted.

Reviewing the group

Reviewing the group with the co-worker plays an integral part in the group process. It is an opportunity to share and discuss our observations and decide which key points we want to feed back to the team in the weekly management meetings. As the co-worker interacts with the children at different times of the day, her opinions are often a very useful and interesting insight into how the music is affecting the children. She will be in a good position to judge whether they are behaving in an expected or unexpected way and whether the musical activities engage children more or less than other interventions on the unit.

Each child will be considered separately and a brief paragraph will be included in the ongoing nursing notes which are written up on a daily basis, in individual files for each child. In this review, it is also important to review how the music therapist and the co-worker are working together and to address any difficulties or tensions in a frank and open way.

The co-worker's view of the group

To inform this chapter and also to provide another view as to what the group can offer in providing part of a global assessment of a child, Emma Carter interviewed her co-worker and we will now describe some of her comments.

The co-worker felt that the music therapy group seemed unique in the way that it could often bring out a child's creative side. She commented that she was often surprised by a child's musicality and imagination and, due to their particular difficulty, was not expecting to observe this. She felt that it was important that the group is structured, yet within this there is a certain amount of flexibility, which can allow children the freedom to explore other sides of themselves. Offering the potential to be creative means that we can observe whether children are able to take this opportunity and what they do as a result of it. As part of the assessment of a child, these observations are often a useful contribution to the team.

The co-worker also discussed the fact that the activities used in the group can often highlight the autistic tendencies of a child, for example, difficulties making or maintaining eye contact, stereotypical hand movements, difficulties in interacting with peers, sharing, taking turns, choosing or being unable to tolerate change. It can also highlight attention deficit hyperactivity disorder (ADHD) behaviours, such as difficulties in concentration, a tendency to play briefly and flit from one instrument to another and difficulties in remaining settled. In addition, the group can reveal a child's sensitivity to loud noise or, as in a recent case, show that a child who was previously thought to be oversensitive to noise could actually tolerate very loud and energetic playing.

The group provides an opportunity for the children to express themselves, to interact with each other musically and to have a chance to be free to enjoy themselves. The music group also provides an opportunity to observe the creative, imaginative and musical sides of a child.

Conclusion

In this chapter we have described a music therapy group which is mainly used to help the psychiatric team to evaluate the children's strengths and difficulties. Although this is an unusual purpose for a music therapy group, we feel that this work is immensely helpful to the team at the Croft and a valuable addition to other more conventional methods of assessment.

References

Bean, J. and Oldfield, A. (2001) *Pied Piper: Musical Activities to Develop Basic Skills.* London: Jessica Kingsley Publishers.

Hibben, J. (1991) 'Group music therapy with a classroom of 6–8 year old hyperactive learning disabled children.' In K. Bruscia (ed) *Case Studies in Music Therapy.* Phoenixville: Barcelona Publishers.

Molyneux, C. (2002) 'Short term music therapy within a child and adolescent mental health service – a description of a developing service.' Unpublished MA dissertation at Anglia Polytechnic University, Cambridge.

Oldfield, A. (2000) 'Music therapy as a contribution to the diagnosis made by the staff team in child and family psychiatry – an initial description of a methodology that is still emerging through clinical practice.' In T. Wigram (ed) *Assessment and Evaluation in the Arts Therapies.* St Albans: Harper House Publications.

Oldfield, A (2001) 'Mum can play too – short-term music therapy with mothers and young children.' *British Journal of Music Therapy 15*, 1, 27–36.

Tyler, H. (2001) 'Group music therapy with children and adolescents.' Paper presented at the Fifth European Music Therapy Congress, Naples, Italy, and at the 'Children Need Music' music therapy conference, London. (Awaiting publication by the British Society for Music Therapy.)

CHAPTER 11

Combined Efforts

Increasing Social-Emotional Communication with Children with Autistic Spectrum Disorder Using Psychodynamic Music Therapy and Division TEACCH Communication Programme

Ruth Walsh Stewart

Introduction

Psychodynamic music therapy and Division TEACCH might seem like an unusual combination. The first centres around moment-by-moment emotional shifts experienced through improvised music making. The second relies on careful adherence to structures and schedules. What happens when process and programme are brought together? This chapter describes how this particular combination helped to increase social-emotional communication with children with autistic spectrum disorder (ASD).

It started when a school-based speech and language therapist approached me. She had a particular interest in the assessment tools and interventions available to children with ASD. The Division TEACCH communication programme (Treatment and Education of Autistic and Communication Handicapped Children) had already begun to be introduced to schools in Northern Ireland in the mid-1990s as a method of developing communication and relating with these children. However this speech and language therapist wanted to find other ways of enhancing these skills. She had heard a little about music therapy and was curious about its relevant potential. Between us we devised a music and communication group structure. It was piloted over a ten-week period with a group of ASD children. It combined the techniques of psychodynamic music therapy and the structure of Division TEACCH. A rating scale was also devised to assess change in the areas of social skills and emotional communication. Levels were seen to increase over time. It was hypothesized that this observed improvement reflected an increase in each child's sense of autonomy, capacity for intersubjectivity and emotional relatedness. This was seen to be related to the provision of a specific facilitating environment within the music and communication group (Winnicott 1965).

This chapter will introduce ASD, psychodynamic music therapy and Division TEACCH and describe the set-up, format and outcome of the group project. It will then focus on the progress of one randomly chosen group member, 'Harry'.

Autistic Spectrum Disorder

Autism is a disorder of mental and emotional development affecting the ability to engage with other people, be aware of their feeling states and develop emotional relationships. Due to the wide range of apparent symptoms and abilities, it is also known as autistic spectrum disorder. Kanner (1943, p.250) said that autistic children 'come into the world with innate inability to form the usual, biologically provided affective contact with people'. Many theorists have provided variations on this theme. Alvarez and Reid (1999) describe it as a cognitive deficit where 'lack of emotional relatedness to others is the core and primary symptom' (p.5). Baron-Cohen and Howlin (1993) further hypothesize a 'theory of mind' (Leslie 1987) deficit which affects the ability to be aware of one's own and other people's mental states and to understand the relationships between these states and behaviour. Stern (1985) underlines this when he describes how a child, in face of potential danger, would not look to his mother to judge her response to a specific situation unless he could attribute to her 'the capacity to have and to signal an affect that has relevance to [her] own actual or potential feeling states' (p.132). This social referencing (Hobson 1995) guides the child in his assessment of and response to the situation. It also reflects intersubjectivity (Hobson 1993; Trevarthen *et al.* 1996) and interaffectivity (Stern 1985), a sense of another person's feeling states.

Hobson (1993) describes how the notion of intersubjectivity applies 'between and across individuals [where] one person's subjective experiences are both linked with and differentiated from the experiences of others'. In this way a child can build a sense of his own internal world in relation to the external world. In the case of autism he suggests there is an impairment in intersubjectivity where there is a 'sufficiently profound disruption in [these] forms of patterned interpersonal interchange that affect sharing, conflict or other modes of co-ordinated experience between the child and others' (Hobson 1993, p.14).

The route to greater awareness of self in relation to others is through the experience of accurate affect attunement (Stern 1985). In the first pre-verbal parent–infant relationship, the parent must initially be able to read or intuit the infant's feeling state. Second, she must reflect it back, not through imitation, but in a way that matches in vitality affect. This corresponds to the 'momentary changes in feeling states involved in the organic processes of being alive' (Stern 1985, p.156). Third, the infant must be able to read the response and understand it as corresponding to his own experience. 'It is only in the presence of these three conditions that feeling states within one person can be knowable to another and that they can both sense, without using language, that the transaction has occurred' (p.139).

In the case of ASD, difficulties lie in the third social and emotional referencing stage of affect attunement. However, there is potential for change provided a specific developmentally attuned approach is employed. This is done 'sometimes by meeting [the patients] wherever they are, at other times by tugging on the lifeline of human communication to get their attention and interest' (Alvarez and Reid 1999, p.49). What is important is the concept of the child/patient *in relationship* to other – 'cognitive and communicative "skills" can arise through emotional relationships' (Alvarez and Reid 1999, p.6). In therapy, therefore, the route to change is via the development of an affective relationship. This is the central tenet of psychodynamic music therapy. Additionally, recommendations for treatment of ASD, which correspond to the principles of Division TEACCH, are:

- formulation of simple contracts with detailed work schedules

- prompting and reinforcing to improve social and communication skills

- group work to focus on social tactics (Baron-Cohen and Howlin 1993).

Psychodynamic Music Therapy

Psychodynamic music therapy recognizes the importance of affect attunement with regard to the pre-verbal development of an emotional relationship. Stern (1985, p.146) operationalizes attunement by identifying three features of behaviour that can be matched without being imitative. These are intensity, timing and shape. They can be further broken down into the six categories of absolute intensity, intensity contour, temporal beat, rhythm, duration and shape. The musical equivalence of these terms is obvious in light of the rhythmic and affective dynamics of music. Improvised music provides the flexibility for reflecting the moment-by-moment dynamic shifts of a person's internal, emotional world and the interface of that with another person. It offers the opportunity for intersubjective attunement and adaption at an appropriate developmental level. This relates to one aspect of Winnicott's (1965) concept of holding, when he speaks of mother–infant interaction: 'it follows the minute day-to-day changes belonging to the infant's growth and development, both physical and psychological' (p.49). It provides the dependent infant with a line of continuity so that he is not just reacting to unpredictable events and 'for ever starting again' (p.141). He has a sense of 'going-on-being' (Winnicott 1958) which fortifies the experience of self.

In psychodynamic music therapy the organic nature of the medium of improvised music attends to the subtle vitality affects of intensity and time. In it lies the 'special potential for contact and communion' (Bartram 1991, p.6), a facilitating environment where the unshareable can become shareable and the internal world of the patients can 'mix with another's and be known to another' (Bartram 1991, p.17). Thus, the musical interchange reflects the dynamics of emotional relating and can help 'forge an affective relationship' (Sobey and Woodcock 1999, p.136).

In addition to improvised music making and focus on the relationship, clear boundaries with attention to consistency of time, place and duration of each session, are an essential part of psychodynamic music therapy. This reliable structure serves a holding and containing function. It increases the sense of predictability of the session and consequent agency and ability for interchange for the patient. We can appreciate the importance of this in relation to the potentially precarious world of inter-relations experienced in autism. This consistency of structure links with Baron-Cohen and Howlin's (1993) recommendation of simple timetables and schedules.

Division TEACCH

Division TEACCH is a structured communication programme devised for use with children with autism. It helps them by 'organizing their environments and providing clear, concrete and meaningful visual information' (Mesibov 1997, p.25). This takes the form of line-drawn pictures or photographs (depending on the child's ability to focus on an image without being distracted by dimension or lighting variation). These are used to indicate activities such as worktime, lunchtime, music, playcorner. A schedule is set out to sequence these activities. In this system the adult determines *what* work the child does, *how* the child works, for *how long* the child works and what follows.

Scheduling the work combined with psychodynamic boundaries was seen to provide a specific holding environment. This facilitated creativity, flexibility and a space for dynamic process. Here was the opportunity for developing emotional relationships and consequently each child's sense of himself.

Procedure

As outlined above, the project combined psychodynamic music therapy and the Division TEACCH programme. It ran for ten weeks with a group of five children. A scale of measurement was devised to assess change over time and was piloted on the project. It was hypothesized that the children would show change in a range of areas and that the measurement scale would provide evidence of this. The combined package was to offer both *a structured and a flexible environment* for the children. The structure took the form of:

- psychotherapeutic boundaries
- the use of visual cues for arriving at the session, indicating what task to carry out and when – photographs were used to help the children choose which instrument to play
- simple musical structures: specific songs with piano accompaniment marking the beginning, middle and end sections of each session.

Flexibility was offered in the following ways:

- some personal choice of musical instrument – encouragement of the child to play in his/her own way
- duration of each turn determined by the child (within reasonable limits of the group setting)
- improvised vocal accompaniment to the final activity
- adaption to suit the '*in relationship*' mental and emotional developmental level of each individual.

The 'how' and 'for how long' parts of the work were not pre-determined. This represented an adaption of the TEACCH method to fit the dynamic music therapy approach. Group participants were chosen as follows:

- each child group member had to be on the autistic spectrum. (Aarons and Gittens Autistic Continuum 1992)
- they had to be on a TEACCH programme before the project commenced
- they could not have had music therapy before.

Five boys were selected ranging in age (to nearest month) from 4 years and 5 months to 9 years and 11 months.

Adult members were consistent throughout the project. They included one music therapist, one speech and language therapist, two teachers and one classroom assistant. Apart from the music therapist, they all worked with at least one of the children in their professional capacities. The session structure was designed in consultation with the staff team and had the following format:

- Lively and brief 'hello to everyone'.

- Hello song where each child was offered a drum to play.

- Each child was invited, in turn, to choose a photograph of a musical instrument from a choice limited to their level of ability. They had to fetch the instrument and play it. There was a song structure with piano accompaniment. This activity was repeated, so that each child could choose a second instrument. As the children became more familiar with the song, it was increasingly varied and improvised on to reflect the creative and emotional quality of each child's music.

- A rainstick was played for the child and/or he played it. I vocalized to reflect the child's perceived experience of the sound.

- A chart mapping out the ten sessions and holiday breaks was marked off.

- From the piano, I sang and waved goodbye to each child and to the whole group.

Each session lasted approximately 40 minutes. All sessions were video-recorded.

Results (1)

For auditing purposes some composite results for the whole group were drawn up by the speech therapist and a colleague of hers and were confirmed by me, with reference to video recordings of the first, third, seventh and tenth sessions. These measured skill level over time ranging from 'no evidence' through 'emerging skill' to 'appropriate skill'. This was a limited design as the video was not always in a suitable position to pick up on every child's response within each session. Therefore, certain responses which may have been noted in personal records of the session would have registered as a non-score because they were not observable on video. The general areas covered were attention, social skills and musical response. Overall improvement was observed. See Figure 11.1 for the composite result for each child.

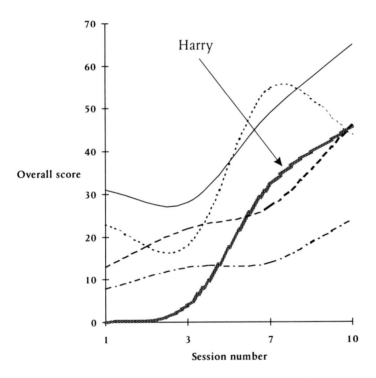

Figure 11.1 Composite scores for skill level over time

I then mapped the trend of increase for each skill area per child, indicated in Figures 11.2, 11.3 and 11.4. It is to be noted that there was no triangulation of these results nor statistical analysis. In addition, whilst there was an obvious trend of general improvement for each child causality is not inferred.

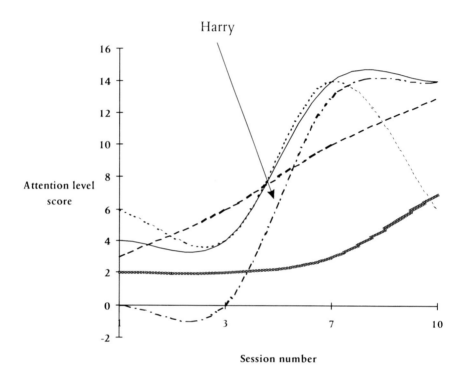

Figure 11.2 Levels of attention over time

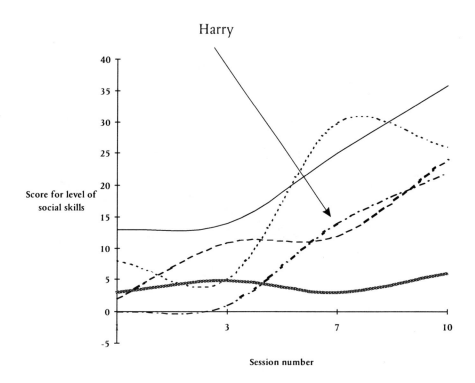

Figure 11.3 Level of social skills over time

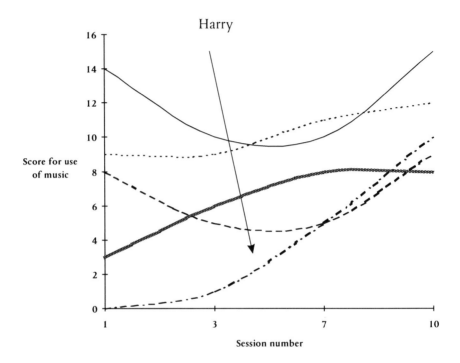

Figure 11.4 Use of music over time

Focus on one group member

Encouraged by the composite outcome results, I decided to revisit the data and look in more detail at the specific points of change for one randomly selected boy, Harry. A scale of measurement was drawn up to cover a broader range of areas: attention, communication, language, participation in the music, interaction, emotionality. The scale was devised with reference to the Autistic Continuum (Aarons and Gittens 1992) and the Pragmatics Profile (Dewart and Summers 1995), although measurement of emotions was not part of these. In addition, teachers of a school exclusively for ASD children were asked what measurements they would be interested in. The scale originally had 53 questions covering depth and breadth of information. This was reduced to 19 questions preferring to address a *range* of categories rather than depth. Where at least one instance of an event occurred it is marked one.

Harry's progress in the group music therapy

In the first session Harry was either in tears or on the verge of them throughout. He kept his arms firmly folded or pushed away instruments offered to him. He reportedly watched me while I played the piano, but not when I directed my attention to him. In subsequent early sessions he progressed to looking at the instruments and participating by repeatedly pushing at the instruments. I understood this to be music on his terms. In the middle sessions he became increasingly involved, tolerating my attention, giving eye contact, occasionally reaching for instruments, although maintaining a 'sulking' attitude throughout. He began to pass instruments to other group members and to wave goodbye.

In session eight, for the first time, there were no tears. Harry's music changed. He played for the duration of his turn and, significantly, in a new way – his music was gentle and quiet, with varied rhythms. There was a different texture and intensity to his music. It felt as if there was another part of Harry emerging through his music, no longer resistant or guarded, but open to being creative, exploratory and perhaps more vulnerable. By the final session his skills of social and emotional interaction were more apparent. He took a lead, he followed other's music, he more obviously played with the musical structures. He watched and waited for my accompaniment and it felt comfortable for me to be more improvisatory with his music. There was an exchange socially, musically and therefore, I think, emotionally – a sense of connection and relationship, wherein Harry felt sufficiently emotionally secure to risk interaction.

Video analysis was carried out on all of the first, sixth and last sessions. This was to test if there was observable and measurable, other than anecdotal, change over time. In scoring the questions, the observed occurrence of at least one instance of an event was marked one. There was no interrater reliability sought, nor were statistical tests carried out.

Results (2)

Change was observed in all categories, though not for each component. Harry's focus of attention moved away from other children in the group when they were acting out and became more channelled on to me. His control of attention moved up a stage, indicating an increase in receptivity to others' actions (Aarons and Gittens 1992; see Appendix at chapter end), see Table 11.1.

Table 11.1 Attention			
Attention	**Session 1**	**Session 6**	**Session 10**
Focuses on:			
Significant adult	0	1	1
Activity/musical instrument	0	1	1
Person carrying out activity: adult, peer, whole group	1, 1	1, 1, 0	1, 1, 0
Single channel attention:			
Difficult to control	1	1	0
Can control own attention	0	0	1

Harry became less self-absorbed and increasingly oriented towards the relevant activity or adult (Table 11.2).

Table 11.2 Communication			
Communication	**Session 1**	**Session 6**	**Session 10**
Orientates body towards:			
Activity	0	1	1
Significant adult	0	0	1
Requests assistance	0	0	0
Responds to:			
Greeting	0	0	1
Goodbye	0	0	1
Displays lack of body language	n/a	n/a	n/a
Displays spontaneous body language	0	0	1
Repetitive activities:			
Aimless	0	0	0
Purposeful	1	1	1
Creative	0	0	0
Seeks physical contact	0	0	0

Harry's level of engagement moved from a self-oriented physical response to the music to being more engaged with the musical instruments and in shared music making. His level of creativity also increased (see tables 11.3 and 11.4).

Participation in the music	Session 1	Session 6	Session 10
Table 11.3: Participation in the music			
Responds to musical stimuli:			
Moves body	0	1 taps arm	1 taps foot
Moves eyes	1	0	0
Reaches for source of sound	0	0	0
Grasps instrument	0	0	0
Holds instrument	0	0	1
Pushes instrument away	1	1	0
Selects instrument:			
By photograph	0	1	1
By instrument itself	0	0	0
Receives instrument from adult, peer	0, 0	1, 0	1, 1
Matches photograph to instrument	0	0	1
Plays instrument:	0	1	1
Range of volume	—	Quite loud /loud	Quiet/quite loud
Range of intensity	—	Rough/ rigorous	Hard/gentle; uncertain/ deliberate
Range of duration	—	Limited time/set song	Set song
Range of apparent affect	—	Resistant/ engaged	Determined/ thoughtful

Plays in relation to other:	0	0	1
Waits for beginning	—	—	1
Keeps beat	—	—	0
Stops when music stops	—	—	1
Plays in a range of ways	0	0	1
Requires musical structure to play	n/a	1	1
Plays with improvised music	0	0	1

Table 11.4: Interaction			
Interaction	Session 1	Session 6	Session 10
Initiates interaction: With adult, peer	0, 0	0, 0	1, 1
Verbally	—	—	0
Musically	—	—	1
Maintains interaction: Verbally	n/a	0	1
Verbally	—	—	0
Musically	—	—	1
Imitation	—	—	0
Own ideas	—	—	1
Exchange of ideas	—	—	1
Can tolerate being imitated	n/a	n/a	n/a
Terminates interaction:	n/a	1	1

Verbally	—	0	0
Musically	—	1	1
Draws to a close:			
Naturally	—	0	1
Abruptly	—	1	0
Gets distracted / loses interest:	—	0	0
Stops when accompaniment stops	—	0	1

Harry was always expressive in his body language and facial expression. He displayed a broader range of emotions when he played music (Table 11.5).

Table 11.5: Emotionality			
Emotionality *Expresses emotions:*	**Session 1**	**Session 6**	**Session 10**
Verbally	0	0	0
Non-verbally	1	1	1
• facial expression	1 – pouts	1 – pouts	1 – serious
• body language	1 – hands on hips; head in hands; arms crossed	1 – arms crossed	1 – hands on hips
Vocally	1 – cries	0	0
Musically	0	1 (see music)	1 (see music)
Apparent emotional experience	upset; resistant to change	upset; resistant; curious	indignation; surprise

Discussion

The scale of measurement

The purpose of devising and applying a scale of measurement was to investigate and give evidence of change in a range of areas for ASD children in a combined music therapy and Division TEACCH programme. There were deficiencies in the scale of measurement of the nature of operationalization of certain terms, e.g. 'significant' adult as music therapist or person holding instrument, offering photographs. There were also difficulties with overlap of categories, e.g. communication, interaction, emotional expression and musical play. The scale, however, did measure change in all areas. Questions are raised regarding the reason for these changes and are a result of context research rather than running a controlled experiment. It would be difficult to run an ethically sound experiment and to take account of the variables of human personality, developmental shifts and familiarity effect, amongst many others. Some context-related issues include the following:

- Harry's focus of attention was measured as moving away from other group members except when it was their turn. This could reflect his skills of attention to the activities, but we do not know the nature of the other children and if they were highly distractible in the early sessions and more settled in later ones.

- Chairs were used in the final three sessions (instead of beanbags). This physical change to the environment may have influenced Harry's focus and control of attention and his body orientation towards the activities.

The scale observed apparent level of affect and noted an increase in range of emotions. It would be useful to use a pre-existing category of emotions in a move towards objectifying the record of observation. As interrater reliability was not sought, the involvement of an outside source of reference on a retest would test the reliability of the scale.

The combined music therapy and TEACCH input

This was seen to effect change with increase in the following areas: focus of attention, involvement in the group structure and music making, interaction with others, creativity in the music and observable range of non-verbal and musical expression.

The TEACCH programme provided a work schedule for the structure of the group session – getting to the music therapy room, what work was involved, e.g. hello song, instrument choice, etc., leaving the room and 'what next'. Musical structures, mostly in the form of songs or the use of specific instruments, were employed to demarcate the beginning, middle and end sections of each session. The application of these structures provided a coherent and predictable framework and the opportunity to address social tactics (Baron-Cohen and Howlin 1993). They also related to the psychodynamic concept of provision of a holding and facilitating environment offering consistency, reliability and responding adaptively to the needs of the child. This adaptive response called on the techniques of accurate affect attunement, containment and countertransference. Through the use of improvised music – a flexible and creative medium – the moment-by-moment dynamic shifts of the child's internal emotional world and its relation to another's could be attuned to in an ongoing organic and supportive way. In this way the child could develop an emotional capacity to play and relate to other people (Walsh Stewart and Stewart 2002). This helped to identify and reinforce a sense of subjective self and contribute towards the development of individuation. From this point, the child could become aware of another person as separate, just as a young baby leaves the state of experience of merging of minds with the mother and gradually recognizes the space between them.

Within this transitional, holding space lay the opportunity for intersubjective and interaffective relating. In Hobson's terms, the musical interplay provided the opportunity for social referencing and the development of understanding. In this instance the combination of the structure and the inbuilt dynamic flexibility at a musical and emotional level facilitated the opportunity for cognitive and emotional learning and development. As Alvarez and Reid say: 'it is the emotionality in the contact which promotes change in social relatedness, communication and thoughtfulness' (1999, p.6). Harry may have had the experience of emotional relating and containment through the shared music making. This contributed to a developed sense of internal cohesion and emotional self-awareness and therefore the ability to engage in the unpredictable arena of social interaction. For example, when he pouted and crossed his arms firmly he seemed to resist anything to do with another person touching his inner world. When he engaged in music making he opened himself up to be interacted with in a more creative way. From this it was evident that he developed a sense of agency within the interaction, an increase in intersubjectivity and interaffectivity.

The engagement of a multidisciplinary team

Through regular feedback, the engagement of a multidisciplinary team offered opportunities for learning about other approaches and for questioning, adapting or reinforcing one's own techniques. As Sobey and Woodcock say: 'a [music] therapist may treat as meaningful and significant sounds which perhaps initially are spontaneous and unintentional. Becoming aware that these are being treated as communicative may lead to them being used as such' (1999, p.148).

This project provided a unique time and space in the educational setting to think about all sounds, silences and behaviours of the children as meaningful communications. This opportunity, in some instances, informed the approaches used in the classroom. Staff said they were encouraged to transfer some of the ideas from the group sessions back to the classroom e.g. adapting more child-centred interactional approaches, such as waiting for the child's creative response and using flexible musical structures to assist with group work, the development of social skills and self-agency.

Validity of the project

This project was valid as a research pilot in that it answered the questions it set out to investigate. Change was measured and noted to be in the direction of social and emotional individuation and consequent interaction. The cause of the change was not measured, although it is suggested that the facilitating environment of a developmentally attuned, structured approach combined with the musical and emotional relationship with the music therapist were contributing factors. Making this into more than a suggestion is dependent on being able to measure how much the child is attuned to and making an in-depth measurement of his/her capacity for social referencing and for experiencing emotional containment. A much larger scale of research could investigate the link between emotional development and the development of social skills in the context of psychodynamic music therapy, Division TEACCH and autistic spectrum disorder.

Conclusion

Ten sessions of group music therapy combining a psychodynamic approach and the structure of Division TEACCH brought about change in the areas of social-emotional communication for children with ASD. This was a new and innovative project at a multidisciplinary level carried out in Northern Ireland. It succeeded in stimulating a fresh and creative approach to complement existing resources available in the treatment of children diagnosed with ASD.

Appendix

Attention control

STAGE 1

Approximate age 0–1 year.
Can pay fleeting attention, but is highly distractible.

STAGE 2

Approximate age 1–2 years.
Pays rigid attention to an activity of own choice.

STAGE 3

Approximate age 2–3 years.
Single channel attention.
Can attend to activity of adult's choice but is difficult to control.

STAGE 4

Approximate age 3–4 years.
Integrated attention.
Can attend fully, but for short spells only.

STAGE 5

Approximate age 4–5 years.
Integrated attention.
Can attend fully, but for short spells only.

STAGE 6

Approximate age 5+ years.
Integrated attention.
Can pay well-controlled and sustained attention.

Acknowledgements

The author would like to thank the Armagh and Dungannon Health and Social Services Trust for funding the original project. Thanks are also due to Professor Noel Sheehy, Queen's University Belfast, for his supervision on the further research aspect of this project.

Particular and special acknowledgements are due to Mrs Grainne Smith and Mrs Angela Coulter (specialist speech and language therapists) for their invitation to introduce music therapy to the children on the autistic spectrum and for their subsequent resourcefulness regarding the finer details of the application of Division TEACCH.

Final thanks go to the children and staff members of Lisanally Special School (Armagh) who participated in the project.

References

Aarons, M. and Gittens, T. (1992) *The Autistic Continuum.* Windsor: NFER-NELSON.

Alvarez, A. and Reid, S. (eds) (1999) *Autism and Personality – Findings from the Tavistock Autism Workshop.* London: Routledge.

Baron-Cohen, S. and Howlin, P. (1993) 'The theory of mind deficit in autism: some questions for teaching and diagnosis.' In S. Baron-Cohen, H. Tager-Flusberg and D. Cohen (eds) *Understanding Other Minds.* Oxford: Oxford University Press, pp.466–480.

Bartram, P. (1991) 'Aspects of the theory and practice of psychodynamic music therapy.' Paper presented at the November conference of the Scottish Music Therapy Council, Edinburgh.

Dewart, H. and Summers, S. (1995) *The Pragmatics Profile of Everyday Communication Skills in School-Age Children.* Windsor: NFER-NELSON.

Hobson, R.P. (1993) *Autism and the Development of Mind.* Hove: Lawrence Erlbaum.

Hobson, R. P. (1995) 'The intersubjective domain: approaches from developmental psychopathology.' In T. Shapiro and R. W. Emde (eds) *Research in Psycho-Analysis – Process, Development, Outcome.* New York: International Universities Press.

Kanner, L. (1943) 'Autistic disturbances of affective control.' *Nervous Child 2,* 217–250.

Leslie, A.M. (1987) 'Pretence and representation: the origins of theory of mind.' *Psychological Review 94.*

Mesibov, G. (1997) 'Formal and informal measures on the effectiveness of the TEACCH Programme.' *Autism 1*, 1, 25–35.

Sobey, K. and Woodcock, J. (1999) 'Psychodynamic music therapy – considerations in training.' In A. Cattanach (ed) *Process in the Arts Therapies.* London: Jessica Kingsley Publishers.

Stern, D. N. (1985) *The Interpersonal World of the Infant.* New York: Basic Books.

Trevarthen, C., Aitken, K., Papoudi, D. and Robarts, J. (1996) *Children with Autism: Diagnosis and Intervention to Meet Their Needs.* London: Jessica Kingsley Publishers.

Walsh-Stewart, R. and Stewart, D. (2002) 'See me, hear me, play with me: working with the trauma of early abandonment and deprivation in psychodynamic music therapy.' In J.P. Sutton (ed) *Music, Music Therapy and Trauma – International Perspectives.* London: Jessica Kingsley Publishers.

Winnicott, D.W. (1958) 'Primary maternal preoccupation.' In D. W. Winnicott *Collected Papers: Through Paediatrics to Psycho-Analysis.* London: Tavistock.

Winnicott, D.W. (1965) *The Maturational Process and the Facilitating Environment.* London: Hogarth Press.

CHAPTER 12

Preparing a Potential Space for a Group of Children with Special Needs

Julie Sutton

This chapter describes group work undertaken in a special school. Twelve children from two classes attended weekly during the second term of the school year. A collaborative approach with staff was central to this work, because the idea for the group came out of discussion with teaching staff based in a classroom where children with challenging behaviour were placed. In order to emphasize the significance of this approach, the preparation for the collaboration forms the major aspect of this chapter. The aim is to show how the collaboration was achieved, demonstrating why such preparation is essential in group therapy work in schools. In the chapter I explore the issues that arose during the work in five main sections:

1. The story of the group.

2. The thinking behind the music therapy group.

3. Running the group.

4. What was learned.

5. Final thoughts about working in schools.

The story of the group

This work was a departure from previous music therapy group sessions in the school, which were aimed either at meeting the needs of small groups of two to six children (selected from more than one class), or based on single-class groups of up to eight or nine children. In this case, a class of children who had previously attended group sessions was joined by three children from a special unit. These children (A, B and C) presented with behaviour on the autistic continuum and, in different ways, had severe difficulty in forming relationships and coping with everyday social situations. One of our aims was to provide a space where these three isolated children could be offered a group experience. We also intended to explore the potential within both structured and improvised music making for this diverse group. Finally, the work depended on the support and active involvement of five members of staff drawn from each classroom.

This multipurpose focus presented challenges. There were not one but three groups – the three isolated children, the previous class group and the staff members. The features holding these elements together were the room in which we met, the regularity of sessions, the time boundary and the musical focus. I also thought of the group membership in terms of meeting some of the issues that related to the three children in the larger school community.

The group size was another important factor. Compared to my usual clinical practice, this was a large number, with up to 12 children, 5 members of staff and myself present. It would be important to be clear about the purpose of meeting together and I felt that an agreed approach would make this manageable. With a smaller number there could be more focus on the individual. The larger size, however, would concentrate on the social nature of spending time together. As Ettin has noted, there can be both 'closeness' and 'anonymity' in such a setting (1999, pp.17–19). This concept provided the best fit for the differing needs of the trio of small groups within the whole.

The thinking behind the music therapy group

In the school at this time there was a tendency to group 'difficult' children together in one classroom. A behaviour programme was undertaken, based around a highly structured approach relying on visual cues, reward and punishment. The predictability of the structure had a calming effect on some children and they conformed relatively readily to their assigned tasks. The programme was considered a means of reducing 'difficult' behaviour and seemed to provide an answer to how to manage these children. Yet segregating the children into one classroom also had an impact. Their problems were classified through their behaviour. Denial of the reality of difficulties underlying the behaviour left the children isolated and outcast. They were considered problematic members of the school community as a result of behaviour which was challenging to those around them. As Strange has noted previously: 'In the educational setting a hyperactive, aggressive, nervous or withdrawn child tends to be seen by staff and children as a problem for the group' (Strange 1987, p.30).

Strange recommended that these children be incorporated into music therapy groups specifically in order to address the impact of challenging behaviour, resisting the natural urge of staff to protect other children from this. With the group I was organizing, the physical reality of A, B and C attending a working music therapy group had an effect on the rest of the staff. It was rather like giving permission for the recognition that these children had potential to share a working space with their peers. Each week that the group met without the (unspoken) feared disaster and destruction proved that it was not only possible, but a positive event that held its own value.

Before the group began there was the opportunity for discussion with the teachers from both classes involved. We spent time thinking together about our expectations and hopes for the group, as well as the needs of the children. We agreed that, as well as our own attendance, we would involve staff members from each classroom. Their responses and observations would be essential in the development of the group as a whole. Their supportive presence would help us create a safe atmosphere in which the group could take place. In defining these adult roles, we placed particular emphasis on becoming engaged and interested in the group music, while not being actively directive. We aimed not only to encourage the children's involvement, but also to give them the space in which to make their own responses: for instance, we wanted to avoid the well-intentioned action of taking a child's arm and making them play an instrument. We established a 'house style', viewing each child's response as unique and valid. We set simple ground rules about acceptable and unacceptable behaviour for the children, to make this approach safe for staff members and children. We suggested ways in which boundaries could be set. We introduced the concept of a child acting out a bad feeling and the necessity for not sending out a message that the child was 'bad'. These preparatory discussions enabled the adults involved to identify common goals, the usual practice when establishing working groups in schools.

I described the central aspect of our thinking about the group as containment. With particular reference to A, B and C we explored what I understand to be Bion's concept of a 'psychic container', where the responses and feelings from the child are attended to, held onto, thought about, assimilated and then reacted to by parents (Bion 1962, pp. 306–10). The child senses this containment and is enabled to experience difficult and overwhelming feelings safely. Without this, such terrifying feelings remain unbearable, unable to be thought about and are projected outwards. In our discussion we were able to think about our roles in the group combining to provide a 'psychic container'. We agreed how easy it could be to become caught up in an outburst from a child and then accentuate the tense and frightened feelings that might be in the room. It was important to hold our idea of container in mind during the sessions and we hoped to pass on this approach to other staff members. We were aware that any explosive events in the room would also need to be talked about afterwards. In this particular school, staff coffee and lunch breaks were often used for this purpose. For instance, it was helpful that there was a general understanding that anyone experiencing a physical attack would be given space to talk before the end of the day. The necessity for staff to process stressful experiences was acknowledged.

It has been my experience that the idea of processing and assimilating the emotional component in collaborative group work can be difficult in the educational setting. In this instance, there was a group of staff members who had agreed to explore a different way of working. I became more aware of the impact of my work in a curriculum-orientated context because, as well as staff incorporating my perspective, I was able to learn more about their approach to the children in the classroom situation. This process reminded me of the huge impact that a music therapist can have in joining a school staff. Our approach and theoretical training can be at odds with the ways that children's educational progress is measured. While able to think developmentally and in terms of types of behaviour, we focus on the psycho-emotional aspects of a child's life. This is not the focus of a school curriculum. The arrival into a school of a music therapist can therefore be seen as a radical move, leaving bewilderment, suspicion or hostility in its wake. An undercurrent of our work in schools is the task of holding in mind a sense of identity as a music therapist. We know from experience that this is not always an easy undertaking. Clinical supervision and contact with our peers is therefore vital.

For this new group, I suggested that there should be a predictable, structured approach to the sessions, but that this structure could be actively challenged with improvisation. There was an agreed format that could be presented to the children from the beginning. In this sense I thought of the structure as a container. I have come to understand that my suggestion for structure also reflected my anxieties about running the sessions. These concerned my ability to contain this disparate and challenging group, along with the expectations of its accompanying adults. Even before we began, it was a highly charged situation. We were not only taking on the group, but the wider implication for the school of the unconscious material projected onto these children. I was reminded of the observations of Towse and Flower:

> Overall, the group started from the position where there were two sets of anxious people: the therapists and the others. In an attempt to alleviate anxiety, the therapists were very active, setting the agenda and taking responsibility for the 'success' of the session. (Towse and Flower 1993, p.76)

I see now that my use of structure aimed to alleviate the anxiety of the adults to some extent, giving us a solid musical place to start from.

Running the group

The group ran for a school term, using a structured approach based around activities bounded by songs. At the beginnings and ends of the sessions there was an identifiable greeting and goodbye. A ritual of arriving and leaving the room with the instruments accompanied this. The middle part of the session focused on activities such as playing together, taking turns, copying or accommodating any particular request a group member had. While the session was structured we departed from predictability through picking up different group responses. The following two examples illustrate occasions where this was possible:

The 'hello'

> We begin the 'hello' song, where group members can nominate who we will sing to if they wish. Everyone is included and can choose whether or not they participate actively. We engage in this for several minutes. Suddenly, the dinner lady puts her head around the door, looking for some information from a teacher about the number of dinners required that day. Child B vocalizes anxiously in response to the intrusion, while another calls out the dinner lady's name with some excitement. The music had now petered out, but we agree to sing 'hello' to her, also incorporating the information she needs into the song. During this child B becomes visibly relaxed and vocalizes part of the dinner lady's name. The song finishes, the dinner lady smiles and tells the children that she will see them at lunch. She then leaves the room quietly, we wave and then continue with the 'hello'.

This example began with an unexpected intrusion into the room, causing Child B to become agitated. This agitation resonated with the shock felt by other members of the group. The use of the song enabled the focus to shift back to the point at which the session was interrupted. Child B was sufficiently reassured by the return to the familiar activity to add his contribution. By incorporating the interruption into the music the session was brought back into focus.

This brings up the issue of potential boundary problems in the therapy setting, which can be particularly difficult in schools where classrooms can be visited frequently during the day. The powerful effect of visitors upon those in the room cannot be underestimated: some children welcome visitors, while others will experience the opening of the classroom door as an intrusive and frightening event. In using a classroom for a session the therapist is faced with challenges on many levels. There are the problems of making the space as free as possible from outside distractions, whether within the room (for example, equipment and furniture) or outside it (sudden interruptions). Establishing the confidentiality of the setting is essential, but can be difficult to maintain if the 'Do not Disturb' notice on the door is disregarded by a forgetful staff member or a child who cannot read. Therapists in schools are usually working in what is regarded as a public, social space. The safeguarding of the private space necessary for therapy work is undertaken in relation to this. The above example demonstrates an occasion when a dinner lady's appearance caused a private space to become public. The reaction and subsequent actions of the group re-established the sense of ownership.

The problem of unexpected interruptions is not uncommon in settings where space is at a premium and where the general running of the institution becomes paramount. Nevertheless, impact of these intrusions is powerful for the child in a vulnerable state. Again, the agreed approach of the adults in the group enabled this to be dealt with calmly, as well as retaining the focus of the session. This reminds me of a point raised in a recent paper by the Portugese therapist Teresa Paula Leite (2001). While based on work with a different client group (using an improvisatory approach to psychodynamic group therapy within an adult psychiatric setting), it has relevance to the example. Leite also stressed the importance of retaining a space that is separated from the general running of the institution:

> The music therapy session should be prepared in a way that we provide the patient with an organized frame to help him/her organize their thoughts and behaviour, with a time and a place that are consistent throughout and clearly differentiated from other activities on the unit ... It is through the consistent features of their own environment that they will regain the capacity to control their

internal experience of chaos, relate to the world around them, and distinguish themselves from it. (Leite 2001, p.93, 95)

The adult response to the dinner lady's intrusion into the group can be seen as a response related to reclaiming the group space that was destroyed by the interruption. This underlies the recovering of privacy when the space had been made public by the intrusion of the visitor.

The drum

> We are taking turns to choose an instrument. For the first time Child C is able to choose, but does not play. Placing the instrument near him, I play and sing softly about his choice. Other children begin to vocalize and I improvise with them. As the music changes from the group song to the group's own music and then back to the song, Child C gently strokes the instrument. There is a feeling of Child C receiving the music made spontaneously by the group out of and returning to the original structure.

This was a pivotal moment for Child C. Staff could have taken C's hand and played the instrument with it, but by tolerating the uncertainty of C's reaction and not expecting him to participate as other children had done, staff had enabled something else to take place. This was a way of holding onto and thinking about C's response. This became a form of containment. In not acting on their own wish for Child C to perform by playing, a space emerged within which other children both contributed to and led the developing music. While emerging from a structured approach, the music became the group's creation, held in mind by the adults.

Another important factor for the group was the impact of the three children upon the other nine. These nine children had attended group sessions during the previous school year. The sessions were run with the active co-operation of their teacher, who took on a co-therapist role with me. I was fortunate that this teacher was a sensitive musician who had established a safe and creative classroom environment for the children. The group sessions fitted easily into this setting and had at their base creative play and improvisation, within an overall structure that formed the basis for the later, larger group work. Therefore the nine children from the original group were familiar with the format and the therapist. It was also explained in simple terms that three other children would be joining us in this new group. We added that their behaviour would show us how difficult it was for them to share the music with others. We were there to support them in their efforts, as we had already done with each other in the previous sessions. The final example illustrates this:

Waiting

> We have sung 'hello' and the session has reached a stage where we are taking turns to choose an instrument. The children have also chosen whether or not they will play on their own, with the therapist, or with another group member. The mood of the group has been one of expectation of each next choice, along with acknowledgement of the effort and achievement of each musician.
>
> It is Child A's turn. When offered the choice of either a drum or a cowbell (his usual preferences), A looked excited and tense, but pushed away both instruments, while still holding onto the drum. Knowing that he could throw objects when under pressure, his teacher held the other side of the drum. It was apparent that A indeed wanted to play the drum, but, provocatively, was not going to. I noted that perhaps we had kept A waiting for long enough and now it was our turn to wait. One of the class group wondered if A didn't want to take his turn today anyway, a comment that could have been at least partly motivated by her own desire to play, as she was the next to take a turn. Her teacher reassured her that everyone would have a turn, but maybe A needed a little more time to 'get ready'. We could all see that A still held the drum and was now beginning to relax. The mood in the room had changed from one of expectancy, to a relaxed companionship. It was OK to wait and we were all ready for A to make his own choice, rather than urging him to begin. As the tension dropped further, A gently tapped the drum, beginning the music.
>
> The group listened intently to A's music and after he had finished there was spontaneous applause from several members of the class group. Rather than a reflex action after a performance, this

applause reflected an acknowledgement of A's choice to actively participate. A pushed away the drum and folded his arms.

This example demonstrates a major impact of the three individual children upon the other nine children. It can be interpreted in a number of ways, but central to what took place was the ability of the whole group to wait to see what A might choose to do, and to wait in a non-judgemental manner. The difficulty of his long wait for his turn had been voiced and indeed shared by others. For A, a pattern of something being expected of him was broken. Rather than having to 'perform' for someone else, perhaps he had an experience of his peers accepting his contributing, as he was able. The response of the adults was to reinforce this attitude of shared responsibility, while recognizing differing needs. The preparation for the sessions enabled us to provide models of how to respond that could in turn be taken up by the nine children who formed the class group.

The three examples illustrate the significance of the preparatory work with this group which facilitated a change in approach by the adults based in the educational setting. While the preparation was detailed and included different ways of thinking about the children and their responses in the sessions, this directly affected the course of the sessions. As well as informing the group work, the result was a supportive setting in which to work.

What was learned

A major purpose of the sessions was to plan a time in the school week when three isolated children could be offered an experience of them-selves as part of the larger school community. In the title for this chapter I have used Winnicott's term 'potential space' (1971). This was in order to indicate the way in which the group was thought about from the very beginning. Winnicott uses the term *potential space* in order to think about a stage in development during which the baby is at first merged with and then separates from the mother. The term describes where this develop-mental shift can occur between the baby (me) and the other (not me). Placing this in a broader context, Winnicott has this to say:

> It could be said that with human beings there can be no separation,
> only a threat of separation; and the threat is maximally or minimally
> traumatic according to the experience of the first separatings.
> (Winnicott 1971, p.108)

With these words, Winnicott places cultural experience as something
taking place between the individual and the environment. Using the term
'potential space', this cultural experience is said to be rooted first in play,
the significance of which is described in the following way:

> The potential space happens only in relation to a feeling of confi-
> dence on the part of the baby, that is, confidence related to the
> dependability of the mother-figure or environmental elements ...
> Given the chance, the baby begins to live creatively, and to use actual
> objects to be creative into and with. If the baby is not given this
> chance then there is no area in which the baby may have play, or may
> have cultural experience. (Winnicott 1971, p.100–101)

The adults in my group appear to have taken on collectively a role of
dependent figure in order that the children had the confidence to begin
to play. Along with cultural experience as expressed in Winnicott's terms,
for Child A, Child B and Child C this was essential. These three children
had an experience of being segregated from the immediate school
community. This was also of significance for the other children, outside
mainstream education, within the special school system.

Final thoughts about working in schools

As the sessions evolved, this was an exciting process to be part of. I feel
that the large amount of pre-session preparation that I undertook was significant in the development of this group. I was also fortunate to be
working with colleagues who were open to exploring a different way of
working. The issues we faced in deciding to combine children with
differing needs from two classes can be summarized as follows:

- conscious awareness of the challenge of running the group

- having a common purpose

- issues of containment and safety

- a sense of group ownership
- staff process
- feedback
- maintaining a space separate from the rest of the school day
- importance of thinking together about the space – encouraging a reflective stance.

Finally, this was by no means a group without difficulties. In schools, like other settings, adults can look to the therapist and project onto them any number of roles. We can find ourselves cast as rescuer, or someone with all the answers – the expert, the concert performer and therapist to all. In schools we can sometimes be assigned other difficult roles – the inter-loper or the revolutionary, because we bring theoretical approaches outside those mostly used in educational institutions. An active awareness for the therapist that her role is separate from herself is of course important, as is the task of holding onto therapeutic effectiveness in an environment that is not focused primarily on the psycho-emotional state of pupils. This all takes energy, particularly when there are projections onto the therapist that can be undermining. It was possible to confront these issues in a collaborative way because of the initial preparatory work in the form of a pre-group comprising the adults who were to be working together.

There was also an unexpected outcome of making a political statement about general perceptions of a segregated class of children. As Winnicott wrote:

> It is creative perception more than anything else that makes the indi-vidual feel that life is worth living. Contrasted with this is a relation-ship to external reality which is one of compliance, the world to be fitted in with or demanding adaptation. (Winnicott 1971, p.65)

Our collaborative work had aimed to provide a potential space where the children were able to experience themselves as a group. When the sessions ended we felt that our creation of such a space had proved useful for both children and staff. In preparing a potential space for the group it was necessary to accept first that there was potential for the group to co-exist. We then prepared the space within which this could take place.

We recognized that we had to contain in different ways what might be presented in the room. We offered the music to the children for their use as a potential means of containing what could not be expressed verbally.

Our thinking about the group provided another form of container. Here we assumed the responsibility for holding onto and then what Sobey and Woodcock describe as 'digesting' some of the anxiety brought into the space by the three individual children (1999, pp.146–7). When talking about their child psychotherapy work with violent children and adolescents, Parsons and Dermen echo this way of working (1999, p.337). They placed the importance of seeing children's challenging behaviour as attempts and then failures to find a way of feeling safe under stressful circumstances. The role of the therapist is to provide a containing environment, thinking about what cannot be thought about by the child. In my group it was the adults in the room who shared increasingly the responsibility for this task. Our discussions about what had taken place in the room also served as a supervisory space within which our own responses to situations could be aired and thought about. In writing about a different setting in a psychiatric ward, O'Connor has described how important team thinking can be and how this in itself can safeguard acting out in response to countertransference (O'Connor 1994, p.111). This is relevant to the example I have given, because the thinking we adults did together acknowledged that our feelings and actions had a direct impact upon what happened in the room. In the educational setting it can be difficult to find this type of space. Much is focused upon aims, goals and attaining targets, through that which can be measured.

In the group sessions this approach also enabled the nine children from the class group to experience the three isolated individuals in a different way. Rather than be segregated or avoided, the children were welcomed and valued. These responses had an impact upon the children for whom the group was originally formed. As they felt continually safer in the setting, the aggressive behaviour of A, B and C diminished and they were able to offer more of themselves to and receive from the group.

This also had an impact upon the larger school environment. The classroom where A, B and C were based became more accessible to others. The group sessions themselves served the function of containing what had been unable to be thought about by the rest of the school.

Other staff members expressed interest in what was happening in the room. It is possible that some of the earlier interruptions to the sessions were attempts to discover more about what had been taking place privately. The positive impact of the collaborative work was demonstrable when the adults concerned were to be observed talking intently and often with excitement outside the sessions. We had evolved a good model for working with the 'difficult' children. Furthermore, these very same children had not only responded to this approach, but with their peers had been able to contribute constructively to the group. For all these reasons I feel that the long and careful preparation for the potential space was worthwhile and of great benefit, and rewarded the initial effort.

References

Bion, W.R. (1962) 'A theory of thinking.' *International Journal of Psychoanalysis* *43*, 306–310.

Ettin, M.F. (1999) *Foundations and Applications of Group Psychotherapy*. London: Jessica Kingsley Publishers.

Leite, T.P. (2001) 'Psychodynamic group music therapy with acute psychiatric patients.' In D. Aldridge, G. di France, E. Ruud and T. Wigram (eds) *Music Therapy in Europe*. Rome: ISMEZ/Onlus, pp.89–101.

O'Connor, S. (1994) 'Countertransference: some clinical aspects.' In R. Ekins and R. Freeman (eds) *Centres and Peripheries of Psychoanalysis*. London: Karnac, pp.94–111.

Parsons, M. and Dermen, S. (1999) 'The violent child and adolescent.' In M. Lanyado and A. Horne (eds) *The Handbook of Child and Adolescent Psychotherapy. Psychoanalytic Approaches*. London: Routledge.

Sobey, K. and Woodcock, J. (1999) 'Psychodynamic music therapy: considerations in training.' In A. Cattanach (ed) *Process in the Arts Therapies*. London: Jessica Kingsley Publishers.

Strange, J. (1987) 'The role of the music therapist in special education.' *Journal of British Music Therapy 1*, 2.

Towse, E. and Flower, C. (1993) 'Levels of interaction in group improvisation.' In M. Heal and T. Wigram (eds) *Music Therapy in Health and Education*. London: Jessica Kingsley Publishers.

Winnicott, D.W. (1971) *Playing and Reality*. London: Routledge.

CHAPTER 13

A Children's Group

An Exploration of the Framework Necessary for Therapeutic Work

Katherine Grogan and Doris Knak

Introduction

While many clinical areas of the music therapy profession are well established and have increasing amounts of research and writing informing them, the area of children's groups, particularly in the field of child and adolescent mental health, remains, in comparison, unmapped territory. Some methods and styles of working have been documented, such as Bryan's work with autistic children (1989), or Friedlander's approach to paediatric inpatient music therapy (1994). Hughes (1994) and Oldfield and Bunce (2001) illustrate different ways of working with children and their families, but there has been relatively little written or discussed about children's groups in the field of outpatient child and adolescent mental health and, in particular, psychodynamically informed non-directive children's groups. While papers about music therapy groups with adults (Davies and Richards 1998; Stewart 1996; Woodcock 1987) can be most helpful for music therapists working in the field of child and adolescent music therapy, there are, nevertheless, some issues which remain specific to this client group which we feel would benefit from discussion.

In this chapter we describe and elaborate on some of our experiences of organizing and running non-directive children's groups. It is first and foremost a descriptive account of our personal learning, which is very much an ongoing process.

Context

The work we would like to discuss took place in an outpatient music therapy department, in an NHS child and adolescent mental health service. The service receives referrals for children and young people aged 2 to 17 with a variety of needs. These include developmental issues and communication disorders, emotional and behavioural difficulties, specific life events such as bereavement, and particular mental health diagnoses such as conduct disorder, obsessive compulsive disorder and anorexia nervosa. Referrals come from GPs, health visitors, school nurses, speech and language therapists and teachers as well as psychiatrists, psychologists and other mental health professionals within the multidisciplinary team.

For many years most of the service's work was with individuals, but more recently group work has become an increasingly important part of the treatment offered. This development arose not only because of pressures to see increasing numbers of children, but also because of a growing awareness within the team that group work had much to offer. We began offering group work to children who were assessed as having needs in the area of social interaction, and we ran a number of groups with different emphases. Some contained a significant amount of structure directed toward particular developmental skills, while others were less directive and focused more on the emotional needs of the children referred. The children we selected for the latter type of group tended to be those who were quite withdrawn, lonely, had little self-confidence or belief in themselves, or little awareness of the impact they had on other children.

Very early on it became apparent that group work in this setting not only presented different challenges from those encountered in individual work, but that non-directive groups raised different issues from structured groups. Most significant among these was the importance of the framework surrounding the therapy when working with emotional issues. Many music therapists will be familiar with ideas concerning therapeutic boundaries such as stability of time, duration and place which frame and contain the therapeutic process. Additionally, however, we increasingly found ourselves needing to engage with the logistics of the group's organization; that is to say the wider context of the group's membership and the drawing together of those contexts.

This was relatively unknown territory to us and this chapter discusses our learning process in developing a framework around psychodynamically informed non-directive children's groups. Some of our ideas arise from our own experience, some from supervision and reading, and some from Doris Knak's attendance at a group workshop at the Tavistock Centre. This chapter falls into two parts:

- a description of one particular group, to be referred to as Group X, including the group's composition and process and our learning from the experience of running the group

- our current thinking about framework, based on Group X and subsequent groups.

Group X

This group consisted of four boys, Max (7), Paul (8), Liam (8) and Michael (9), all of whom had expressive and/or receptive language disorders and who attended a language unit attached to a local school. Both Liam and Michael had received several months of individual music therapy – Liam with Doris and Michael with Katherine – and we felt that both boys would benefit from further music therapy, but this time within a group setting.

Our starting point with regard to the composition of groups was the belief that groups work best when they consist of children of a similar age and with similar needs. As there were no other children on our waiting list with similar language disorders, we decided to contact the school's speech and language therapist, who suggested that Max and Paul might benefit from some input. We then saw both boys and their families for an assessment and felt they would be suitable participants. Following this we set some general aims for the whole group, which were related to the boys' speech and language and social difficulties.

The group was initially set up to run for three months but, as things seemed to be going well, was extended twice so that the group actually ran for an academic school year. This was agreed both with the boys and with their families.

Group process

Attendance was initially good. After some early anxiety about what to do and what was expected of them, all four boys were very eager to come to the group, and to engage with the instruments and with us. The general atmosphere was one of busyness, with very little silence or room to reflect. The music was used in a different way by each boy: Max was loud and forthcoming, Paul was more hesitant, using subtle sounds, while Michael was loud, seeming to cry out for attention with his very physical play and use of his voice. Finally, Liam was shy and somewhat on the edge of the interactions between the boys, rather directing his verbal and musical communications to the therapists. The main themes visited in the first term included exploring the setting in terms of instruments and roles and negotiating rules, which were written down and added to each week.

During the second term there was less enthusiasm from the boys and attendance became a little irregular. The main themes centred on differences between the children and we felt challenged to see and respond to each child as an individual. It seemed that the children were competing for our attention and for their space in the room and that a question was being asked: could we, as two women, provide boundaries that were safe for this group of boys? For example, the rules for the session were challenged many times, by taking the instruments apart.

At the same time, the boys seemed to experiment with different aspects of themselves. Michael showed a vulnerable side, while Liam became more actively involved with the other children and less focused on the adults. There were phases without any music that we felt were linked to anxiety in the room, perhaps about the fear of the group falling apart. It became an important part of our role to help the children focus their energy, by initiating musical ideas to which the children could contribute and which helped create a feeling of togetherness. However, towards the end of this term Max became extremely reluctant to attend sessions and, despite meetings with both him and his mother, he dropped out of the group.

The group was further reduced when, at the beginning of the final term, Michael was withdrawn from the sessions. The trigger for this seemed to have been confusion about session dates. Unfortunately it was not possible to talk this through with Michael's family. Consequently only Paul and Liam attended the remaining sessions and while they made good use of the setting, they struggled to orientate themselves in this new situation. Inevitably the material centred on coping with the loss of two group members. Mourning, confusion and guilt were expressed by both boys. As the group drew to a close, they used the image of going on a long and adventurous journey to think about their experiences and how only two of them had stayed until the end. A large part of our role at this time was to help Liam and Paul to cope with the changes in the group and to try and understand their feelings. Verbalizing our own impressions of how things felt in the room seemed helpful and served to release the group to play expressively. Both boys seemed to find a sense of their own identity in surviving the departure of two other group members.

After the sessions had come to an end, we both had a strong conviction that the group had been a useful setting for these four boys to explore particular aspects of themselves. Even though only two boys were present at the end of the group, different phases in the group's life were certainly evident. The presence of what Whitaker (1985) refers to as formative, established and terminating stages indicated that the setting had been secure enough for the group to mature and develop. We felt that we wanted to continue this type of group work, but we were also disappointed that, despite our best efforts, not all the children had been able to follow the process through to the end. We spent a lot of time thinking about what might have contributed to the group's disintegration. It was easy to feel that we had failed to provide a safe enough space for difficult things to be expressed and thought about, and we felt responsibility and even guilt towards both the children who dropped out and those who remained. While there were certainly learning points for us from the therapeutic process, there were a number of issues concerning the framework that we felt were important to consider further.

Learning

First, although we had thought hard about extending the group and the impact this might have, the decision to do so may have been more unsettling than we realized. It is interesting that Max stopped attending at the end of the second term while Michael was withdrawn at the point at which the group was informed that it would definitely finish by the summer. Although we had taken pains to negotiate the extension both with the boys and the parents, it seems that there were issues around this that remained unspoken. Another possibility is that the punctuations in the group's life provided the children and/or their families with an opportunity to opt out of a difficult process. With hindsight it might have been more helpful to set a time scale that was not dependent on how well the group was going.

Second, we realized that parents found it hard to support their children's attendance through the difficult phases of therapy. Several parents said to us that they were happy to bring their children as long as they were willing to come. Although we had met with parents at the beginning and had explained that therapy often raises uncomfortable issues, they still did not seem to find it easy to bring their children when the therapy was no longer that much 'fun'. We also reflected on our decision to set group aims rather than to agree individual aims for each boy with both the child and his parents. We wondered if a joint process of setting specific aims for each child would contribute to a framework where parents felt connected and were then able to see the relevance of the group to their particular child. We realized that we needed to examine and change the way in which we conveyed information, and to help parents understand more of what the group was about so that they were more able to support their children in using the group.

At about this time Doris Knak attended the groups workshop that forms part of the child psychotherapy training at the Tavistock Centre. One of the issues raised at this supervision and discussion group was the issue of the diversity of membership of the group. In this case all four members were boys with speech and language difficulties who attended the same school. It was suggested that our task was to allow all of them to be observably different from one another and that this was difficult for us to achieve because of the specific composition of the group. Similarly, it made it difficult for the children to assert their individuality within this membership. As a result, they all tried very hard to attract our individual attention, sometimes in creative ways and sometimes in ways that felt more destructive. One could argue that Max's departure from the group was actually a powerful way of claiming individuality. It was suggested that it might have been more helpful to put children of different ages and genders and with varying needs together, so that a setting could be created where children could bring their differences and thus increase their learning from each other.

A related point was the fact that the boys knew each other not only at school, but also in other settings. Michael and Liam played together outside school, for example, and shared lifts to the music therapy sessions. This raised issues among the boys, but also for us, as the boundaries of the music therapy setting felt blurred and fed into the idea of music therapy as a 'fun activity'. In such a therapeutic group, we felt it would ultimately be more helpful to group children together who do not already know each other.

It was clear from the earliest stages of the process that two of the boys already had established relationships with the two of us, while the other two boys were entering a completely new experience. For Paul and Max, who had not come before, there seemed to be some insecurity about why the others had had therapy and they had not. Michael and Liam both seemed to mourn the individual time they had lost while making efforts to claim back their individual therapists; for example, Michael addressed all his communications to Katherine. It was also difficult for us to hold a lot more information about these two in our minds while trying to consider the needs of the group as a whole, although this became easier as time went on. We felt it would have been better to start with all the children on more of an equal footing. In summary, the main issues from this group which we took forward into future work were:

- to discuss and agree the duration of therapy

- to spend more time with parents at the beginning of the group and to be available to them throughout the group process

- to agree individual aims for each child in consultation with his/her parents

- to bring together children with *different* needs

- to choose children who had not had individual therapeutic work with either therapist.

Our current thinking

This section looks more closely at these issues in order to discuss how our thinking has evolved with regard to providing a containing external frame for non-directive children's groups. Our thinking has been informed by our experiences with subsequent groups we have run, both with each other and with other members of the music therapy team.

Duration of therapy

It is our experience that, in a closed group, agreeing the duration of therapy from the start and keeping to the original time scale is the most helpful way of providing a secure container within which the therapeutic work can take place. Particularly when working in a non-directive way, we have found that children, their parents, and indeed the therapists, can then pace themselves throughout the course of the group. In this way the emotional process is easier to contain and so is the ending, which often raises complex issues of its own. We have found that negotiating the duration of therapy term by term can be very effective when working with individuals, but we would argue that in group work, where the process is multifaceted the duration of therapy should not be extended, but needs to be clear from the start.

Engagement with families

It is an obvious but important point that children are completely dependent upon adults to make the arrangements for therapy to take place. In our outpatient setting we have found that engaging families is therefore crucial not only to ensure that children attend, but also to create an environment where families feel valued and supported and where difficult issues can be thought about.

It has been a longstanding part of the way we work to meet with parents at the beginning of therapy and to use these meetings to gather information about the child's needs and to tell them about music therapy. Following our first group, we wanted to make sure that parents had a better understanding of how a particular group could be beneficial to their particular child. We have therefore involved the parents in deciding on the aims of the work and have discussed in greater depth how the group will be run. We have also shared ideas about the likely group process, including difficulties that children sometimes encounter.

Some parents are much more receptive to these ideas than others, and we have struggled with whether we should involve a child in a group or not if the parents are not able to embrace the commitment that is necessary for the group to work. Perhaps it is ultimately unhelpful to offer this input to families who are less likely to see the process through. These decisions can be hard as this sometimes means that children who may benefit are not offered a place.

Making alliances with parents and establishing practical frameworks for the work to take place require skills that are complementary to, but different from, clinical music therapy. We have been able to attend further training on this subject and have also been fortunate to observe other professionals within our multidisciplinary team. We have learned to listen to parents and to think together with them about how a music therapy group might help their particular child. Parents are then able to make a more informed choice about whether they wish their child to be part of a music therapy group.

We have also found that putting time and thought into engaging with families at the beginning of the work has enabled us to move towards our goal of working in partnership with parents. We have seen that it is easier for parents to be committed to the work and to support their children throughout the process when they have a strong alliance with us. When children have experienced difficulties, we have felt more able to work with parents and they with us.

The issue of confidentiality is also important. We feel it is crucial that a child knows that what takes place in the session will not be passed on to others and that this is an integral part of the therapy process. However, this also has to be balanced with the parents' needs and rights to be informed about their child's therapy. We have found this a difficult question and do not feel that we have found the definitive answer. We tend to speak in generalities to parents unless there is a specific area of concern, in which case it will be negotiated with the child that specific information will be shared with others. Group work raises questions as to where this negotiation should take place. Should the therapists meet with the child outside the session, or use the group session time?

In the future we would like to run a discussion group for parents in parallel to a children's group. This might offer a forum where parents can give each other support and also enable them better to support their children. This may be more effective if run by another professional within the multidisciplinary team who is not working directly with the children, as this type of work would necessarily change the therapeutic alliance that we as therapists have with the parents. We have found that the greater the contact with parents, the more the relationship between therapists and parents becomes a part of the work with the children. This has been something to acknowledge and accept as a factor within the therapy.

Selection of children

We have tried hard to group children together who not only have different needs but are also of different ages and genders. This can be problematic as many of the children who are referred to us present with very similar needs. We also receive many more referrals of boys than of girls. We have found that working more collaboratively with our wider mental health team by asking for referrals to specific groups has been a useful way to increase diversity within groups. Wherever such a group has been possible to compile, we have found it much easier to hold each child in mind, distinct and separate from the other children. This increased capacity on our part to maintain a thinking space for each child seems to mean that, while children still claim their right to our individual attention, they do not have to fight so hard to be noticed. Instead, our attention can be drawn to each child's strengths and needs and to how these have an impact on the group. At the same time, it has been helpful to ensure that no child feels isolated in the group because of gender or race. The only black child in a group of white children may become scapegoated or the only girl in a group of boys may find it hard to hear feedback from the group as all issues may seem related to her difference from them. Useful feedback about her as an individual may then become lost.

We have found that bringing children of different ages together can be useful in that the older children have the freedom to access and explore issues from earlier in their childhood and, if necessary, can play in a younger way. Similarly, a child who is the youngest in his or her family may find that (s)he is the oldest in the group and is therefore presented with the opportunity to explore what this feels like. This can raise issues such as taking responsibility or being the leader. The widest range of ages we have brought together has spanned five years, although we have not mixed children and adolescents together as we feel that the issues of each age group are too diverse for the process to be beneficial to either.

We have tried to ensure that the children who are seen in this context have not had any other input from the therapists who are running the group. In contrast to our experience with Group X, we usually find that the question of who has been to music therapy before and with whom they worked is quickly thought about and the group can then move on to other issues. Another crucial factor is being able to find suitable children who are all able to attend a group at the same time and at a time when we are available to run a group. On occasion we have found ourselves working at times which were less convenient to us, for example, right at the end of the working day, in order for a group to take place.

All of these practical factors mean that, despite a long waiting list, the number of children available to select from can actually be very limited. In addition the question of which children are able to make use of a non-directive setting has been another key area to consider when compiling a group. This issue was highlighted for us when a child stopped attending a subsequent group that we ran together. In this instance the child felt that the therapists had 'just sat there' while he felt attacked and excluded by the other children. This particular child thought quite concretely and would perhaps have benefited more from direct intervention rather than a reflective approach. We considered whether we had misjudged this child's suitability for a non-directive group, and assessment of whether children can manage to make use of this setting is obviously most important. However, in all the groups we have run there has been a tension between the needs of each individual child for differing amounts of structure which emerge at different times in the group's life. Perhaps it is helpful to view the need for structure as a creative tension that can occur in a group, and which requires us as therapists to find a balance between structure and a more free environment which enables all the group members to feel safe enough to use the setting.

These thoughts about selection of children relate to an ideal world and it is our experience that it is very difficult, even impossible at times, to create an ideally composed group. However, while aiming for the ideal, we also need to be realistic and to engage with the children we have rather than endlessly search for the 'right' children. We have chosen to form groups that we hoped would be 'good enough' and to be open and responsive to the issues which arose.

Most significant in our learning in setting up this type of music therapy group for children has been the importance of planning which, although time consuming and frustrating at times, reaps its rewards when the children arrive and the sessions begin as the process feels contained by the preparation that has taken place. In addition we feel that setting up times to evaluate how the group is going and developing clear criteria for measuring how the process of the group relates to each child's individual aims of therapy can be most helpful. Similarly supervision helps the therapists to make sense of the session content and to think about each child and the process as a whole. These different spaces for reflection serve to create a framework of thought, which support and work alongside the practical frameworks discussed in this chapter.

Conclusion

Writing this chapter has had an impact upon us in several ways. First, it has been valuable to recall some of the groups we have run and to remember how particular children made use of the group setting. It has also made us want to write further about the therapeutic processes of some of our groups and to discuss in greater depth such issues as the use of music and words or the role of the therapists. It has brought back memories of some of the frustrations and the difficulties we encountered, while reminding us once again how hard it is to work with emotional issues and the challenges raised when feelings are the focus of the work. There can be no doubt that non-directive children's groups require particularly high amounts of energy from the therapists, not only to engage with the therapeutic process, but to engage with the outer framework necessary for the work to take place. Most powerfully, however, we find ourselves believing that, despite the groups that have fallen apart and the lessons learned about time scales and group composition, non-directive children's groups have a great deal to offer in this area of child and adolescent mental health and can be the treatment of choice for some children.

We are aware of how much there is to learn in this clinical area and how very experimental some of our ideas are. We have been struck by how every group raises new opportunities for learning and by how our ideas continually evolve and change. We hope that other music therapists working in this and related fields may be encouraged to share their experiences and thoughts, and so increase the body of literature in this intriguing and valuable clinical area.

References

Bryan, A. (1989) 'Autistic group case study.' *Journal of British Music Therapy 3*, 1, 16–21.

Davies, A. and Richards, E. (1998) 'Music therapy in acute psychiatry. Our experience of working as co-therapists with a group for patients from two neighbouring wards.' *British Journal of Music Therapy 13*, 2, 53–59.

Friedlander, L.H. (1994) 'Group music psychotherapy in an inpatient psychiatric setting for children: A developmental approach.' *Music Therapy Perspectives 4*, 92–97.

Hughes, M. (1994) 'Groups with down's syndrome children and their mothers.' Unpublished dissertation.

Oldfield, A. and Bunce, L. (2001) 'Mummy can play too: Short-term music therapy with mothers and young children.' *British Journal of Music Therapy 15*, 1, 27–36

Stewart, D. (1996) 'Chaos, noise and a wall of silence: working with primitive affects in psychodynamic group music therapy.' *Journal of British Music Therapy 10*, 2, 21–33.

Whitaker, D.S. (1985) *Using Groups to Help People.* London: Routledge.

Woodcock, J. (1987) 'Towards group analytic music therapy.' *Journal of British Music Therapy 1*, 1, 16–21.

CHAPTER 14

Working, Playing and Relating

Issues in Group Music Therapy for Children with Special Needs

Helen M. Tyler

In this chapter I want to look at some of the issues which can arise in group music therapy for children with special needs and to show how a combination of practical musical resources and psychodynamic under-standing can help the music therapist to work effectively. I will share some thoughts arising from my experience both as a music teacher and as a music therapist, with reference to Nordoff and Robbins's (1971) concept of 'work' in therapy and to Winnicott's (1986) theory of 'play'. Two case vignettes will introduce the issues, followed by a longer case study of a group which develops some of the ideas previously discussed.

Children, even more than adults, spend most of their waking lives in groups, first at home in the family, then at school and frequently in after-school or weekend group activities. Music in particular draws children together in groups, whether through organized singing and playing in choirs, orchestras and bands or in activities where music is sig-nificant such as dancing, from ballet to pop. As Hargreaves and North write (1997, p.1): 'Music has many different functions in human life, nearly all of which are essentially social.' The music therapy literature, however, is generally biased in favour of children's individual clinical work, despite the fact that music therapy, particularly within special education in the UK, frequently takes place in a small group setting. This comparative shortage of literature follows the precedent set by other forms of therapy for children, as suggested by Canham and Emanuel (2000, p.282), who write: 'Psychoanalytic group psychotherapy for children is a comparatively rare form of treatment and has received little attention in the literature.' There is also an ongoing debate about the relationship between music therapy and music education (Ockelford 2000; Robertson 2000; Warwick 1995) which addresses the perception that group music therapy for children is an extension of music teaching. In the following pages I hope to show that group music therapy has a specific contribution to make for children with special needs, diagnostically, as an intervention which can complement and support the work of teachers and as a treatment in its own right.

Andrew: mainstream primary school

A class of 9-year-old children in a primary school is having a music lesson. They are in small groups planning musical improvisations based on the theme of 'The Haunted House'. Most of the children are deeply involved in making up a story and composing appropriate music using a variety of percussion instruments. One boy, Andrew, has not settled into a group. He grabs the biggest drum and bangs it deafeningly until the teacher takes it away, giving him a very small tambourine to play. He then wanders disconsolately round the classroom, making raucous 'ghost' noises and generally being disruptive. All the teacher's efforts are taken up with managing his behaviour, rather than concentrating on the other children's creativity. As a part-time visiting music specialist, she does not know Andrew well and wonders why he seems determined to sabotage the lesson which the other children are enjoying. Eventually her patience runs out and she sends him back to his classroom so that his teacher can deal with him. This leaves the music teacher feeling inadequate at having been unable to handle the situation herself. Most of her classes contain children like Andrew and she is drawn to involve them in the lessons, feeling that their difficult behaviour masks vulnerability and a plea for help. However, the numbers of children in the class and the demands of the curriculum prevent this from happening in the way that she would like.

Discussion

This vignette reflects one aspect of my experience as a specialist music teacher in mainstream education some years ago. Before training as a music therapist I taught classes of children of all ages, from pre-school groups to 18-year-old A-level students in a grammar school. The scenario above, with the disruptive pupil, was not uncommon, particularly in a school where I delivered music for the entire primary school in one morning. The teachers generally were only too glad to hand their classes over to me for half an hour and, apart from a register of names, I had very little information about individual pupils. The freedom and emotional stimulation of the music lesson with its noise, creativity and self-expression was too difficult for some children to manage.

Further investigation usually revealed that the most disruptive children were also the most distressed, as Greenhalgh writes: 'Children and young people who are troubled and suffering emotional distress not only trouble others with whom they come into contact, but find it difficult to be available for learning' (1994, p.1). There are echoes of the pioneer play therapist, Virginia Axline, here: 'A teacher whose mind is beset with anxieties, fears and frustrations cannot do a satisfactory teaching job. A child whose emotional life is in conflict and turmoil is not a satisfactory pupil' (Axline 1989, p.133). Despite the compassionate attitude of most teachers to children under stress, the predominant approach was a combination of threats, sanctions and punishment, to prevent the work of the class from being disturbed by the disturbing minority.

Since training as a music therapist I have again worked with children, both individually and in groups, with a similarly wide age range, 2 to 18 years. Far from behavioural or management issues belonging exclusively to teaching, I soon discovered that they occurred equally in music therapy. In the music therapy group, however, difficult behaviour could be understood as a communication from the child about his inner state rather than as a problem to be eradicated. As a therapist I could respond with a different and more flexible set of tools, both in my thinking about the group and in the musical resources which I could call upon. Aigen supports this view in his research into music therapy with a group of adolescents. He describes how 'confrontations between group members were not treated purely as 'management' problems by the therapists, but were instead used to address clinical goals such as increased verbal and musical expression of feelings, interpersonal contact, and self-awareness' (Aigen 1995, p.351).

Nordoff and Robbins, too, stress the emotional and psychological potential of music therapy:

> It is the music therapists' role to supplement the educational and classroom activities of the teacher with a programme aimed at providing special experiences that have central psychological significance for the children, and which can be therapeutic for their whole development. The strengthening of ego-function, the liberation from emotional restrictions and the alleviation of behavioural problems, all make for happier, more fulfilled children who can participate more fully in their school life and derive greater benefit from it ... Working in this way we invite and hold the children's attention, then intensify their capacity for concentration. They begin to *work*. (Nordoff and Robbins 1971, pp.135 and 139)

Aigen has written that 'work, even more than play, appears as the process most central to the early formation of the Nordoff-Robbins approach.' He goes on to write of 'the core belief that not only is therapy work but that *work* is also *therapy*' (Aigen 1998, p.285). This concept can be seen to some extent in the individual case studies re-examined by Aigen, but is even more apparent in the group work. For example, one of the musical plays was called 'Pif-Paf Poltrie, a Working Game' which Nordoff and Robbins described as an 'activity therapy'. It is based on a folk tale which has at its climax the hero, Pif-Paf, sweeping up a roomful of leaves. Nordoff and Robbins they noted improvements in children's social relationships, concentration, self-confidence and emotional stability after taking part in the game (1983, pp.218–21). It is interesting that none of these gains are in the area of musical skill, and yet the music is integral and vital to the play. This links with Foulkes's description of therapeutic groups where 'the occupation may be of secondary importance therapeutically, whereas active participation in the group setting may be the essential therapeutic agency' (Foulkes and Anthony 1984, p.35).

Winnicott, in his seminal work *Playing and Reality*, writes:

> It is play that is the universal and that belongs to health: playing facilitates growth and therefore health; playing leads into group relationships; playing can be a form of communication in psycho-therapy; and, lastly, psychoanalysis has been developed as a highly specialised form of playing in the service of communication with oneself and others. (Winnicott 1986, p.48)

This statement can also be used to make a comprehensive and convincing case for group music therapy when we consider that growth, health, group relationships and communication with the self and others are all attributes to be found through the universal experience of playing music with others. Winnicott makes it clear, however, that play is far more complex than its dictionary definition of 'fun, recreation and amusement (Penguin 2000). He describes it as a potentially frightening occupation, which belongs to 'the interplay in the child's mind of that which is sub-jective (near-hallucination) and that which is objectively perceived' (Winnicot 1986, p.61). The therapist's role is to provide the facilitating environment in which this subjectivity can be explored. Similarly, Nordoff and Robbins were committed to addressing the serious or fright-ening themes which may emerge in therapy. They improvised words and music which expressed the mood or preoccupations of the children and could therefore act as a container for their powerful feelings. One song was improvised to acknowledge an inconsolably crying child in the group, while another was a response to the children's fears and distress after the assassination of President Kennedy. Although these songs were later written down and published, they originated in the immediacy of the group session.

Beverley: emotional and behavioural problems

Beverley is an 8-year-old girl with moderate learning difficulties who is under-achieving in class. Her mother, too, has learning difficulties and has a chaotic lifestyle and her father is in prison. Beverley takes part in a music therapy group with three other girls from her class, who were referred by their teacher to work on issues of peer relationships. Beverley is naturally musical, with the ability to play and sing freely and creatively. However, she finds it impossible to share the therapist's attention or to wait for a turn on a particular instrument. She frequently rushes out of the room, shouting and crying. Her volatile and sometimes aggressive behaviour disrupts the group and creates a tense atmosphere. The group therapists wonder whether Beverley would benefit more from one-to-one therapy with a colleague. After discussion with the class teacher and the group, it is agreed that at the end of the school term she will leave the group and begin individual music therapy.

Beverley was delighted to have a therapist and all the instruments to herself, playing and singing with energy, in an exaggerated imitation of pop-stars. She was very controlling of the therapist's participation, ordering her to 'stop the music' or banging down the piano lid. Soon she invented a game in which she was the punitive teacher of a class of unruly children. The percussion instruments were given the names of the other children in her class, as though the group she had left had come to join her.

As she projected all her feelings onto the instruments she gave a clear picture of her emotional state. The drum was usually the 'best behaved', while the windchime, erratic and hard to control, was the naughty one. The cymbal was frequently sent out of the room for being noisy, swearing or fighting, and the session sometimes ended with no instruments left in the room. Beverley's rage at the instruments was intense and real to her as she screamed, 'I hate you all. I've had enough.' Beverley's mother was pregnant at this time and knowledge of this confirmed the therapist's sense of Beverley's powerful need to be the only one and to obliterate all her rivals.

The symbolic use of the instruments was part of her exploration of relationships within the 'as if' parameters of therapy and illustrates Winnicott's comment that 'it is in playing and only in playing, that the child or adult is able to be creative' (1986, p.62). Beverley's issues of poor peer relationships, lack of self-control and aggressive outbursts, could be contained, understood and worked on during the sessions through playing.

Gradually, as the game developed, there was generally a calmer more constructive atmosphere. Beverley decided that each 'child' could choose a song to sing and those that were good would get a prize of a drumstick or a shaker. The songs ranged from nursery rhymes like 'Old Macdonald had a Farm' and 'Three Blind Mice' to 'When I'm 64' and 'Waltzing Matilda', songs enjoyed by any 8-year-old. Now Beverley wanted the therapist's close support in playing the songs and her voice was authentic and childlike, no longer imitating the pseudo-emotionality of a pop singer.

Beverley's individual therapy lasted two years, the 'group' remaining until the end. In her last session she enacted a school assembly in which she, the teacher, was leaving to go to another school. She was able to acknowledge the sadness of ending in an improvised song with the words 'I'm leaving, I'm leaving, you gotta cry because we have to say goodbye'. According to her class teacher, although her home situation was still difficult, she was far more able to deal with the stresses of school life, she was making better relationships within the class and was beginning to fulfil her potential for learning.

My final case study draws together many of the issues from the preceding vignettes. The therapeutic frame, boundaries, issues of rivalry with peers, the wish to have the therapist's exclusive attention, the balance between structure and freedom, order and chaos, work and play – all these and more were explored in the ten months that I and my colleague Donald Wetherick (DW), worked with this group.

The group

The group consisted of four boys with moderate learning difficulties aged between 14 and 17. Their school provided 'talking groups' with a psychotherapist to address emotional and behavioural issues, but these four had not been able to use them because of their difficulties in verbal communication and language problems – three came from families where English was not the first language.

On the referral forms their teachers identified difficult peer relationships, low self-esteem, poor concentration and anger management as issues to be addressed. In addition, J had partial hearing loss, for which he wore hearing aids while M, the oldest in the group, had difficulty with attention and memory. S had stressful home circumstances, living with his family in cramped hostel accommodation, and was prone to noisy, emotional outbursts. T was described as depressed; at school he barely made eye contact or spoke, except for muttered swearing.

Starting the group: co-therapy issues

My music therapy training had focused on working in a team with a co-therapist who was also a music therapist. Nordoff and Robbins's way of working was that Paul Nordoff played the piano while Clive Robbins facilitated the group's musical participation, offering instruments and assisting children who needed help or encouragement:

> When therapy is undertaken by a team it is essential that the abilities and efforts of both therapists combine closely and freely to attain these aims. This requires that the relationship between the team members is one of partners sharing in the creativeness, the events and the responsibilities of therapy. The role of the pianist is to engage the child musically in a developmentally effective way, while the role of the assistant is to support the pianist's work, to supplement it resourcefully in whatever way the situation calls for. (Nordoff and Robbins 1977, pp.91–2)

Davies and Richards also describe the value of a co-therapy relationship in their work with an acute psychiatric group. Again, one therapist plays the piano while the other has a supporting and facilitating role, but they aim for flexibility, moving between roles as the situation requires. They compare this way of working to a verbal therapy context where 'one therapist may be more concerned with overall direction and process of the group while the other may be more immediately engaged in specific exchanges' (Davies and Richards 1998, p.57).

DW and I found that working as equal co-therapists in a mixed gender partnership provided a model of a parental couple and therefore the possibility of the group being experienced as a family, with the potential for both harmony and conflict. It also provided valuable support and what Turry describes as 'a built-in peer supervision process' as we struggled at times with the complex relationships within the group (Turry 1998, p.191).

Issue: therapeutic frame / boundaries

The sessions took place in a large music room with a grand piano and a variety of tuned and untuned percussion and ethnic instruments. At first we had anticipated using the piano, feeling that it could draw together the disparate responses of the group. In the first session however, we found that the piano as the largest instrument in the room seemed to be a compelling instrument of power for the group. All except T wanted to play it, but in so doing they became absorbed in their own music and isolated from the rest of the group. We therefore suggested that we should sit in a circle, using percussion instruments and our voices, without using the piano. Foulkes describes the psychological representation of the circle as 'a static compromise, an equilibrium, of peripheral movement to and away from the centre' (Foulkes and Anthony 1984, p.63). It felt important to aim for equilibrium through the use of the circle and to encourage a spirit of compromise, while remaining alert to the issues of power, rivalry and envy which the piano had evoked.

When DW and I suggested setting the boundary of not using the piano, it was accepted without difficulty and perhaps with relief. Clarifying the group norms and the frame of the session seemed to help the group to settle down. Another boundary issue which needed work was establishing the difference between sound and silence, as there tended to be continuous noise in the room. We introduced the idea of starting each improvisation with a moment of silence, which was very hard for the group at first but was gradually accepted.

Issue: relating in the group

The tendency of the group members was to play without listening to each other. J, choosing the tambour, played loudly and perseveratively, so that the other boys would shout at him to be quiet or complain that the noise was hurting their ears. It seemed that J was projecting his hearing problems onto the others in the group. S would sit on the floor and vocalize freely, playing a small lyre tuned to an Arabian-type scale. It was as though he was bringing his personal musical identity into the session but did not wish to integrate it with the others' music, in the same way that his family was alienated from its homeland and culture. M hid his lack of confidence by playing at being the clown of the group, crashing the cymbal unexpectedly or teasing the others by taking their instruments. T often pushed his chair backwards, out of the circle, or sat with his head down, avoiding eye contact. In a group improvisation he almost disappeared musically, choosing a small instrument such as a triangle. As therapists, we made musical links with individual boys, but there seemed little desire for them to communicate with each other. They played the instruments freely but there was little of the sharing and reciprocity which is the hallmark of people playing together. We decided to address this by introducing games at the beginning of each session to enable the group to experience elements of musical interaction. We hoped that this would help to develop their confidence and that this in turn would enhance their capacity to relate to each other, musically and personally.

We had begun the first session by playing the tambourine in turn and introducing ourselves and this became a ritual that remained constant throughout the lifespan of the group. We then developed the tambourine introduction further in three stages:

1. Pass the tambourine round the circle, playing and saying one's own name.

2. The first person plays, then says another's name and passes it to them to play.

3. The 'turn' is passed by eye contact rather than by speaking.

This was quite challenging for the group at first, as they all found difficulty both in communicating verbally, remembering and pronouncing everyone's name or in reading non-verbal cues. In his account of group psychotherapy with disturbed children and adolescents Anthony describes a similar situation:

> In the children's group, concrete group structures are created by the therapist prior to any psychological group formation as if in anticipation of what is to happen. The motley collection of children, unrealistic and unrelating, are encouraged to act like a group, hold hands like a group, play games like a group ... even though there is a complete absence of real group feeling. The therapist's expectation and anticipation are fulfilled in that group structures are eventually filled in by genuine group responses. (Foulkes and Anthony 1984, p.231)

Work and play in the group

A further development came in the tenth session, when the passing of the tambourine was spontaneously extended into stamping, singing and clapping, so that the activity became a free-flowing improvisation, as work and play merged. In another variation we encouraged the boys to pass round whatever vocal sound they liked, as all except S were reluctant to use their voices. The contributions ranged from 'Tarzan' calls to 'raspberries', giggles and swear words in different languages. This playfulness helped the group to relax and to feel less anxious about using their voices.

We introduced other musical games, for example, improvising in pairs on the gato drum. It was hard for those not playing to be attentive, but we encouraged a respectful, listening stance and this served to build up confidence in playing in front of each other. Another activity involved taking turns in leading the group, playing a large drum. The aim was to follow the leader's tempo, dynamics and rhythmic patterns as closely as possible. This gave J the chance to be the leader and to play as loudly as he liked, but he soon took pleasure in using his musical ingenuity to make changes in rhythm, tempo and dynamics, testing the alertness of his peers. For many weeks T did not want to take his turn to lead, but shortly before the end of the group the others persuaded him to try. Although self-conscious about being the centre of attention, he nevertheless managed to lead the whole group for a short time.

As the group developed, the listening skills built up in the duet work and in the turn taking became more apparent in the free improvisations and there was an increased awareness of and respect for each other's playing. The group's tendency was to play continuously, so DW and I would come in and out of playing, sometimes introducing a change of timbre when we felt the music had lost its direction and this led to brief but significant shared silences occurring within the improvisation. It seemed as though the boys, who generally lacked confidence in communication, were becoming aware of the impact that sound or silence had on others.

Throughout the group's life they were eager to play, but as time went on they were also able to reflect on the music and the feelings it evoked: for example, 'That sounded like someone being chased', and 'That was like jungle music', or 'Let's play being lost in the maze'. This led to conversations on more personal matters, such as one boy's experience of being racially abused and chased after a cricket match. They were also able to talk about their reactions to each other, for example, J' s loud playing. They became more tolerant, recognizing each other's need for musical and personal space.

Group process

We saw our role initially as making the therapeutic frame safe and secure by establishing boundaries; second, as promoting the boys' awareness of themselves as musical individuals as well as group members, and finally facilitating shared, free improvisations which were satisfying emotional and expressive experiences for the group. The free improvisations, which each generally lasted between 10 and 15 minutes, seemed to fall into three stages. The opening was usually tentative, unsettled and exploratory. The middle section became more energetic and often confused, chaotic and competitive, while in the third stage the group would come together into a shared place where there was listening and mutuality.

These three stages can be seen as relating to Winnicott's three stages of the development of play, when he describes 'the direct development from transitional phenomena to playing, and from playing to shared playing, and from this to cultural experiences' (Winnicott 1986, p.60).

A further analogy can be drawn with Yalom's analysis of the formative stages of a psychotherapy group expressed as follows:

1. The initial stage: orientation, hesitant participation, search for meaning, dependency.

2. The second stage: conflict, dominance, rebellion.

3. The third stage: development of cohesiveness (Yalom 1985, pp.301–10).

This analysis can be applied both to the microcosm of each improvisation and to the overall development of the group. Over the ten-month period, the four individuals, initially dependent on the adults to make sense of their utterances, moved through the struggles of sibling rivalry and conflict to a state where there were the beginnings of cohesive and healthy relating.

Conclusion

My opening vignette introduced Andrew, a child who could not work, play or relate satisfactorily within the music lesson. The music could not contain his emotions, and neither did the lesson provide an environment which could facilitate him exploring his creativity. In the second vignette, Beverley's outbursts in the music therapy group were heard and understood, which led to her need for one-to-one attention being addressed. After confronting the same issues in individual therapy, she was able to work, play and relate more effectively within her peer group. In the final case study J, like Andrew, had a demanding musical voice, which both concealed and revealed his difficulty with hearing and being heard. Within the small music therapy group this became part of the process of finding a place where he could feel heard and valued. Similarly, M's teasing, S's singing and T's non-participation were each treated as important communications about their inner state which needed to be understood as part of the work of the group.

I finish with a reflection from Ockelford who writes that group music 'provides a secure framework for the risky business of reaching out into the far from predictable world of other people' (Ockelford 2000, p.213). Because of their cognitive, behavioural and emotional needs, the children and young people I have described in this chapter face a particularly unpredictable world. Group music therapy, using structured musical activities as well as free improvisation and bringing together concepts of work and play, within a framework of psychodynamic understanding, can make a real contribution to the individual child's growth, health, communication and relationships with the self and others.

References

Aigen, K. (1995) 'Principles of qualitative research.' In B.L. Wheeler (ed) *Music Therapy Research: Quantitative and Qualitative Perspectives.* Phoenixville: Barcelona Publishers.

Aigen, K, (1998) *Paths of Development in Nordoff-Robbins Music Therapy.* Gilsum, NH: Barcelona Publishers.

Axline, V.M. (1989) *Play Therapy.* Edinburgh: Churchill Livingstone.

Canham, H. and Emanuel, L. (2000) '"Tied together feelings." Group psychotherapy with latency children: the process of forming a cohesive group.' *Journal of Child Psychotherapy 26*, 2, 281–302.

Davies, A. and Richards, E. (1998) 'Music therapy in acute psychiatry.' *British Journal of Music Therapy 12*, 2, 53–59.

Foulkes, S.H. and Anthony, E.J. (1984) *Group Psychotherapy: The Psychoanalytic Approach.* London: Karnac.

Greenhalgh, P. (1994) *Emotional Growth and Learning.* London: Routledge.

Hargreaves, D.J. and North, A. (1997) *The Social Psychology of Music.* Oxford: Oxford University Press.

New Penguin English Dictionary (2000) London: Penguin.

Nordoff, P. and Robbins, C. (1971) *Therapy in Music for Handicapped Children.* London: Gollancz.

Nordoff, P. and Robbins, C. (1983) *Music Therapy in Special Education.* St. Louis, Missouri: MMB Music.

Nordoff, P. and Robbins, C. (1977) *Creative Music Therapy.* New York: John Day.

Ockelford, A. (2000) 'Music in the education of children with severe or profound learning difficulties: issues in current UK provision, a new conceptual framework, and proposals for research.' *Journal of Psychology of Music 28*, 2, 197–217.

Robertson, J. (2000) 'An educational model for music therapy: the case for a continuum.' *British Journal of Music Therapy 14*, 1, 41-46.

Turry, A. (1998) 'Transference and countertransference in Nordoff-Robbins music therapy.' In K. Bruscia (ed) *The Dynamics of Music Psychotherapy.* Gilsum: Barcelona Publishers.

Warwick, A. (1995) 'Music therapy in the education service: research with autistic children and their mothers.' In T. Wigram, B. Saperston and R. West (eds) *The Art and Science of Music Therapy: A Handbook.* Amsterdam: Harwood.

Winnicott, D.W. (1986) *Playing and Reality.* Harmondsworth: Pelican.

Yalom, I.D. (1985) *The Theory and Practice of Group Psychotherapy.* New York: Basic Books.

CHAPTER 15

'Could I Play a Different Role?'

Group Music Therapy with Severely Learning Disabled Adolescents

Tuulia Nicholls

Introduction

Working in a secondary school for adolescents with severe learning disabilities, I have often been struck by how many individuals, who function quite well in a one-to-one setting, struggle considerably in a group. Something powerful happens to those adolescents when they encounter themselves in groups. Some of them appear suddenly to lose all confidence and independence, unable to make any constructive contributions to the group. Others seem to find it intolerable not to be the centre of adult attention.

According to family systems theorists (e.g. Gorell Barnes 1998; Jones 1993) people tend to relate to others and the wider world in a way that they have learnt to be in the context of their first primary group, namely in the family. Thus in other groups, individuals typically adopt the role according to his or her own family system. What kind of role might a child with severe learning disabilities have in a family? It has been noted by many authors that the relationships between a disabled family member and his or her 'normal' siblings tend to differ from that between normal siblings. According to Begun (1989), the more dependent the disabled family member is, the more the relationship is affected. For example, it is not uncommon for the 'normal' siblings to adopt a 'teacher role', leading and looking after their less able sister or brother (Wilkins 1992). Although this kind of caring is undoubtedly very useful, one cannot help wondering how it might affect the disabled child's understanding of peer relationships. The disabled child is also likely to be left out of the more sophisticated play of the other children. Furthermore, where normal siblings widen their peer group experiences outside home, this is understandably more difficult for disabled children. Parents of adolescents I have worked with have expressed sadness regarding the social isolation in which their child lives. For some this experience has been magnified by the whole family becoming isolated within both the extended family and its community.

What does it feel like to be a person with a learning disability in today's society which so highly values achievement, independence and competence? How often are disabled people viewed by the majority of the public with rejection, as useless individuals with little to offer to the wider network of people? According to Szivos and Griffiths (1992) many people with learning disabilities are acutely aware of stigmatization by society, to a degree where they view other disabled people as inferior candidates for social activities. Against this background it is hardly surprising to find that many, although obviously not all, people with severe learning disabilities lack self-confidence in social situations, feel depressed and are unable to make full use of their capabilities.

However, it is not only the conscious stereotypes that may affect people with severe learning disabilities. Klein (1975) has written about unconscious psychological mechanisms that people use in order to rid themselves of feelings and thoughts that they do not wish to feel. Basing her theory on her study of young children, she maintains that young infants are not capable of managing strong emotional experiences. In order to cope, they split off such emotions from being their own feelings and project them onto others whom the baby then experiences as 'bad/persecutory' or 'good/ideal' according to the nature of the projected emotion. Typically, the tendency is to get rid of undesirable feelings although more positive qualities may also be projected. According to Klein, these kinds of primitive unconscious mechanisms are not confined to infancy. Rather she sees them as being characteristics of a certain kind of emotional mental state (the paranoid-schizoid position in her terminology) which is present in us throughout our lives. Under increased anxiety, such as in many group situations, people tend to be in a less mature mental state.

In some families the disabled member may become a sponge for all the unwanted feelings in the family. Family life may become organized in such a way that the disabled person carries all the loss, low self-esteem and inability to function, so that the rest of the family can feel strong and able. Although anyone may become a receptacle for split-off feelings, disabled children are particularly vulnerable to receiving such projections as they have fewer cognitive resources to understand what might be going on. The danger is that one may become so used to being in this role that it gradually becomes an essential part of one's identity.

Adolescence is typically regarded as a process of change, a time for re-examining one's identity. It is a time when most adolescents struggle to break free from anything that constrains them, become more independent and feel an intense need to 'belong'. It is a period when one's peer group becomes of the utmost importance (Kroger 1996). So what is adolescence like for a person with severe learning disabilities?

Rationale for having group music therapy

In my experience people who mainly encounter problems in group settings can best be helped in group therapy. For severely learning disabled adolescents, music therapy groups can be powerful. It can help them in their search for a 'healthier' way of relating to others, and help to develop both the confidence and the skills for interacting with others. Using improvised music as the medium of exchange can offer the possibility of a different experience in a group, finding freedom of movement and exploring new ways of being. Expressing oneself and relating to others musically is often experienced as easier and less frightening than through impaired verbal communication.

Context of the work

The setting is a secondary school for adolescents with severe learning disabilities. Many of the students have additional emotional and behaviour difficulties. My role as a part-time music therapist is complementary to the educational provision: to help address the students' emotional difficulties and to facilitate the development of their communication and social skills.

Issues to consider before starting a music therapy group in a school

1. *Group composition*: how homogeneous should it be? It is important to liaise carefully with school staff about the composition of the group. If possible one should have a balance of both sexes, ability levels and types of difficulties. It is also important to think about how prone to acting out the members are and how could this be managed in the group.

2. *Group size*: many psychotherapists (e.g. Spitz and Spitz 1999) view groups with less than five members as too small and lacking the potential for interaction. In my experience this does not seem to be the case in music therapy groups with severely learning disabled adolescents. I have found four adolescents to be the ideal number with a learning support assistant. Perhaps this is due to music being such an interactive medium and to the fact that many of the adolescents I work with are developmentally at very early levels of group interaction, more typical of young children.

3. *Duration of the group*: I usually run each music therapy group in the school for the whole academic year, with the possibility of continuing either with the same or altered membership the following year.

4. *Time and length of the sessions*: it is important that therapy fits into the adolescents' school timetable and that they do not

miss out on core lessons, or on something that they particularly enjoy.

5. *Space*: the group needs a physical space free from distraction. The group members need to feel safe and secure enough to explore their feelings.

6. *Goals*: it is important to have realistic expectations both for the group and the individual.

7. *Group style*: this may vary from completely free to a clearly structured approach.

8. *Boundaries*: these are particularly important when working with adolescents. The testing of boundaries will almost inevitably be part of music therapy group work with this client group.

9. *Co-running the group with an assistant*: learning support assistants often come with a different way of thinking from that of music therapists. It is important to have enough time for discussion about the approach in the sessions before one starts the group. In my experience they bring invaluable expertise into the music therapy groups, and usually know the children much better than the therapist ever will. I believe that a psychodynamic approach, and more educational and cognitive-behaviour approaches do not necessarily need to be mutually exclusive. I think that group work is a place where it may be possible and even desirable to combine aspects of different approaches.

10. *Consent from parents/carers*: this should be obtained both for the actual music therapy and for potential audio and video recording of the sessions.

11. *Liaison*: close liaison with other professionals is crucial for effective group work and contributes to a greater understanding of the adolescents' strengths and weaknesses amongst all staff. Regular liaison is particularly important for music therapists working in schools where the need for privacy in the sessions can often be perceived as secrecy.

Case study

Background information

The group described in this chapter was a closed music therapy group with four members. It met in the school once a week for one school year, each session lasting 45 minutes. I ran the group together with a learning support assistant, Katie, who had no previous experience of being involved in a therapy group. Three of the group members (Sarah, Tom, Louisa) had been in the same music therapy group with me the previous year. Peter was new to the group.

Group members

All the group members were severely disabled and experienced marked difficulties in functioning in groups. Sarah was a 16 year-old girl. She was referred for music therapy because of her communication difficulties and emotional problems. She found it very hard to manage her emotions, share adult attention and interact with her peers.

Tom was 17 years old. He was a rather anxious boy on the autism spectrum. He was referred because of his severe communication problems, high levels of anxiety, low self-esteem and avoidance of social interaction.

Louisa was a 16-year-old girl. She had fairly good speech but found it hard to communicate with others. She was referred for music therapy because of her challenging behaviour and immature ways of relating.

Peter was 17 years old and had Down's syndrome. He was referred for music therapy because of emotional problems, insecurity in social situations, low self-confidence and difficulty in self-expression.

The aims of the music therapy group

The aim of the music therapy group was to provide the group members with an experience where they could explore their identities and begin to find new ways of functioning in a group. Focus was on the interaction in the 'here and now'. The group was not looking at the group members' functioning in the past or elsewhere, nor was it aiming at members gaining intellectual insight into their problems. Rather, the aim was that in the musical relating in the group members would begin to find a 'healthier', more assertive way of interacting with others. In particular this meant:

- to encourage the expression of emotions within a contained framework
- to facilitate the development of social and communication skills
- to improve the students' self-confidence and sense of self and identity
- to reduce isolation and give a sense of 'belonging'.

The long-term aim was that these changes would not only happen within the music therapy group, but also gradually transfer to other group settings. Working together with learning support assistants can facilitate this as individuals may experience their presence in other group situations as reassuring and supportive.

Description

Naturally in any group there are many levels at which interactions and developments take place. In this chapter I have chosen to focus on the music therapy group's processes insofar as they relate to the members' sense of independence, roles and identity. My theoretical framework is psychodynamic, with an educational aspect. With the group I have described, it was often important to think not only about the dynamics of the group as a whole, but also about what was going on for each individual in the group.

Phase 1: Beginnings

The early sessions were characterized by fragmentation and dependency in the group. The group members sat with their heads down, avoiding eye contact. When playing the various instruments, there seemed to be no musical connections between them. Tom was shifting and jerking uncomfortably, asking me once in a while in an anxious voice what the various instruments were called, and finding it hard to choose anything to play. Louisa played some shakers with her head almost buried between her knees – her playing was highly tentative, copying rhythms that I had played. She did not say anything. Peter's playing was quite loud, but 'mindless'; he did not seem to listen either to himself or to the others. Sarah wandered from one instrument to the next and seemed to want all my attention.

The group members seemed preoccupied with themselves, unaware of each other's playing. Everyone seemed to play to a different pulse and the music was monotonous. I experienced a strong sense of heaviness and 'stuckness' in those sessions. It was very hard for me to link the members' contributions together musically. I found myself being easily drawn into 'duets'. However, even these duets felt rather passive, with the individuals expecting me to take the lead musically, looking at me for approval. There was a strong sense of the group being completely incapable of doing anything without me. I experienced a desire to create structure and musically lead the group. It was hard to resist being completely pushed into this role.

I found Bion's (1961) concept of Basic Assumption Dependency (baD) helpful at this point. According to him, groups sometimes function in basic assumption mentality, by which he means that the group behaves in certain ways in order to meet the unconscious needs of its members by reducing anxiety. In Basic Assumption Dependency (baD) the group members behave in pathologically dependent ways. They expect the group leader to make all the decisions. By behaving in such ways the group members become even more disabled and dependent. In Kleinian (1975) terms, it seemed that the group members were splitting off their capacity to think, and projecting that onto me. For these individuals, it was probably the most familiar and maybe the most comfortable way of being in a group.

When working with severely learning disabled children and adolescents, it is important to take into account the group members' level of cognitive and emotional development. There is a danger of seeing all behaviours as an expression of unconscious difficulties and forgetting where the person is developmentally. Were these adolescents at the level of very young children, only able to relate to others on a one-to-one basis and seeing others as unwanted rivals? Or were they more like children of latency age, beginning to explore imaginatively the social world as long as it stayed within regular routines? Or were they functioning at the level of adolescents with a creative capacity but with explosive adolescent feelings?

It seemed to me that with this group the difficulties in functioning as a group were due to a number of factors. It appeared that the group could benefit from an approach which combined both containing the various feelings in the group musically and developing skills that are essential for group interaction, and thus more mature ways of being in a group. I thought it important that the group members felt that their individual musical contributions could be heard and built on, but without the fear of the experience becoming too chaotic and frightening. The long-term aim was that little by little they would internalize the experience and thereby be able to work as a group with less help.

Phase 2: Beginning to make connections

Katie and I decided that our approach should combine both structure and freedom. The group needed us both to attend to emotional issues and to facilitate the development of some of the social and communication skills necessary for group interaction. There is sometimes a misconception amongst staff in schools where the assumption is that music therapy groups with adolescents simply aim at cathartic emotional expression. My view is that although catharsis may be part of therapy, it is by no means its only component.

The early sessions were thus structured around a number of improvisations. Some of these improvisations were on pre-selected instruments in order to promote musical cohesiveness. Some incorporated solo time for each member, in order to develop confidence, listening, sharing of attention and turn taking. In others the music's duration was determined by each member in turn, enabling group members to feel in control but also needing to listen to one another. This helped to build the group members' ego strengths and their beliefs in their capacity to relate to others. Within these kinds of simple structures it was possible to work more within the music, on both cognitive and emotional levels.

In the group improvisations one of my main roles was to contain musically (Bion 1962, 1967; De Backer 1993; Stewart 1996) the various feelings expressed in the group, ranging from timid expressions to rather explosive adolescent emotions. Katie and I attempted to link musically the group members' playing together, attuning to their sounds and movements and encouraging the group to develop their intentional and unintentional sounds and musical ideas further. At this stage I found myself often struggling to find a balance between musically reflecting on and contextualizing the group members' contributions on the one hand, and actively suggesting new musical possibilities and directions for the group on the other. I was constantly asking myself whether they could arrive in a new place musically by themselves, with me just supporting them, or whether they needed to have some experience of such possibilities before they could get there by themselves. It was often difficult to know whether more 'directive' and varied musical output from me would be experienced by the group as helpful, or as overwhelming and stifling to the members' freedom of musical expression – a danger that Woodcock (1987) has highlighted. I think my dilemma relates to the area of development that Vygotsky (1978) calls the 'proximal zone': what can the child do by himself and what can he do with the help of an adult?

During this phase there began to arise moments when the group members were finding ways of functioning as a group, starting to be more confident and showing more initiative. But these moments were usually hard to sustain and relied quite heavily on Katie and me actively supporting the group. On a more emotional level the group struggled with many different issues, such as trying to exclude one person from the group, frustrations about personal limitations and challenging boundaries.

EXCLUSION

The group struggled considerably over the months with the issue of exclusion: who belongs to the group and who is an outsider? For example, there were times when the group members did not want to sing 'hello' or 'welcome' to Katie, but wanted her to play the smallest possible instrument, and refused to let her have any authority in the group. I wondered if the members feared being excluded and found this feeling hard to bear. It seemed that they projected the feeling onto Katie. Maybe by unconsciously making Katie into the unwanted outsider, the group members could themselves feel insiders. It seemed that Peter, who was the newest member to the group, was particularly determined to make Katie feel unwanted.

Although exclusion is potentially an issue in all groups, I wonder if it might be particularly so for adolescents with severe learning disabilities. According to Stokes and Sinason (1992) they have often experienced severe trauma through a shocked reaction to their birth, through abandonment or in their early relationships. Perhaps the feeling of not being wanted has been a painful issue for their carers to think about. Perhaps this could explain why the feeling of 'not being wanted' was split off and projected with such force in this group. I felt a need to convey to the group that this issue could be thought about in the 'here and now' of what was happening in the group.

FRUSTRATIONS ABOUT ONE'S OWN LIMITATIONS

When group members began to feel more secure and confident in the group, they began to express frustration about their limitations. For example, Peter got angry if he accidentally dropped a beater, or a chime bar came apart and he was not able to fix it. Our approach was to acknowledge and not deny the disability and feelings about it, while also working with the more 'able' part of the self. If the disability is denied, the painful feelings about it tend to get split off and displaced to some other target. There were some sessions when the disability in the group appeared to be projected onto Sarah, both in her lack of music and in terms of relating to others.

It is important not only to acknowledge the negative aspects of the child's life and the limitations that s/he faces, but also to build on strengths and capabilities. As Stewart (1996) has pointed out, it can be valuable if the music therapist in a group focuses on the experience of 'having' as well as 'losing'. A therapist who feels pity towards people with disabilities — and this is not uncommon among helping professionals (Cobb and Warner 1999) — may only focus on the negative aspects of the person's life, and thereby prevent the person from achieving greater awareness of his or her potential.

CHALLENGING BOUNDARIES

There were times when the boundaries of the sessions were heavily tested and it was difficult to concentrate on working musically with the group: for example, when Peter and Sarah wanted to use the session for kissing and cuddling; Tom kept getting instruments that we had agreed not to play; Peter wanted to leave the session and use staff toilets. Our aim was to acknowledge their need to test the boundaries, yet remain firm about them. We conveyed to the group that their sometimes destructive impulses could be contained.

Phase 3: Towards a more independent workgroup

After about six months the group seemed to move on to another phase: beginning to function as a more independent group. The following vignette is from session 24:

> Louisa suggests at the beginning of the session that the group starts by improvising vocally as we had done the previous week. She looks very excited when the group picks up on her idea and members begin to clap their hands on their knees. The group quickly develops a common pulse and there is a sense of anticipation with everyone looking at each other, waiting for someone to start vocally. After a few minutes Sarah makes a rising crescendo sound, accompanying this with arm movements. Tom and Peter immediately copy this and after a while Louisa, Katie and I join in. Sarah seems delighted about the group following her lead and initiates many new sounds. Tom and Peter begin to introduce new musical ideas, too and the improvisation develops into a free-flowing vocal piece. There is an underlying pulse with a lot of variety in the rhythmic configurations and dynamics of the vocal sounds.
>
> After some time Peter suggests playing some instruments and the group decides that we can include them in the music. Tom chooses bongos and plays them standing up, while Louisa chooses maraccas, Peter a drum, and Sarah small shakers. I choose castanets and Katie chooses a tambourine. Everyone plays standing up and the music develops gradually into a Latin-American style dance. I

notice that Tom begins to move to the music and seems really to feel rhythm in his body. Louisa begins to dance while playing and improvising vocally. Her voice seems to grow stronger during the improvisation and she is responding to Peter's rhythms on the drum. Peter's voice and movements seem to have a strong adolescent, sexual feel. When Peter sits down and says that he does not want to dance any longer, Sarah tries non-verbally to encourage him to join in. I notice myself thinking that the group could function at this point without Katie and myself.

The group seemed to be able to function quite independently at this point. The members were clearly aware of the value of each other's musical contributions, responding to and developing one another's ideas. They appeared to own responsibility for what was happening in the group in a constructive way and were able to be creative. The improvisations had energy and freedom for exploration with a range of dynamics, tempo and pitch. The members also seemed more confident in saying what they would like the group to do. Perhaps they had internalized a 'positive' way of being in a group, had gained some sense of how they could relate in a group, and were now able to draw on that internalized experience themselves. Maybe one could also think of the group members here in terms of the concept of the 'Music Child' (Nordoff and Robbins 1977), being able to reveal their authentic musical selves through the shared group improvisations.

For me, this change in the group felt both a great relief as well as slightly unsettling. There was now more space for me to 'stand back' and observe what was happening. The feeling of being made 'redundant' made me ask what my role now was in the group? Perhaps this could be compared to how a parent might feel 'letting go' of her small child, feeling not only relief and pride but also uncertainty. There was naturally a danger at this stage of the group that Katie or I might make a musical or other intervention, not because the group needed it, but in order to make ourselves feel needed.

This kind of group functioning, which Bion (1961) called the workgroup mentality, is not a fully achievable state of mind. Although the group tended to function generally quite independently at this stage and there seemed to be little need for planned structure in the sessions, there were times when the group suddenly seemed to experience more anxiety and reverted to less mature ways of functioning. This happened, for example, around anticipated breaks and when Katie was absent from the group. This resonates with Klein's (in Segal 1973) idea that throughout our lives we fluctuate between less and more mature ways of functioning (the paranoid-schizoid and depressive positions in her terminology).

Concluding thoughts

What might the group members have gained from the experience?

Obviously one can only speculate as to what the experience of being in the group might have meant for the group members. It seems that the group developed in substantial ways over the year. Rather than simply being 'the handicapped member', individuals began to experience being more able and independent. Through their involvement in the dynamic communications in the group, each member became more confident and began to trust that he could make a valuable contribution, owning responsibility and finding musical freedom. They were able to explore their roles in the group and develop some important social skills through a medium where verbal limitations were set aside. At the same time, the group worked on many difficult emotional issues, such as feelings arising from being disabled and fears about 'not being wanted' in the group. It seemed that towards the end of the year the group members were, at least temporarily, able to find a different, less 'handicapped' sense of self.

Our intention was that the experience of feeling more able and independent in the music therapy group could help these young people to resist slipping so easily into the 'helpless follower' role in other groups. Feedback from school staff seemed to indicate that this was, indeed, happening. These four adolescents had clearly become more confident and more co-operative in other group settings in the school, and had began to show more initiative and independence.

References

Begun, A. (1989) 'Sibling relationships involving developmentally disabled people.' *American Journal of Mental Retardation 5*, 566–574.

Bion, W.R. (1961) *Experiences in Groups and Other Papers.* London: Tavistock.

Bion, W.R. (1962) 'A theory of thinking.' *International Journal of Psychoanalysis 43*, 306–310.

Bion, W.R. (1967) *Second Thoughts. Selected Papers on Psychoanalysis.* London: Maresfield.

Cobb, H.C. and Warner, P.J. (1999) 'Counselling and psychotherapy with children and adolescents with disabilities.' In H.T. Prout and D.T. Brown (eds) *Counselling and Psychotherapy with Children and Adolescents: Theory and Practice for School and Clinical Settings,* 3rd ed. New York: Wiley.

De Backer, J. (1993) 'Containment in music therapy.' In M. Heal and T. Wigram (eds) *Music Therapy in Health and Education.* London: Jessica Kingsley Publishers.

Gorell Barnes, G. (1998) *Family Therapy in Changing Times.* London: Macmillan.

Jones, E. (1993) *Family Systems Therapy. Developments in the Milan-Systemic Therapies.* Chichester: Wiley.

Klein, M. (1975) 'Notes on some schizoid mechanisms.' In M. Klein *Envy and Gratitude and Other Works 1946–1963.* London: Hogarth Press.

Kroger, J. (1996) *Identity in Adolescence: The Balance between Self and Other,* 2nd ed. London: Routledge.

Nordoff, P. and Robbins, C. (1977) *Creative Music Therapy.* New York: John Day.

Segal, H. (1973) *Introduction to the Work of Melanie Klein.* London: Hogarth Press.

Spitz, H.I. and Spitz, S.T. (1999) *A Pragmatic Approach to Group Psychotherapy.* Philadelphia: Bruner/Mazel.

Stewart, D. (1996) 'Chaos, noise and a wall of silence: working with primitive affects in psychodynamic group music therapy.' *British Journal of Music Therapy 10,* 2, 21–33.

Stokes, J. and Sinason, V. (1992) 'Secondary mental handicap as a defence.' In A. Waitman and S. Conboy-Hill (eds) *Psychotherapy and Mental Handicap.* London: Sage.

Szivos, S. and Griffths, E. (1992) 'Coming to terms with learning difficulties: the effects of groupwork and group processes on stigmatised identity.' In A. Waitman and S. Conboy-Hill (eds) *Psychotherapy and Mental Handicap.* London: Sage.

Vygotsky, L.S. (1978) *Mind in Society: the Development of Higher Psychological Processes.* Cambridge, MA: Harvard University Press.

Wilkins, R. (1992) 'Psychotherapy with the siblings of mentally handicapped children.' In A. Waitman and S. Conboy-Hill (eds) *Psychotherapy and Mental Handicap*. London: Sage.

Woodcock, J. (1987) 'Towards group analytic music therapy.' *Journal of British Music Therapy 1*, 1, 16–21.

Part 3

Group Work
in Supervision and with
Music Therapy Students

CHAPTER 16

Supervising A Music Therapy Group

A Seriously Non-Musical Problem

Esmé Towse and Cath Roberts

I feel like a conductor but I don't know in the least what the music is which will be played. (S.H. Foulkes 1948, p.292)

The writings of S.H. Foulkes, founder of group analysis, abound with musical imagery. The group is described as the instrument of therapy, the group therapist as the conductor. Other authors have used musical form to describe groups and group processes, likening them to symphony (Powell 1983) or to fugue (Towse 1997).

One of the fundamental concepts of group analysis is that of the matrix. Foulkes described it thus:

The group matrix is the operational basis of all relationships and communications. Inside this network the individual is conceived as a nodal point. The individual, in other words, is not conceived as a closed but as an open system ... As is the case of the neurone in the nervous system so is the individual suspended in the group matrix. (Foulkes 1964, p.118)

The matrix can be thought of as operating on two levels, namely the 'foundation matrix' which is created by the features common to the members from the start, and the 'dynamic matrix', the flow of themes, exchanges and events which materialize as the group develops in intimacy and maturity. The task of the group conductor is to facilitate this process by attention to management and boundaries and by intervening at times with interpretations.

Foulkes also suggested that there is a set of five levels of experience and discourse in the group as follows: Current, Transference, Projective, Body and Primordial. One of the tasks of the conductor is to choose the level in which to pitch an intervention/interpretation. He constantly stresses the identity of the *group as a whole* and the importance of the conductor having an empathic relationship with the group as a single entity.

If we take the view that the matrix is constantly operative, we must assume that this is also so in music therapy groups. The model which is most akin to an analytic group is one in which the group is essentially unstructured within its set boundaries which are maintained by the conductor. When the members of a music therapy group have sufficient verbal and cognitive skills and ego strength, the here and now can be explored in a similar way to that which would occur in a verbal analytic group. However, many music therapists work with people in settings where the more limited verbal skills or psychological-mindedness of their clients may preclude (verbal) exploration and analysis. Yet it may be that music therapy groups, and musical improvisation in groups in partic-ular, could provide an effective form of group analysis for those people who might otherwise not be offered this form of therapy.

But what is it about groups which is therapeutic and allows *an individ-ual person* to feel better in some way? Caroline Garland (1982) suggests that this question needs to be asked in two parts:

1.   What causes change?

2.   What makes the change a change for the better?

Garland points out that change is a necessary prerequisite for therapy rather than the reverse, although change in itself is not necessarily thera-peutic. She states that a 'change-producing factor co-exists with what is therapeutic in the analytic group but is distinct from it' (1982, p.4). She goes on to argue that a fundamental producer of change in a group is the move away from discussion of the group members' presenting problems to the area she calls the 'Non-Problem', that is the attention to the interactions taking place in the here and now of the group itself. Thus the individual group member moves away from the intrapsychic system which is dominated by the presenting problem into a new system in which there is the possibility of exploration, play and growth.

We suggest that engagement in a musical improvisation is a form of engagement with Garland's 'Non-Problem'. Thus the task of the music therapist is first to foster the situation in which a group of people can engage in the process of improvising musically and second to consider how to try to enable the change to be therapeutic.

In considering the application of group analytic theory to those clients who would not have access, through the nature of their difficulties, to verbal therapies, we will consider some of the issues explored in the supervision of a group run by C for children with severe learning difficulties. We will also look at the style of the supervision provided in relation to this group and consider how this informed the supervisors and supervisee's understanding of the dynamic factors within the group.

The setting

The group takes place in a school for children with severe learning difficulties. C is the only arts therapist employed at the school and takes referrals for children who could benefit from therapeutic interventions of various kinds.

The group takes place in a playroom attached to a classroom. It is free from distraction and the walls are bare apart from a fixed, long mirror. A variety of percussion instruments is available but there is no piano.

The members

There are three members in the group: J, K and L. When the group began there was also another member, W, who attended the first session but did not return. After a period of seven weeks, during which he had the opportunity to attend, he was considered to have left the group and was not replaced. J, K and L are all 9 or 10 years old and have severe learning difficulties, which include, among other characteristics, limited use of verbal language. L has a diagnosis of autism and J and K are classed as having global developmental delay. K is also disabled by being grossly over-weight, which severely impairs her movement, and J has a history of sudden aggressive behaviour. Both K and J constantly seek attention from staff, whereas L is often withdrawn and tends to defend herself against interacting with staff or children. All three are members of the same class, which is a class of four, including W.

The group

The group is run as a closed group and as far as possible along group analytic lines. It meets weekly during school term time. The group is facilitated by C and P, an assistant. P participates in the 'hello' and 'goodbye' songs which mark the boundaries of the group. The main focus of the session is then musical improvisation, in which the children are free to choose instruments, to change instruments, or not to play at all. C also takes part in the improvisation, sometimes using her clarinet and sometimes the percussion. The group members have contact with each other at other times, but no other contact with C. They were referred for music therapy by their class teacher. Whilst they do have a choice about attending, they are aware that there is an expectation from the staff team and the therapist that they attend. Their pre-existing relationships with one another and with P, together with their established relationship with the space within which the group takes place, create the foundation matrix. One might think, however, that this could inhibit the possibilities of engaging with a new system which, as Garland writes, is essential for change and hence for therapy to be possible: 'In a group ... we cannot change directly the rules governing the individual's pathological transac-tions within his own system, but we can bring about change in the indi-vidual by making him part of a powerful alternative system, in which a different set of rules is operating' (Garland 1982, p.5)

Two sessions

In supervision two consecutive sessions which occurred eight months into the group were discussed.

Session A

All three members, C, and P were present. J began by handing to C the tambourine which is always used as part of the hello song. In doing this he immediately demonstrated his desire for special attention from C. L observed this taking place. After C had sung to L and she had used the tambourine to play hello, L was reluctant to return it to C, protesting that someone else (K) would now get C's attention. When we began improvising, L, who usually sits in a corner and is very withdrawn, came to sit next to P, leaning on her shoulder in an affectionate way. The theme already emerging in this session seems to be one of sibling rivalry. K, who finds physical movement difficult and tends to expect people to come to her rather than motivate herself to move, began shuffling across the room towards L and P, clearly wanting both to be a part of something she may have felt excluded from, and to gain P's attention for herself. Both K and L seemed angry and expressed this by throwing their instruments away. Whilst continuing to play, J, who is consistently preoccupied by performing for himself in front of the mirror, came to join C, seeing an opportunity where she had been left 'unattended'.

At this point the group felt very fragmented and seemed to have split into two corners. K, who was physically closest to the middle but also seemed torn between wanting to be part of both corners, managed to resolve the situation and reunite the group by turning to face J and C and imitating J's music with exaggerated body movements. At the end of this session J and K were continuing to taunt each other, finding it difficult to let go of some of the angry, rivalrous feelings that all three had expressed. All three were reluctant to leave and there was a sense that something important had come to light in the group. There was perhaps anxiety, however, about what might happen next.

Session B

The next session seemed initially to suggest a retreat from the confrontation and rivalry expressed in the previous session. L appeared to withdraw completely from the group, having had a central part in it the week before. She responded to the hello song, but very shortly into the improvisation she curled up in a corner and went to sleep, in spite of the level of noise around her. The strong message seemed to be one of absolute need for withdrawal from a challenging group situation. The improvisation which took place between J, K and C and seemed to be divided into two clear sections. The first consisted of J dominating the music, playing loudly using beaters on a drum. He had again positioned himself directly opposite the mirror and his dominance of the group seemed reinforced by the reflection of himself he received back from it. K had chosen to play the maracas, but despite her best efforts she was no match for J's drumming. Clearly K's choice of instrument was significant: she had set herself an impossible task in seeking to challenge J. She began shouting loudly, trying to rise above the drumming. During this first section of improvisation C was supporting and responding to the group's sounds using the clarinet. However, C felt unable to challenge J as, it seems, did K, so C changed instrument in order to play the drums, choosing a small conga drum played with the hands.

At this point the intensity of feeling in the group seemed to increase. In the use of the conga C felt more able to challenge J. K, sensing this shift, also increased her use of her voice, trying to find a way in to the improvisation or musical group discussion. J responded to this by allowing himself to join the group more fully. He turned away from the mirror and moved to sit beside C. Noticing how she was playing her drum, he put down his sticks for a few minutes and also began to play using his hands. In this way he was able to engage with the group and respond musically to the challenges presented to him. K also responded to this heightened sense of engagement in the second section of music by holding onto her maracas. She often appears ambivalent towards the instruments and hence the group, wanting to play but soon appearing bored and throwing them away only to want them back again. Now she held on tightly to the maracas.

There was a strong feeling of engagement and that we were indeed a group. Throughout this, however, L remained asleep in the corner, perhaps struggling with her own ambivalence about the group. After a few minutes J returned to his place by the mirror. Having tried out this different way of engaging, he now needed to retreat to familiar territory. The group was left with a sense that a new level of engagement with the group process had been reached, but each member was clearly continuing to express the difficult emotions experienced by all in relation to being in the group.

Supervision

C is an experienced music therapist who has additional training in group analysis. The supervisory relationship is one of two colleagues who discuss case work, rather than one in which there is an assessment function. Supervision often does not include tapes of the clients' music.

The group at ten months (at the time of writing) is as yet relatively immature. It is also small by analytic standards. It may be, however, that when the modality is one in which the group members are invited to be more active and are, as it were, free to 'talk' simultaneously, smaller groups can develop satisfactorily. There may be a greater sense of equality between the conductor and the other members, as each person is engaged overtly in a shared task. This will be controlled to a large extent by the group conductor as it will be influenced by factors such as her choice of instrument (does she have exclusive use of an instrument?) and by her musical interventions.

There is no piano or keyboard in the room and other than C's clarinet the only instruments available to the group are a variety of percussion. The clarinet and its impact on the group was discussed at length in supervision. C had felt a strong pull in the early stages of the group to use the clarinet throughout the sessions as a way of containing the group's anxiety. However, as the group progressed and a new system was established, C and E (the supervisor) began to feel that C's use of the clarinet was perhaps holding the group back in some way. In choosing to use an instrument that clearly needed some degree of skill and was not available equally to all group members, C was set apart from the others in a way that prevented the group from engaging fully on an equal footing.

An important factor in the dynamic matrix of C's group is the loss of W and the fact of his place not having been taken by a new member. How is this likely to re-emerge? On hearing a verbal report of session A, E realized that the information about the children's behaviour was vital. C had been struck by the positions each child had taken up, both physically within the room and in relation to the two adults in the group. The fact of

J's preoccupation with his reflection in the mirror seemed important, as did K's usual immobility, but her capacity to move when sufficiently motivated to do so. C was concentrating on Foulkes' Level 1, whilst at the same time thinking about Level 2, in which the two adults in the group might represent the parental couple in a family. C was adopting a group analytic stance in which she facilitated the group process and allowed material to unfold in its own time.

We discussed the three children as individuals who are part of the group matrix, looking in particular at those aspects of their characters which lead them to resist engagement in the group musical improvisation. L, it seems to E, is the most enigmatic in the group. Sometimes she withdraws into her own world. She could easily be overlooked, as she appears not to make any demands on the group. Does she come to the group actively, because at some level she wants to, or passively, because she will not protest in an assertive way? Her behaviour in the 'hello' section suggests the former. We therefore have to consider a paradox: in order to change and develop, L will have to be able to behave in a way which may not be welcomed by others, as she will have to be able to express feelings such as anger, protest or jealousy. It is her expression of 'I won't' in her reluctance to give up the tambourine for K that gives C and E some hope that she does want to be involved in the group.

K is a much more dominant presence, as exemplified by her size. Her obesity, which results in immobility and therefore having people come to her, wheel her about in a wheelchair and generally wait upon her, characterizes a system in which she passively controls her objects. Psychically, she remains in a state of babyhood in terms of having adults attend to her and might be seen as attempting to hold on to the gratifying aspects of infantile dependence. Whilst people around her continue to allow themselves to be dictated to by her, will she ever change? Why should she? Again the paradox emerges that K perhaps needs to feel some emotional discomfort in order to move out of her paralysing system. She uses the activity of the group and the freedom to move in the room, as well as the instruments (perhaps representing L's toys or, at a more unconscious level, C and P's babies), to express her jealousy and rage. In doing so, she mobilizes her aggression and acts positively.

J's psychological system appears narcissistic. He is more attracted to the reflection of himself than he is to the group. What is the impact of the full-length mirror in the room? Were it not there, would J be constantly seeking mirroring by the group? Would that be more or less difficult to manage than the present situation? One advantage of the mirror is that it is distinct from the group, so that when J does turn away from his own reflection and towards the group, it is apparent immediately.

Developmentally, J and K have things in common, although at first sight they appear very different. Both have put themselves at the centre of the universe. Neither is able to interact with others as separate, individual people, only as objects, which they attempt to control. One of C's tasks will be to manage the situation in which two of the three children will battle to be 'number one', whilst L will opt out and may be the second casualty of the group. But what of W? How might his exclusion be seen? One possibility is that his departure from the group will be regarded not as a loss which might evoke feelings of sadness or guilt, but as a triumph, a successful killing off of a rival.

Session B, which was taped and heard by E, appears to illustrate the dynamics outlined above. So was C right to let L sleep? The danger is that she is colluding with the forces of destruction. The image that comes to E's mind is that of the cuckoo in the nest. But who is the cuckoo, J or K? E suspects K. An alternative view is that L needs to be allowed to utilize her defences in order to maintain her place in the group and that she is simply following the pattern of 'two steps forward and one back'. C's intervention , in which she placed herself next to the sleeping L, makes an important statement that, for her, L is still very much part of the group. Meanwhile, important interactions are taking place between J and K in relation to C and the group as a whole. It is a battle for domination. J, in line with his capacity for self-admiration, equips himself with the loudest, most potent object, which even C's clarinet cannot rival. K, in line with her capacity for passive aggression, takes a quieter, more dif-fuse-sounding instrument and then shouts in an attempt to take control. Each is behaving according to their fixed systems. The noises they make are either cacophonous or musically sterile, when the improvisation is dominated by J's relentless, monotonous beat.

Again, C concentrates on Level 1 whilst keeping Level 2 in mind. Her move to the conga drum is extremely effective. First, it is a move into the shared music, as it is an instrument available for shared use. Second, she chooses an instrument which is capable of matching J's, yet is small and does not threaten his fragile potency too much. At the same time, it is sufficiently different from J's to enable K to experience support, rather than overwhelming domination (two drums against her). The music changes. There is a sense of attentiveness, of some listening to each other. It feels like a musical improvisation in which voice and instruments are used creatively in the service of the group's musical expression. J and K, by engaging in this, have become 'unstuck', albeit temporarily, and have moved into a way of being in which each person is allowed a voice and no one person has to be in absolute control. Sadly, L was not ready to make that move on that particular day, choosing instead to retreat into her known and safe system.

Discussion

We suggest that engagement in a musical (i.e. musically coherent, creative and flexible) improvisation is equivalent to Garland's idea of engagement in the non-problem. As such it is both the cause and the effect of a change, a shift from the system in which the patient is otherwise stuck. We are not saying that any group in which the participants do something with musical instruments will be necessarily therapeutic. Just as Garland asks the fundamental question about how a group can be therapeutic, so we must ask ourselves why might improvising musically might be a form of therapy?

It will be noted that, of the two sessions described, only one was available, musically speaking, to E. The authors deliberately set up this situation, in order to try to think about the importance or unimportance of the music produced. E needed to have a mental picture of the children, including their positions in the room, their preoccupations, their ways of relating to each other and to C and P, their choice of instruments, when they played or were silent, and how they played in terms of leading, following, listening, disregarding, volume, intricacy and creativity. She also needed C's opinion of the musicality of the improvisation at various times. All this could be conveyed verbally by C, although listening to the tape together brought additional richness. It also allowed E to think about her own understanding and interpretation of the group process, rather than one which was necessarily coloured by C's description (and therefore by C's choice of what to report and what to leave out).

It was also important that one of us should hear the difference in quality of the sounds in session B from non-musical to musical, following C's change of instrument. Listening to the tape gave us a better chance to do so, and for that part of the session to be considered in greater detail. Following session B, C began to use the clarinet less as both C and E noticed that the true moments of engagement and cohesion within the group seemed to occur when C was also playing percussion. This gives rise to thoughts about the instruments used by conductors of improvisation groups. The use of one's own instrument or of a piano or keyboard is likely to set one apart from the group in a physical way. Additionally, the use of any instrument not available to the rest of the group will have a significant impact on the dynamic matrix of the group. It may be making the statement, 'I am different from you. I can do something you cannot'. This is not quite the same as the unspoken statement of the group analyst, which is one of 'I am like you but here I have a particular role'. Groups will often try to make the conductor different or set him/her apart. It becomes harder to work with these dynamics if, at the same time, the conductor is acting them out.

When considering the use of tapes in supervision, what seems unimportant and indeed counterproductive is any attempt to pick out an individual's playing and then to try to guess what that might symbolize or represent. Foulkes constantly warned against over-enthusiastic attempts at 'deep' interpretations:

> A therapist with a sense for depth may agree that, in the general run of our profession, there is a false idea of depth and surface. Depth is always there: it is always possible to get hold of it on the surface, it is there all through, visible and tangible. It depends on who is looking, who is listening; one need not jump from what is going on to what is behind it. (Foulkes 1990, p.280)

Foulkes also stated that 'group analytic psychotherapy is *not* a hunt for unconscious meaning'. Detailed analysis of the content of the individual's music, or indeed the group's music, would draw us into these same realms and away from the group as a whole and its mood at any particular time. However, the form of the music – its rhythms, harmony and counterpoint and, above all, its sense of cohesion as opposed to randomness – is of the utmost importance, although not necessarily to be analysed. There is a quality, hard to put into words, but obvious to the listener both in the room and in the supervision setting, which is present in the improvised music of players who are aware of each other to some degree. It is quite different from that of a number of individuals remaining in their own worlds and disregarding all around them. In our view, music should not be analysed, only recognized as having been achieved. What needs to be analysed is the struggle to get to the point at which the music can be created. Thus we also find that one of the 'problems' often considered by music therapists, namely, how to balance music making and talking in groups, simply disappears, as Garland describes. Indeed, talking about the *meaning* of the music could be regarded as resistance to engaging in the group process, creating a form of anti-group. Talking about *responses* to the group music would be a different matter, as that would involve continuing engagement with the group. In other settings, for example, in those situations in which group members have greater verbal fluency than the children in C's group, it may be part of the foundation matrix that the group discourse includes speaking to each other. Our point is that it is not either necessary or indeed desirable to search for insight into the 'deeper' meanings of the music.

Another legitimate question is whether it is necessary for the group members to gain conscious insight or whether it is enough to experience being part of a creative group process. It is certainly the case that insight in itself does not produce change. People can be insightful, but can either choose to remain in their system or be too afraid to give up what is known and feels safe in its own way. In C's group, J, K and L have all demonstrated that they can move, literally and metaphorically, and that they are therefore able to change. There can be no guarantee that they will continue to do so, only optimism.

Perhaps another way of finding out whether the engagement in musical improvisation can in itself bring about lasting change would be for music therapists to experience personal group music therapy as part of training, just as the group analysts engage in personal group analysis. In this way we as individuals would know whether or not we were able to gain insight and/or to effect change in ourselves. E's experience in the early Guildhall training of the improvisation group led by the late Alfred Niemann has had a major beneficial impact on her, both personally and professionally, leading to her belief that engaging in improvised music making in a group must necessarily involve a break from one's fixed system and a move into something new. C's experience of group analytic experiential groups as part of her training with Group Analysis North both challenged and enlightened her understanding of the powerful medium of the dynamic matrix, and this in turn profoundly affected the music therapy groups which she facilitates. The fundamental principles of group analysis present themselves to the authors as being extremely available to music therapy groups. However, clarity of thinking on the part of the conductor as to his/her own understanding of the concept of the dynamic matrix seems essential if the groups with whom we work are to gain some positive benefit and change from the interventions which we offer.

References

Foulkes, S.H. (1945) 'On group analysis.' *International Journal of Psychoanalysis 27*, 46–51.

Foulkes, S.H. (1948) *Introduction to Group Analytic Psychotherapy.* London: Karnac.

Foulkes (1964) *Therapeutic Group Analysis.* London: Allen and Unwin.

Foulkes (1990) *Selected Papers.* London: Karnac.

Garland, C. (1982) 'Group analysis: taking the non-problem seriously.' *Group Analysis 15*, 1.

Powell, A. (1983) 'The music of the group: a musical enquiry into group-analytic psychotherapy.' *Group Analysis 16*, 1, 3–19.

Towse, E. (1997) 'Group analysis and improvisation: a musical perspective.' *British Journal of Music Therapy 11*, 2, 51–55.

CHAPTER 17

Some Observations on Music Therapy Training Groups

Elaine Streeter

Introduction

This chapter aims to outline themes which may be of help to anyone embarking on running a training group. Each of the groups I have convened have offered me a fascinating, moving, testing experience. Some groups happened rather easily, whilst others were more complex, depending upon the fit between group members, training institute and my particular style of working. Groups have been quite individual in character each engaging in the process at a different level.

The purpose of each group has been somewhat different according to the particular training course in which it has taken place. The needs of the trainees have also varied according to what other forms of support have been available. However there have been some common factors and I would like to share some of my observations of how these themes may affect the work and development of such a group.

A little about groups

We gather our experiences of groups at different stages throughout our lives, and on the whole quite imperceptibly. It is so much part of our experience that we take it for granted. We need different sorts of groups at different times. At the time of writing I am both a lecturer within a university faculty and a student within another university. My role in these two groups is very different; what I can ask for and expect to receive, what the rules of engagement are and what influence I can have. I enjoy the fact that my participation in both groups enhances and informs my experience of the other. So some parts of my week are spent guiding, others are spent in seeking guidance.

Groups change and move on. Members come and go. Comfortable endings are usually thoughtfully anticipated, prepared for and perhaps experienced as a subtle shift in tempo or harmony. The participant is able to look back over the past whilst imagining his place within a new group in the future, safe in the knowledge that endings and beginnings can be negotiated.

On the other hand, group membership can end abruptly. It is not easy to forget the image of a tiny man in a business suit tumbling from the World Trade Centre; one minute a company executive, the next in free fall about to become one of a group of victims; likewise the fireman going up instead of down the stairs; one moment part of a team, the next a hero. Between these two extremes lies the middle ground where we make mistakes, leave and come back without too much disruption to others, get what we need enough of the time and manage to hold our heads high at least some of the time. Usually it is not until one decides to become a therapist that these kinds of continuous, relatively unconscious experiences of group membership are thrown into relief.

Conditions of Music Therapy Training

Training to be a music therapist requires the trainee to observe certain personal and creative processes which will on the one hand be specific to each individual and on the other share some commonalities with others; for example, examining the role of the performer. Defining one's unique individuality as a creative therapist is as important as finding congruence and fit within a theoretical orientation. How we nurture both possibilities for students is complex when many post graduate music therapy training courses are full time, relatively short and intensive. Hardly has the student managed to settle into her own therapy before she is expected to apply her learning to others. At the same time, individual personal therapy for trainees is very often not required to be music therapy, but may be verbal psychotherapy and this itself can be confusing.

Trainees occasionally find themselves at sea sooner than anticipated. They may well have moved from one city or even from one country to another. They may have accommodation worries, financial worries, or family demands. In addition they find themselves part of an intense new group. Within the first few weeks it is usually the case that one or two people may be wondering what they have got themselves into. I am painting a somewhat bleak picture for a reason; experiential learning is not easy and is not without risk.

Defence mechanisms

People's reasons for training as therapists are usually complex and often sensitive. Training can sometimes provide an opportunity to park certain personal difficulties in a holding environment for a while. Even though on the face of it students are there to learn how to help others, in doing so they may in some way be trying to find support for themselves.

Training courses are designed to produce music therapists, so defending against the experiential aspects of the process can be pretty exhausting. A variety of different 'experiential' learning situations is offered, ranging from one-off individual workshops with visiting specialists to week-on-week experiential training groups. Even though trainers may have designated the experiential training group meetings as a particularly useful time for trainees, a good deal of time and space may be needed before trainees can orientate themselves towards the purpose of the training group and find a level at which they can function comfortably. In finding help for oneself, one does not necessarily want to unravel the defence mechanism which is serving to hold one together or keeping difficult feelings at bay. Experiential learning inevitably proposes possibilities for change and this is why personal therapy is so important as an adjunct to experiential learning in a training group so that issues arising in the training group can be explored in more depth elsewhere.

Power and confidentiality

In Stanley Kubrick's film *Eyes Wide Shut*, the protagonist finds himself led, partially as a result of his own curiosity, into a secret group from which he can find no escape. It is with a similar sense of trepidation that some trainees experience the powerlessness of belonging to an experiential training group even though they themselves have decided to undertake such a journey. Issues of power and confidentiality often need to be aired. Inevitably the training group is part of a wider training course which requires the trainee to 'succeed' at experiential learning. Even though most training groups are not formally evaluated, trainees are usually expected to attend regularly. The dual purposes of such a group may cause trainees some confusion. If your experience tells you that you do not wish to attend the group, then why go along? Surely that must mean you are not experiencing it? Such conundrums bring further confusion and to a certain extent increase levels of anxiety.

Fantasies about communications between group convenor and other staff are inevitable. How confidential is the group? It is important that trainees know whether or not their group convenor is likely to communicate with the director of training and under what circumstances any communication might take place. Communication varies from course to course and from therapist to therapist; perhaps in the form of termly staff meetings where students' general progress rather than specific communications are discussed. Whatever the arrangement, trainees need to know to what extent the confidentiality of their expressions is likely to be contained so that they can judge for themselves how they wish to make use of the group and at what level.

Confidentiality issues do not however simply rest between group members and group leader, although these will at first perhaps be easier to identify. Members of a training group go on communicating outside the boundaries of the group during seminars, lectures and of course socially. This is a learning point for trainees. They need to test out the difference between boundaries of confidentiality related to their training group and those different boundaries of friendship outside the training group. Whether it is possible to manage all these roles and relationships with the same group of people may prove to be the subject of much exploration.

Testing

The convenor of an experiential training group will usually be an experienced music therapist who is able to manage strong projections from a group. Flexible, fluid thinking processes are required and will be tested. In high seas, students tend to hang on to what they consider a safe harbour; sometimes just staring at the horizon is about all that they can do. At least the training group is a place where one is not judged or evaluated. As trainees slowly begin to come to terms with their new role as therapist and all the new boundaries which that entails, basic boundaries in the training group are likely to be tested and retested.

When I was a member of a training group, the subject of the group convenor's shoes from time to time took up our interest. How was it possible to take him seriously when he wore soft cotton shoes? Even though we knew he arrived at the training institute on a motorbike wearing leather boots and therefore quite sensibly wanted something comfortable to change into, the fact that he continued to wear soft cotton slip-ons was read as an indication of some kind of weakness and possible unprofessionalism. I often used to find myself defending him. In the end I experienced his ability to maintain his stance as a form of stamina from which I learned a great deal. The fact that he seemed comfortable with himself in a role which we were finding difficult to manage with our own clients showed me it was possible to survive being a therapist. Surviving the training group's tests is part of the ongoing job of convening such a group.

Some participants will apparently be uninterested and unimpressed by your presence, your music and what you say. More or less anything you may try to explain can easily take on a hollow sounding emptiness when placed in the resilient silence of a training group in test mode. Naturally, proof is required by members of such a group that you are (a) a capable role model; (b) an inspiring musician; (c) know what you are doing. After several weeks you are probably lucky if you have gained much ground. As one group member announced to the group at the end of his second session, 'By the way this isn't the way groups are run.' This in turn proved to be rather a useful comment because it allowed that particular group to explore differences between the ways in which music therapists work with different client groups.

There are certain groups in which one might be required to remain in an imagined state of incompetence throughout. At the same time, the group convenor usually has patients and supervisees who will remind the therapist that they are experienced and so it is possible to understand these kinds of communication in context. An experiential group may become the container for complex institutional issues. In one such group, the staff team appeared to be in disagreement as to the value of such a group and even whether such a group should really be included in the training. Although everyone tried very hard not to let this affect the life of the group, inevitably it did. The group convenor's ability to withstand the tests of the group are likely to be appreciated in the long run and may in the end prove to be the most fundamental aspect of the learning process. So each group has a context and it is obviously helpful to take the intitutional context into consideration when trying to understand the pattern of events within a training group.

Trust, connections and sensitive music

Training groups provide different opportunities for students according to the style of training course. But perhaps common to all trainings is the opportunity for group members to reflect both upon their previous group experience as well as their 'here and now' experiences in the present. Both these connect with the way students interrelate with one another musically. Curiosity helps and some trainees will be full of curiosity with regard to these processes.

One only needs perhaps one or two memorable musical experiences in a music therapy training group to realize the effectiveness of this form of learning. The experiences I am thinking of were moving expressions of group music which members came upon quite spontaneously as a result of some discussion, or as a result of a silence or previous piece of improvisation which in their view was unsatisfactory. All these special musical improvisations involved an equal sharing of group process, not necessarily because each member played as much as any other, but that their part in the music was of equal importance to that of others. These have been moments of intense creative communication when the music seemed just 'right'. Usually there has been little that anyone has wanted or needed to say. The fact that training groups find a way of constructing such music out of thin air and often on instruments that just moments ago were far from stimulating, can provide an additional means of inspiration to the trainees. They discover and remember the significance of an improvisation almost as some kind of proof that music therapy has an effect. Once they have experienced something for themselves which has felt meaningful and expressive, then they seem more able to work confidently with their own client groups.

I would say that at the root of these experiences lies trust: trust in each other to take seriously the expressions of one another, to listen and to try and make sense of sounds and silences; trust in the group co-ordinator to let the music be the way it is, whether or not everyone is playing; trust that whatever happens one will feel safe. So it is not surprising that sensitive musical improvisations may take a long time in coming through. A great deal of testing of the group convenor and of other members will often have taken place. A knowledge of each other's issues and concerns of the day is not necessarily a forerunner of such an experience. A person may remain silent, unaware of how they are feeling and what they are communicating, only to speak after the improvisation about what was concerning them, or about how they felt during the music. The most astonishing times have been when the discussion has been around one particularly knotty topic; the music coming at a completely different angle to the subject, virtually sounding out an answer that no one had previously considered.

Creative loss

There will, of course, be times when silence is very important. However, silent groups do sometimes need encouragement. Exploring why there is a silent patch (when much of the time may already have been taken up with attempts at interresponsiveness which have fallen on hard ground) is not usually helpful. It simply puts more pressure on the trainees to 'perform'. Playing oneself may sometimes be more helpful. But what do you play in response to a room full of silent music therapy trainees? It is a question of allowing one's own creativity to emerge partly as a role model for the group and partly as a means of changing the medium of expression from verbal silence to musical space.

Whether or not group members then choose to play is probably irrelevant. The fact that some music has entered the equation may be helpful. The music may have touched on the feeling in the room, or posed a question or perhaps turned on a light. Depression and despondency can often be present in training groups. Some kind of aliveness is being given up on and is no longer hoped for, perhaps the loss of music as a result of the training experience? This may seem an absurd idea when so much improvising goes on in music therapy courses, but I believe there are some profound experiences of loss (as well as growth) involved in training to be a music therapist. One's musical life outside the realms of music therapy can feel disrupted.

The revival of creativity is certainly possible, but at some junctures in their training year I have heard trainees describe how their music is disintegrating or is in danger of disappearing. The turning away from the self towards the other, for the sole purpose of helping the other, has its dangers. It can lead to the near extinguishing of a creative flame which is central to the expressive life of a person. At the far extreme there are trainees who feel that their music is a gift to be given away to others. These individuals may work extremely hard in trying to 'develop' their music. In the process they can no longer hear themselves. It is possible in a training group to become alert to these sacrificial tendencies and to work with them.

Musical improvisation need not be directed towards an attempt to express what is being emotionally experienced. Certainly in my own work with trainees I have rarely found this useful (e.g. to ask them to play a piece expressing what they have just been discussing). What I have found more useful is to become aware of possibilities for creative expression, usually by suggesting an improvisation might be started at a particular moment in time. Something may be hanging in mid-air unresolved; something may be feeling absolutely immovable in the room; someone may have been silent for a long time or someone may be crying. These interventions I would say are linked to a thought process, but are in themselves spontaneous creative acts on my own part, somewhat like adding a slightly unexpected hue to a watercolour wash. Creative interventions may begin a process of flow and colour within the group.

Sometimes the colours may be very pale and hardly there at all; sometimes they may burst out into brightness. One is allowing music to happen, but not forcing it or controlling it in any way. Allowing is the important part. Giving permission may also be part of these moments. One gives permission to the group to play for themselves, not about anything in particular or for anyone in particular but simply in the 'here and now' for no immediate reason. Sometimes it can be a lifeline. Merely hearing the voicing of an instrument can put a group member back in touch with their creative self.

Overplay

Of course other groups may find themselves producing a mass of sound. Conscientiously following the guidelines that they have picked up along the way, a group may feel compelled to produce material which, however hard they try, never seems to take the form of music. (By this I mean sounds which when connected give rise to authentic creative form, however fluid or unexpected.) This can be an intensely frustrating experience for musicians, who know only too well the intensity of musical expression of which they are capable. Doing, rather than allowing and empathizing rarely has any effect. A group needs to come to its own conclusions about the cacophony produced. Often leaders will emerge in the group who feel the need to take control of the random nature of the music and sometimes other group members will be more than happy to fall in behind them. Repetitive pulses and metres are sometimes the way in which these instances appear to take musical form. However, there is only so much that can be borne. Helping members to work things out for themselves seems to me to be the role of the convenor. Encouraging group communication is often very helpful. As with group therapy in other contexts, it is useful to point out one's observations about the workings of the group as a whole. This is often enough to allow trainees to start their deliberations.

Collapse and recovery

Trainees need to find places where they can 'fall apart' safely at certain points in the week. This may make it hard for a group convenor to feel that their group is progressing. Sometimes the fact that trainees come along and just sit there, tired and exhausted, is enough in itself. To be able to offer this resource is perhaps one of the most difficult things to manage and yet one of the most important functions of such a group. When music does emerge it can provide a deeply nourishing experience, but it may take time. The ability to be there in a way that neither condones such lack of engagement, nor encourages it, is an art in itself. Much processing outside the group may be necessary for the convenor in the form of supervision. It is tempting at times to feel enraged that trainees have been 'made' to feel like this, but of course one is only identifying with their predicament; feeling the anger that they themselves need to get in touch with.

At other times running such a group can feel almost impossible. Often this is related to the extremes of anxiety and exhaustion which are commonly part of a training experience and difficult for trainees to process when they are both expected to 'experience' their responses to the training and produce assignments. Evaluation and experiential learning are not happy partners. On top of having to learn a number of specialist subjects at postgraduate level, trainees are beginning to get a sense of the depths of their clients' difficulties through their own transference relationships. Being inexperienced and in such close proximity to pathology is often profoundly unsettling for trainees. They had perhaps hoped that music therapy would be an inspiring, exciting way of working. Pretty soon they realize that the work is intensive, demanding and challenging in a way that they could never have quite imagined. There are occasional glimpses of something creative and exciting happening, but the day-to-day work is often quite gruelling, sometimes with little reward in terms of musical engagement. They may question why they have chosen to do this work and whether or not they want to continue.

Outcomes

At some point it may be useful to remind members that just because they have decided to train as a creative arts therapist does not mean that they necessarily have to work in the field afterwards. It may be a 'successful' outcome for a group member if in the end they decide the work is not for them. The training group can provide a space to examine other possibilities. Of course most trainees do go on to work in the field and this is also a successful outcome.

Usually by the end of a group, members will have been able to identify aspects of their training group experience that have been particularly useful. It is also valuable to allow space for members to look back over the experience and try to work through any unresolved issues which may have emerged. Ending a training provides many opportunities to look at boundaries.

At the end of training students may dread the loss of the course and feel an emptiness approaching. They may not yet have secured employment in their chosen field. Goodbyes to clients, placements, supervisors and peers take up their attention. For most trainees this will be the first time that endings have been given so much thought . To some it may seem quite ridiculous to keep bringing their attention back to the approaching ending. However, this may also be an opportunity to witness how an experienced therapist deals with such issues. The ending of the training group is an important opportunity for learning.

In one group that I worked with, the tendency of the trainees had been to opt out of the group one by one so that at our last meeting only one trainee attended. Other groups have used the training group right to the very last minute, feeling that something valuable was potentially there in the last few sessions and moments. There is nothing better or worse in these two examples; it is merely that unless the training group convenor maintains very firm boundaries the group itself will lack the opportunity to express itself in whatever way feels right for them.

Conclusion

Training groups require clear boundaries in relation to confidentiality and purpose and this needs to extend to the institutional context in which they are learning. Trainees need to feel free to make use of their group at their own pace and at whatever level feels helpful to them. Testing out the group convenor is more or less an essential part of a training group experience and anxieties may run extremely high from time to time. This means that projections are likely to be strong and therefore will require the time and space for reflection and understanding on the part of the music therapist who is running the group.

Creativity is often at the core of the desire to train as a music therapist and this needs to be sensitively nurtured. Music may not always be possible. Sometimes just finding a place to more or less collapse and then discover one's ability to recover is all that is possible. Intense musical experiences usually happen at some point in the life of a group. Being sensitive to the pace and timing of a group's expression and yet able to offer interventions when necessary are both useful positions to take up. Allowing improvisation rather than directing or guiding music seems an essential component of helping a group to find a music that is a satisfying means of expression.

Finally, by keeping to professional boundaries the group convenor shows the group that it is possible to survive the rigours of therapeutic work. This in the end may be one of the most important learning experience for trainee therapists.

Thanks

It is due to the creativity and participation of the many music therapy trainees I have worked with that I have been able to formulate these themes. Without their participation in the groups I have run this chapter could not have been written.

CHAPTER 18

A Group Analytic Look at Experiential Training Groups

How Can Music Earn Its Keep?

Alison Davies and Sue Greenland

Introduction

In this chapter we discuss student experiential training groups from the perspective of group analysis. We then go on to consider how group analysis can inform our thinking about experiential music therapy groups. Two questions will be held in mind.

1.   What can group analytic thinking give to the music therapy process?

2.   How can words and music be integrated and thought about in this context?

Experiential training groups

Sue Greenland

Our current collaboration on this chapter has arisen through being colleagues as principal adult psychotherapists in the NHS Trust in Lincoln. We have subsequently spent time together exchanging ideas and reflecting on our work in groups. I have benefited from the richness and diversity of ideas that Alison encounters in her additional work as a music therapist and I offer my experience and understanding of group analytic theory from my training as a group analyst at the Institute of Group Analysis.

I have been involved in counselling and group work training since 1988. I have also supervised the running of experiential groups, including an experiential group on a music therapy training. There are many different models of counselling but I am going to restrict my reflections to the psychodynamic model. In this model an experiential group is regarded as an integral component of a therapy training. But to start with I would like to address some key features of analytic theory, drawing on the work of Foulkes, the analyst who pioneered analytic group psychotherapy. This is particularly pertinent to the scope of this chapter.

Foulkes's frame of reference

Foulkes departs from psychoanalytic thinking by placing the group at the centre of theory rather than the individual. Psychoanalytic theory always prioritizes the individual over the group. Whilst he acknowledges the clinical usefulness and relevance of the fundamental discoveries Freud brought to the individual psyche in terms of unconscious processes, Foulkes invites us to look through a different lens and take the group as priority. He argues that: 'each individual – itself an artificial, though plausible, abstraction – is basically and centrally determined, inevitably, by the world in which he lives, by the community, the group, of which he forms part' (Foulkes 1983, p.10).

Here, Foulkes insists on the interconnectedness and interrelatedness of our experience of being in the world. Although it is sometimes useful to separate out the part from the whole, the individual from the group, in isolation they have no meaning. He invites us to keep this in mind at all times and not to fall into the trap of individual versus group. They are like two sides of the same coin. The individual is embedded and permeated by the social. Interactions need to be framed in this context to be seen.

When facilitating an experiential group, I have found this emphasis on relatedness and interconnectedness very helpful. The experiential group is a space for trainees to reflect on themselves and on their capacity to relate. This becomes visible to them in the immediacy of experience which the unstructured nature of these groups offers. It raises trainees' self-reflective capacity and awareness of the therapeutic relationship.

Foulkes's model of psychological development is also useful. For him, the social relation is transmitted through communication within the family network into which the individual is born. Foulkes (1990b) calls this the 'foundation matrix' of the individual. In other words, he uses the concept 'matrix' to describe these relationships and communications. He makes a distinction between the template of relationships which is laid down in the original family, calling it the 'foundation matrix', and the 'dynamic matrix' which is present in an analytic group. The experiential group forms such a dynamic matrix, with its potential for growth and change.

In prioritizing the social over the biological, Foulkes is also highlighting the essential nature of what it is to be human, to be related, to belong, to be a part of something. Dalal notes that 'Foulkes is saying that both the structure and the content of the psyche are profoundly informed by experience rather than inheritance.' (1998, p.49). This is a departure from psychoanalytic thinking and in this Foulkes is being 'radical'. Foulkes believed that to see an individual as a whole, one needs to see the person against the background of a group. Within this 'total situation' Foulkes highlights the creation of a 'new phenomenon' that arises. He speaks of 'transpersonal processes': that is, mental processes which 'like x-rays in the bodily sphere go right through the individuals composing such a network' (1990a, p.224). Foulkes is concerned with the interactive processes that go on between people. He gives communication a critical role in this process of transmission. Everything that happens in a group is a communication, and it is this attention to the communication and relating that is the primary focus of the group analyst.

If we accept that the psyche is formed within the foundation matrix of early relationships, then it may be that change and modification of not only the psyche but the way we relate and communicate can occur in the dynamic matrix of the experiential group.

Ralph Stacey (2001) extends Foulkes's idea of 'something new' being created in the group by seeing in the processes of communication in the dynamic matrix the potential for a transformative experience. This happens as trainees struggle to be understood by the group and to understand others

The function and purpose of the experiential group

It is generally accepted on the majority of therapy and counselling trainings that a period in an experiential group, with no fixed agenda, where trainees can reflect both on themselves and how they affect each other, can be valuable. For example, students can see themselves mirrored in others as well as recognize unconscious aspects of themselves, which may well contradict how they see themselves. Trainees can gain awareness and insight into what part they play in the patterns of group behaviour manifested at any one time. They may want to dominate and lead the group, challenge the conductor, rescue other people, fall into the role of scapegoat or use humour or provocation when there is conflict.

Framed within the dynamics of the group, the trainee reveals his/her capacity to relate and communicate. Disturbances in the capacity to relate, which no doubt arose in the foundation matrix, can be worked on to some degree in the 'here and now' of the group. In becoming aware of perhaps a potential incongruity in their perceptions of self and the perception that others have of them, group members can then be open to experiencing themselves in a different way and learn new ways of relating. Attitudes and assumptions can be challenged and feelings understood and trans-formed.

The experiential group is also useful in providing a confidential setting in which trainees can safely discuss their responses to the content and management of the course. Parallel processes in the different components of the course can be revealed and reflected upon. Group members can also take to their personal therapy sensitive issues and difficulties that arise from their group experience, hopefully without diminishing their group experience. Splitting between the two will inevitably happen at times and the group conductor and therapist need to be aware of this and to handle it appropriately.

The role of the conductor

One of the most important tasks of the conductor, working in an analytic frame, is to pay close attention to the relating and communicating that goes on in the group and to feed this back to the group to think about. As conductor I am more concerned with how something is communicated, verbally and non-verbally, and what response that communication receives than the content of what is said. For Foulkes everything that happens in the group and at the boundary of the group is a communication: 'In talking of communication we are thinking of all those processes, conscious and unconscious, intentional and unintentional, understood and not understood, which operate between people in a group' (Foulkes and Anthony 1957, p.244).

As trainees struggle with uncertainty, they gradually begin to take responsibility for themselves and their contributions. In doing so they become more conscious of their communications. In prioritizing relating and communication processes over content, I do not imply that I never pay attention to content or its meaning for the group. Indeed, content can draw attention to processes going on in the group and can mirror events in the group. For example, a trainee talks about a painful tooth she has had extracted. This leads to a response from another group member to a loss of a part of oneself and eventually the group talks about the absence of a trainee who has left unexpectedly.

Boundaries and containment

We expect a lot of our trainees: to be in personal therapy, to develop their skills as practitioners, to deepen their understanding and experience of the therapeutic relationship, to digest theoretical ideas and to be able to use these ideas appropriately and meaningfully in their own voice. In their clinical work we expect them to develop the capacity to contain their patients within the frame of therapy and to be able to use themselves, their insight and their thinking in the service of their patients.

In accepting trainees onto a training we are acknowledging their wish to belong to a profession. They may or may not in the end meet the criteria. This situation can resonate at a very primitive level and can be seen in the natural anxieties aroused in trainees as they struggle with their fears of 'Will I be good enough?' 'Will I succeed?' 'Will I belong to this family, this peer group and eventually to the profession?' They struggle with uncertainty and not knowing; key elements in the psychodynamic therapeutic relationship. This situation echoes the priority that Foulkes gives to the social over the biological; that the driving force behind human interaction is the need to belong, to relate and to communicate.

Safety, trust and confidentiality are essential to containment. This has implications for the group conductor. It is preferable that the conductor is not a member of the core team but comes from outside the training. It is much easier to maintain boundaries and confidentiality and thereby maximize containment if the conductor is unconnected with the assessment procedures of the training. The group is an excellent forum for members to become aware of the significance of boundaries and confidentiality as they experience them being held and managed on their training. Confidentiality and boundaries are often taken for granted and until we experience a breach and have to take responsibility for them we often do not fully appreciate their significance.

This brings us to the second part of this chapter which asks: 'Does the fact that students play instruments change the focus and task of the conductor in experiential music therapy training groups?'

Experiential music therapy groups: the place of music

Alison Davies

Context

There are, at the time of writing, six accredited courses in England and Wales where students can train as music therapists leading to membership of the Association of Professional Music Therapists. The nature of experiential group work on the various courses differs. Some have an experiential music therapy training group like the one I shall be describing in this part of the chapter. Other trainings have experiential talking groups, separate from a music group.

Towards the end of the 1980s and onwards, group analysis was beginning to have a growing influence on music therapists, just as music therapists were beginning to be interested in psychoanalytic theory and how it might inform their work. John Woodcock (1987, pp.16–21), describes a patient group where he incorporated aspects of group analysis and psychotherapy. This was an important step in considering aspects of group analytic thinking in music therapy. Gradually, many music therapists have incorporated this way of looking at the group process, observing analytically aspects of relatedness and communication within the music.

A group scenario

Let us imagine a group scenario where the students are sitting in a circle around a collection of tuned and untuned percussion instruments. It is the second session of the year. The members have been talking and then, after a short silence, one member leaves her seat and picks up an instrument and begins to play. Other members gradually join her and a period of musical improvisation unfolds. As the conductor, I engage in a number of ways: I note who plays what and when within the music, what particular instruments are being played and whether an instrument is the students own or one from the circle. I note the musical dynamics such as loud and soft, pitch and rhythm, and the quality of sounds; drumming with a beater or with a hand, pizzicato or sustained notes, chords and presence of harmony, atonality or dissonance. I then consider how this music reflects the feeling of this particular group at this moment and how it might also mirror feelings at the beginning of the students' training.

The music stops and members remain where they are or return to their seats. A period of silence or dialogue may follow. I attend to what is happening. Do members spontaneously translate their musical experience into words or not? Do I prompt this? Do I offer my thoughts and reflections? As in a talking group, I would think about what is happening in the 'here and now'. I may think about the feelings or anxieties that are being avoided or support those being acknowledged.

The important factor for the conductor is to process what is happening in the room. At an unconscious level this is part of the dynamic matrix of the group and will inform the group experience. I am also reminded of Foulkes's dictum that the conductor is in the group not to direct or lead but to trust the group to be able to do its own work. I would be cautious about making an intervention in the form of an interpretation at this point.

As the training continues it will become clearer who does what and when in the group and how the trainees use the music both individually and together. Students use it in a variety of ways to express a range of feelings. The music also has this capacity in the same way as a talking group might use content and metaphor to express or avoid feelings, The music therapy training group is bilingual (Cooper 2000) in this respect.

My predominant questions during a group session would be: What does it mean to be in this particular group with two means of expression: words, and music – music in the form of free improvisation? What is the nature of this bilingual communication? In adding music, is communication deepened or more confusing for participants? Does the music mask issues or illuminate them? Finally, can we effectively move between the words and the music in order to have a more balanced understanding of what is going on – a clearer picture of both the thinking and the feeling?

The conductor as music therapist

Foulkes used the term 'conductor' precisely because of its connotations with an orchestral conductor. In this context, Rachel Chazan writes: 'Foulkes emphasised that the group itself is the instrument of therapy, not merely a background.' She goes on to say that 'the therapist's task is to forge and perfect this instrument, not to be the only therapist. A conductor training a choir could not sing all the parts' (Foulkes 2001, p.98).

Woodcock (1987, p.20) reminds us that Foulkes said of the conductor that 'whenever possible he lets the group speak, brings out agreements and disagreements, repressed tendencies and reactions against them ... the conductor's function can thus be compared with a catalytic agent'. Does the role of the conductor change with the introduction of the medium of music? If the task is to bring out what is being communicated in the group, a close observation of how music might mirror the talking is what needs to be closely attended to. Words and music are the shared currency in a music therapy group. This bilingual experience of two languages requires the conductor to move between the music and the words in her observations. This might mean at times the participation of the conductor in the music: a participant observer in both currencies.

The question of whether the conductor should play in the music is often raised. Can she remain within the province of the conductor by doing so? I hold the opinion that playing music does not detract from the role. If I have played, it is to confirm or challenge what is being communicated. My job is to draw trainees' attention to the network of communications that are both present within the words and the music. Care too has to be taken that my contribution, at the times I do play, does not change the direction of the music but is a reflection of an understanding of what is going on. The group's music needs to evolve 'without the nature of that material being directed or suggested by the therapist' (Woodcock 1987).

The music therapy conductor might actively use the music to draw emphasis to a particular group dynamic or draw attention in music to what she feels is being withheld. This might be done in a music therapy group, either by the conductor joining the already existing music or by making a separate statement in a musical gesture of her own.

Movement between words and music

Some student groups very quickly and spontaneously involve themselves in musical improvisation. Other groups present the opposite dynamic and words fill the space. I might be inviting the students to be curious as to why the words or the music is predominant. Sometimes there is a desire to move from words to music by some students but resistance by others, or the reversal of this. Part of the learning process for students is to help them think and to be more attuned to why both consciously and unconsciously they move between the two currencies.

Encouraging students to express their views means acknowledging that they too are therapists in the group. For instance, the music could at a particular time be considered by some as a defence against being thoughtful or by others as a comfort in the face of frustration, or still further a flight towards a healthy moment of order out of chaos. There may be more than one interpretation. The most important aspect of the students' learning is nurturing a culture of thoughtfulness about themselves and their music. There might be times when I would actively suggest a move into music. I will give an example.

EXAMPLE 1

Anxieties and uncertainties together with not having the usual academic goalposts, might present as typical themes in a student group. Here students are on a course where personal self-development and reflection are needed and where to be a therapist often means confronting one's own doubt. Yet students also have to get through various hoops such as exams and placement expectations in order to pass the course. It might be difficult for students to hold this rather contradictory space: on the one hand a place of not knowing, but on the other having things expected of them. In sensing anxiety of unexpressed feelings and moods below the surface, perhaps displaced onto topics outside the group or talked about in an intellectual way, might lead me to suggest that group members could use the music to explore these feelings further. In this case, a suggestion that we move to the music could help the group to bypass the intellectual thinking and focus on the feeling at a more free associative level that perhaps arrives at a more accurate expression of the mood of the group.

EXAMPLE 2

Another example where I might direct the proceedings towards music might be if the group expressed the theme of frustration with angry feelings of being overwhelmed with work, perhaps nearing the end of a term. I might suggest a move into music in order to get another sense of the significant feelings that were being expressed. The music might then have a quality that, for example, expressed angry feelings in loud, disconnected and confused ways, perhaps on drums or with small, edgy percussive sounds significant of frustration. Or specific musical instruments might be chosen that express the feeling of bewilderment and vulnerability in a more essential way than the words. Primitive anxieties aroused on trainings, to which Greenland made reference in her section of this chapter, may be more safely expressed and contained in the music.

Free improvisation focus

Why have no agenda? Perhaps this sense of discovery in the group of how we communicate both in words and music can happen most effectively when there is an absence of what is expected in a formal or structured way. Learning in other contexts is often equated with 'knowledge'. Music students bring with them all sorts of aspects about being a musician. Playing music has associations with mastering an instrument, emulating others and hours of repetitive practice. Free improvisation is often unfamiliar territory, yet a very important therapeutic skill. Helen Odell-Miller describes free improvisation 'as similar to the aspect of free association and free-floating attention in psychoanalytic work' (2001, p.127). Use of music in this way, as well as being a tool for students' future practice, can be a liberating and creative form of being together and learning from each other. The playfulness inherent in free improvisation seems to bring out the possibility of Foulkes's idea of something new being created in the group, and also echoes Stacey's (2001) idea of a transformative experience. For students in experiential music therapy groups, responding in this free way that is not founded on patterns of pre-conceived musical structures may bring to the surface all sorts of anxieties. Can I be heard? Do I want to be heard? Can I risk taking the music in another direction? Is this the moment to accompany or to break away? Do I support? Can I confront? All this has parallels in the talking.

Clinical and artistic aspects of improvisation

During the course of the year, when students experience their therapy practice on placements, the experiential group often reflects on the nature of clinical improvisation and how this relates to the artistic. I see the clinical and the artistic as interwoven. In clinical improvisation, it is not only an artistic and 'musicianship' response that is needed, but also an ability to engage a third ear. This quality of standing back and listening allows the student or clinician to respond in the service of the 'other' – the patient or client. It seems to me that the move back and forth between artistic and clinical improvisation is subtle. These need not be separate entities. Both forms are intertwined in how we respond as music thera-pists.

Final thoughts

At the end of the training, it is always interesting to look back at the group's use of the music and the words. Is there more music? Is there less music? More talking? Less talking? Some music therapists would think in terms of moving from music into words as in a developmental model from non-verbal to verbal, immortalized by Freud's famous lines 'where id was, there ego shall be' (1973) – in other words, the bringing of the unconscious into consciousness. Other music therapists might hesitate in using an exclusively developmental or progressive model, but seek to consider a balance between the words which might bring something to consciousness and letting the music, at a more unconscious level, speak for itself within the symbolic image. Sandra Brown, music therapist, writes about the element of free association as 'a creative process which holds its own process and finds structure within itself' (1999). Rather than thinking of the 'self' in terms of ego and therefore consciousness, the evolving of the 'self' might be the bringing into balance the richness of both conscious and unconscious images. James Hillman, Jungian psychologist, says 'an object bears witness to itself in the image it offers and its depth lies in the complexities of this image' (in Moore 1989, p.100). Carl Jung drew our attention to the need for a balance between conscious and unconscious life: 'both are aspects of life'. In his thinking about individuation he said: 'It is the old game of the hammer and the anvil: between them the patient iron is forged into an indestructible whole, an "individual"' (Jung 1959, p.288).

Conclusion

This chapter has tried to show the various ways in which group analysis can inform our thinking about student experiential music therapy groups. We have described how the music can enhance the experience of being together and express the feelings that the words at times might struggle with. We also acknowledge that bringing the music into words, when appropriate, can generate a place of thinking and thoughtfulness that is important in its own right. However, there are times when the music speaks for itself and needs to remain within the image, thus acknowledging the value of a balance between the thinking represented by words and the feeling expressed in the music.

We would like to end with a metaphor that has come up for students in both an experiential talking group on a counselling training and an experiential music therapy group. The groups liken the experience to a boat at sea, sometimes in high seas, sometimes in calm waters, sometimes in a storm with no land in sight. This metaphor is always associated with feelings of vulnerability, anxieties about survival, danger, threat and uncertainty. Who's got the compass? Often, the metaphor is evoked by significant events on the boundary of the group, for instance, a member leaves the course or there are staff changes. Such events can trigger disturbances and in turn this has the potential to develop creative and imaginative thought through group metaphor or descriptive music.

Halfway through training, provoked by an actual storm outside, one group thought of themselves as a ship that had left its port at the beginning of the year and was now at a point in the ocean of no return. The land was not yet in sight. Feelings of doubt and uncertainty were stimulated by the actual sounds outside on the boundary of the room. The music then came spontaneously with no prompting. The elements of frustration, anger, anxiety of the unknown, the need for comfort and consolation from each other, associated with this metaphor, took another expression in the music. At this moment, playing music together felt like the generating of a 'group courage' in the face of uncertainty.

References

Brown, S. (1999) 'Some thoughts on music, therapy, and music therapy.' *British Journal of Music Therapy 13*, 2, p.67.

Chazan, R. (2001) *The Group as Therapist.* London: Jessica Kingsley Publishers.

Cooper, R. (2000) Personal communication.

Dalal, F. (1998) *Taking the Group Seriously.* London: Jessica Kingsley Publishers.

Foulkes, S.H. and Antony, E.A. (1957) 'Group Psychotherapy. The Analytic Approach.' Pelican.

Foulkes, S.H. (1983) *Introduction to Group Analytic Psychotherapy.* London: Karnac.

Foulkes, S.H. (1990a) 'Psychoanalytic concepts and object relations theory: comments on a paper by Fairbairn.' In S.H. Foulkes *Selected Papers.* London: Karnac, pp.107–111.

Foulkes, S.H. (1990b) 'The group as matrix of the individual's mental life.' In S.H. Foulkes *Selected Papers.* London: Karnac, pp.223–233.

Freud, S. (1973) *New Introductory Lectures on Psychoanalysis.* London: Pelican, p.112.

Jung, C. (1959) 'Conscious, unconscious and individuation.' In C. Jung *The Archetypes and the Collective Unconscious, Collected Works Vol. 9, Part 1.* London: Routledge and Kegan Paul, p.288.

Moore, T. (ed) (1989) *The Essential James Hillman. A Blue Fire.* London: Routledge.

Odell-Miller, H. (2001) 'Music therapy and psychoanalysis.' In Y. Searle and I. Streng (eds) *Where Psychoanalysis Meets the Arts.* London: Karnac.

Stacey, R. (2001) 'Complexity and the group matrix.' *Group Analysis 34,* 2, 221–240.

Woodcock, J. (1987) 'Towards group analytic music therapy.' *Journal of British Music Therapy 1,* 1, 16–21.

The Contributors

Emma Carter trained as a music therapist at Anglia Polytechnic University in 2000. She currently works at a child and family psychiatric unit and child development centre in Cambridge. She also works as Amelia Oldfield's research assistant on a PhD project investigating music therapy for children on the autistic spectrum.

Rachel Darnley-Smith studied music and philosophy at Lancaster University. She trained as a music therapist at the Guildhall School of Music and Drama, where she has subsequently been a part-time member of the teaching staff over many years. Most of her clinical work has taken place in adult mental health settings and she is currently head of the music therapy service for St. Anne's Hospital, Barnet, Enfield and Haringey Mental Health NHS Trust, London. She has become particularly interested in music therapy with older adults and is a member of the older adults section of the Association for Psychoanalytic Psychotherapy in the NHS. She lectures on music therapy training courses in the UK and the USA.

Alison Davies is both a music therapist and a psychotherapist. She trained as a music therapist at Roehampton Institute, London in 1984 and subsequently worked in Addenbrookes NHS Trust in mental health services. She has had a special interest in group work and pioneered the introduction of music therapy at St. Columba Group Therapy Centre in Cambridge where she was deputy director of the service. She has taught on the music therapy training at Anglia Polytechnic University and is currently a member of the teaching staff on the music therapy training at the Guildhall School of Music and Drama. During the 1990s she trained as a psychoanalytic psychotherapist with the Philadelphia Association, London and now also works part time as a principal adult psychotherapist for Lincolnshire Healthcare NHS Trust. She is an associate member of the Philadelphia Association.

Catherine Durham is a music therapist based in Bristol. She holds a research fellowship in music therapy at the University of the West of England, funded by the Music Therapy Charity. She is currently undertaking doctoral research into group work with adults with severe learning disabilities. Before working as a music therapist, she was a freelance cellist in London. She teaches clinical improvisation on the postgraduate music therapy training at the Welsh College of Music and Drama and offers clinical supervision and clinical improvisation for the University of Bristol course. She also has a private supervision practice.

John Glyn trained as a music therapist at the Guildhall School of Music and Drama. He works at the Three Bridges Regional Secure Unit in West London. He is currently completing training as an adult psychoanalytic psychotherapist at The Lincoln Centre.

Sue Greenland is a counselling trainer and a group analyst registered with the UKCP and the Institute of Group Analysis. She is a principal adult psychotherapist for Lincolnshire Healthcare NHS Trust. She has a private practice in Cambridge working analytically with individuals and groups. Her experience includes working extensively with staff groups in a wide range of settings. She is a member of Cambridge Group Work, a private organization offering training, therapy, supervision and consultancy in group work.

Katherine Grogan qualified as a music therapist at Roehampton Institute, London in 1993. She subsequently worked with adults with learning disabilities, adults with autism and children with multiple needs including physical disability. She has worked in a variety of settings including private practice and currently works for South West London and St. George's Mental Health NHS Trust where she is Head of Child and Adolescent Music Therapy services. She manages a service working with children and young people between the ages of 2 and 17 who present with a wide range of mental health needs. Katherine has a special interest in working with families and in using both systemic and psychodynamic ideas. She completed a diploma in applied systemic theory in 2000.

Hayley Hind trained as a music therapist at Anglia Polytechnic University, Cambridge in 1995. Since then she has worked within the NHS with adults with learning disabilities and is now a Senior Music Therapist in the Cambridgeshire and Peterborough Mental Health Partnership NHS Trust. She is an approved supervisor for the APMT. Her MA dissertation, completed in 2000, studies the relationship between words and improvised music in working with adults with learning disabilities. She has a particular interest in group work and has undertaken further training in this area.

Doris Knak trained in music therapy at Roehampton Institute, London. Her clinical experience has developed primarily within various mental health settings for children, adolescents and adults with a range of conditions including emotional/behavioural difficulties, communication disorders, developmental delay and acute mental health problems. She particularly enjoys working with children and young people and her focus at present is upon group work and working with parent/child couples. She attended the groups workshop which forms part of the child psychotherapy training at the Tavistock Centre. She is now enrolled in the MA in observational studies.

Helen Loth is a head music therapist in Barnet, Enfield and Haringey Mental Health Trust, and Senior Lecturer in Music Therapy at Anglia Polytechnic University. She has worked as a music therapist in psychiatry for 15 years and currently specializes in work with adults with eating disorders. She has published and presented several papers on this subject and on music therapy in forensic psychiatry.

Tuulia Nicholls received most of her musical training in her native country, Finland, before completing a BA in applied psychology at University College, Cork, Ireland. Following this, she trained as a music therapist at Roehampton Institute, London. She has gained a Post Graduate Certificate in Working with Groups in the Public and Independent Sectors from the Tavistock Institute. Her clinical work has taken place in education settings mainly with children and adolescents with severe learning disabilities.

Helen Odell-Miller is Director of the MA and Postgraduate Diploma programme in Music Therapy at Anglia Polytechnic University, Cambridge and a senior music therapist and researcher in music therapy at Addenbrookes NHS Trust. She has worked as a music therapist for 25 years and has experience in a variety of clinical fields. In 1989 she completed an MPhil at City University, London, which included a research project about the elderly mentally ill and outcomes of music therapy treatment, particularly in dementia. She has published widely and lectured all over the world, including visiting the USA, Australia and Europe as an invited keynote speaker at conferences and a guest lecturer in universities. She is a founder member of the European Music Therapy Committee, a past chair of the Association of Professional Music Therapists and of its Post Diploma Supervision Panel; she is at present Advisor to the Department of Health on Music Therapy in the UK.

Amelia Oldfield has worked as a music therapist in Cambridge for over 20 years with a variety of client groups. She was the joint instigator of the MA in music therapy at Anglia Polytechnic University, where she is a part-time senior lecturer. She has been involved in three major music therapy research projects and is currently investigating music therapy with children with autism. She writes and lectures extensively, and is co-author of the book *Pied Piper: Musical Activities to Develop Basic Skills.* She has produced four music therapy training videos. She is married with four children and plays the clarinet in various local chamber groups and orchestras.

Eleanor Richards lectured in music history and worked in arts administration before training as a music therapist at Roehampton Institute, London. She is a Senior Lecturer in Music Therapy at Anglia Polytechnic University, Cambridge, and a Senior Music Therapist in the Cambridgeshire and Peterborough Mental Health Partnership NHS Trust. She also works at the St Columba Group Therapy Centre, Cambridge. She is currently completing training with the Centre for Attachment-Based Psychoanalytic Psychotherapy, London.

Cath Roberts trained as a music therapist at Anglia Polytechnic University and currently works at Peak School, High Peak, Derbyshire. She is also Joint Co-ordinator of MusicSpace North West.

David Stewart trained in music therapy at Roehampton Institute, London and has worked as a therapist, trainer and musician since 1990. He has published and presented his work nationally and internationally. A main area of interest is the application of a Winnicottian approach to music therapy within child and adult mental health. Since 2001 he has worked as a psychotherapist for a Barnardo's Northern Ireland project which provides support to individuals, families and communities traumatically affected by the 'Troubles'.

Elaine Streeter is an experienced music therapist and trained counsellor and has worked in a wide variety of clinical settings. She trained with Paul Nordoff and Clive Robbins in 1974. She founded the music therapy training at Roehampton Institute and was the director of this training for some years. She is a visiting lecturer at Anglia Polytechnic and a visiting professor at the Guildhall School of Music. She has a wide range of clinical experience with a variety of client groups. She has written and spoken about her work extensively.

Julie Sutton has worked for over 18 years as a music therapist; her current work is based in Ireland and in the UK. She is Music Therapy Advisor for the Pavarotti Music Centre in Mostar, Bosnia and supervises therapists at the centre, in Ireland and the UK. Her research includes work with children with speech and language impairments and Rett syndrome, Parkinson's Disease and psychological trauma. She has recently completed her doctorate. She is the current editor of the *British Journal of Music Therapy* and the UK representative for the European Music Therapy Confederation. Her first book *Music, Music Therapy and Trauma* was published in 2002.

Esmé Towse trained as a music therapist at the Guildhall School of Music and Drama and as a psychoanalytic psychotherapist with the North West Institute of Dynamic Psychotherapy. She currently co-ordinates an independent psychotherapy service in Manchester.

Helen M. Tyler studied music and English literature at Reading University where she also completed an MPhil dissertation on the harmonic language of Mozart's chamber music. After spending several years teaching music to children of all ages, she retrained as a music therapist at the Nordoff-Robbins Music Therapy Centre. She is now Assistant Director of the Centre and a tutor on the music therapy training course, where her focus is on supervising the students' group work. She has published several chapters and articles and has lectured widely. Her clinical work is with children, individually and in groups.

Linda Vickers is a state registered art therapist and UKCP registered psychotherapist. She has worked for the last eight years in the NHS and in private practice in a range of settings including learning disabilities, mental health and palliative care. She has a special interest in both Eastern and Western philosophical approaches to therapy.

Ruth Walsh Stewart qualified as a music therapist in 1993. Since then she has worked with children, young people and adults with a wide range of communication and mental health needs. Her specialist interests include group work with children with autistic spectrum disorder and trauma work, in particular the areas of early childhood deprivation and the impact of the Northern Ireland 'Troubles'. In addition, she has published, presented and consulted on her work nationally and internationally. She is also a qualified psychoanalytic psychotherapist.

Tessa Watson has worked extensively in adult mental health and learning disabilities. Her current clinical work is in an adult community learning disabilities team in London. She is a course tutor on the music therapy programme at University of Surrey, Roehampton. Her interest in the development of the profession has led her to serve on several committees and project groups within the Association of Professional Music Therapists, most recently the Continuing Professional Development committee.

Subject index

Author index

Printed in the United Kingdom by
Lightning Source UK Ltd., Milton Keynes
141349UK00001B/14/A